Peter

A Life Transformed

JACQUIE HOEKSTRA

Keys to Unlock Your Full Potential in Christ

A Discipleship Journey

Second Edition

GLORY PEAK PUBLISHING

Scripture taken from the New King James Version®. Copyright © 1982 by Thomas Nelson. Used by permission. All rights reserved.

This book is a work of non-fiction. Unless otherwise noted, the author and the publisher make no explicit guarantees as to the accuracy of the information contained in this book. No names or places have been altered.

Glory Peak Publishing books may be ordered through online or local booksellers.

 **GLORY PEAK PUBLISHING**

Brownsville, OR
glorypeakpublishing@gmail.com

Certain stock imagery provided by © Thinkstock.

ISBN: 979-8-9909035-2-4
Library of Congress Control Number: 2025915252
Print information available on the last page.

GLORY PEAK PUBLISHING rev. date: 07/16/2025

USED BY PERMISSION

Brown, F., S. Driver, and C. Briggs. 2003. *The Brown-Driver-Briggs Hebrew and English Lexicon.* Peabody, MA: Hendrickson Publishers, Inc.

Carson, D. A., R. T. France, J. A. Motyer, and G. J. Wenham. 1994. *New Bible Commentary 21st Edition.* Downers Grove: Inter-Varsity Press.

Harris, R. Laird, ed., Archer, Jr., Gleason L. Assoc. ed., Waltke, Bruce K. assoc. ed. 1980. *Theological Wordbook of the Old Testament Words.* Chicago: Moody Press.

Thayer, J. H. 2000. *Thayer's Greek-English Lexicon of New Testament.* Peabody, MA: Hendrickson.

Thompson, ed., Frank Charles. 1997. *The Thompson Chain-Reference Bible.* United States: B. B. Kirkbride Bible Company, Inc.

Youngblood, Ronald F., F. F. Bruce, and R. K. Harrison. 1995. *Nelson's New Illustrated Bible Dictionary.* Nashville: Nelson.

DEDICATION

To my kind and generous husband, Martin, who
never fails to love, support, encourage, and cheer me on
as I follow the call and purposes on my life.

CONTENTS

How to Use This Study

This study is structured over six days, comprising five daily study lessons and a review day. Study days consist of questions and notes. The review day is for reflection and application. This cushion allows for a day to catch up when the unexpected parts of life hit and derail your study time.

I used the New King James Version (NKJV) of the Bible to do this study. It will be helpful to use the same version simply because some questions have clue phrases to help guide you to the answers. However, any version will work because the truths and stories remain the same. If you use a different version and have difficulty finding an answer, I suggest looking it up in the New King James Version.

Before you begin each lesson, take a moment to pray and ask the Holy Spirit to lead you into all truth (John 16:13). For the best impact, read all the scriptures listed at the beginning of a section before looking to answer the questions. This will help you retain what you have read and give you an idea of where the lesson is going for each section. However, you know what your life can handle in this moment, so do what works best for your current situation.

I have broken down the scripture references to save you time, but you can read through a chapter if you prefer. For example, Week One, Day one assigns Mark 1:16 21, 29-32; Luke 5:1 3, 10 to save you time and give focus for the day's theme. If you prefer, read it straight through as Mark 1:16-32; Luke 5:1-10. This is your study, so use it as it suits your life.

Challenge questions are for those who choose to search for their answers beyond the scriptures provided. Avoid using the notes at the bottom of the Bible page and commentaries until you have met with your study group to discuss the questions, or after reading the chapter notes if you are doing the study independently. The reason I suggest this is twofold. One, it shows you how much the Holy Spirit does guide you and you get to see how much you can hear Him; and two, we are not looking for the correct answer, but the God answer, because the God answer is always the correct answer.

"I love those who love Me, and those who seek Me diligently will find Me" (Proverbs 8:17). Hold onto this promise from the Lord and expect Him to show up through your efforts to seek Him through this study. He has promised this to you. I hope you will enjoy this journey with Peter as much as I have. May the Lord bless you as you seek Him.

INTRODUCTION

This is the story of how this study came to life: One morning during my devotional time with Jesus, I distinctly heard Him say, "I want you to study Peter."

"Peter? I'm a Paul person," was my immediate and emphatic response. As the words escaped my tongue, I realized I was talking back to the Lord, something I had not done before. I swallowed, apologized and got on board with His plan. My next thought was, what new thing am I going to bring to the table? Everyone has taught on the highlights of Peter's life. At the time, I thought I was doing a personal study, not writing a Bible study for others.

I had just received a degree in Bible study so I thought it would be a good opportunity to utilize my newly acquired skills to keep them fresh. As I considered Peter and wanting to learn everything about him beyond the highlights, I chose to look up everywhere the Bible says, "the disciples" as well as every reference to Peter by name. I considered every time it says, "the disciples," Peter is included in the group and I can learn about Peter in these references, as well—and that is how this ended up being an in-depth, fifteen-week discipleship study. It is also why some of the weeks, you will wonder why we are not talking about Peter specifically. It is because we are sitting alongside of him learning from Jesus with him. As Peter grows and learns at Jesus' feet, so do we.

I have thoroughly enjoyed following Peter's transformation journey from fisherman to fisher-of-men, from boastful, self-made man to surrendered servant of Jesus. Peter is very much like any one of us. He was lost, and then he was found. He proclaimed Jesus as Lord and Savior, the Messiah, then began to follow Jesus, transforming him from the very core of his being.

In reformatting this study, week one, day one ended up being too, but I did not want to cut any of this foundational information. To make it more palatable, I relocated a significant portion of the notes to the introduction. Since this took away some of your opportunity for self-discovery. I decided to give you the option to do it by adding the questions to the introduction. You can assess how busy your life is and decide whether to complete this portion of the study or read the introduction notes and save your studying for day one.

Bonus Study

From: Matthew 4:18; Mark 1:16–21, 29-32; Luke 5:1–3, 10

1. What was Peter's occupation?

2. Who were Peter's business partners?

3. Where did Peter live, and with whom did he live?

Peter is first introduced in the Gospels while on the shore of the Sea of Galilee (Matthew 4:18; Mark 1:16; Luke 5:1–3). The Sea of Galilee is known in scripture by three other names: Sea of Chinnereth or Chineroth (Numbers 34:11; Joshua 12:3, 13:27), Lake of Gennesaret (Luke 5:1), and Sea of Tiberias (John 6:1, 2:1). Chinnereth/Chineroth is Hebrew for "harp-shaped." This refers to the lake's shape, and it was a name used in Old Testament times. The name "Gennesaret" was given in relation to the Plain of Gennesaret, which was located on the northwest side of the lake (Matthew 14:34). "Tiberias" was used due to its connection with the capital of Herod Antipas, and the Sea of Galilee was synonymous with the name of the region in which it was found.

The Sea of Galilee is located sixty miles north of Jerusalem, is fed by the Jordan River, and is the deepest part of the Jordan. It is 80 to 160 feet deep, close to thirteen miles long, and eight miles wide. Galilee is surrounded by steeply rising mountains on its north, west, and east sides. The east side of the sea rises to twenty-seven hundred feet to the Golan Heights. Cool winds charge over and down the mountainous terrain from the east to the sea and cause sudden, violent storms.

Fishing was the backbone of the economy. Filled with several kinds of carp, the lake supported a thriving fishing industry. The nets were made from rope or cord woven from flax, papyrus, or hemp. They were narrow at one end and attached to the boat. The wider end would be cast off of the boat and sunk with weights. They would fish all night and sell their catch in the morning. They would pickle the fish or make gravies out of them. Just as fishing was central to the economy, fish was a staple of the Galilean diet. Fishermen's wages landed them somewhere between rich and comfortable.

We know Peter lived in Capernaum because "as they had come out of the synagogue, they entered the house of Simon and Andrew, with James and John" (Mark 1:29). The way Mark wrote it causes us to believe Peter lived close to the synagogue. We also know that he did not live far, because an Israelite could only travel a Sabbath day's journey on the Sabbath. This means Peter had to live within a mile of the synagogue. However, the wording of Mark's Gospel causes the reader to assume Peter's home was very close to the synagogue. We also learn Peter lived with his brother Andrew, his wife (implied), and his mother-in-law. It is possible Peter and Andrew inherited the home from their father and then took in Peter's mother-in-law when her husband passed. This would be customary in New Testament Galilee; however, it is not written in scripture but is merely an educated guess.

Capernaum was a large fishing town on the northwest shore of the Sea of Galilee. Situated on a major trading route, many travelers, Jew and Gentile, visited Capernaum. The route, which became known as the Way of the Sea, connected Damascus to the Mediterranean coast. Capernaum was most likely settled after the Israelites returned of from captivity. It was large enough to be called a city in the New Testament. The name translated means "Village of Nahum" (not to be confused with or connected to the prophet Nahum).

Galilee's inhabitants were ethnically and religiously Jewish. We know Capernaum had a synagogue, because Peter lived near it. Mark's Gospel tells us Jesus taught there as well as healed a man who suffered a demonic spirit (Mark 1:21– 26). The most interesting fact about the synagogue in Capernaum is a Gentile built it. Luke 5:1–11 tells the story of a Roman centurion who sent his servants to ask Jesus to come and heal his servant who was sick. As the servants came to Jesus, they told Him the centurion loved the nation of Israel and built them a synagogue. This was the centurion Jesus marveled at and said, "I say to you, I have not found such great faith, not even in Israel" (Matthew 8:10). As we follow the life of Peter, we will see Capernaum as a center for Jesus' ministry.

He did much of His teaching on and around the Sea of Galilee, returning to Capernaum and Peter's home. Jesus spent much time in the synagogue there, teaching and healing. It was Peter's house where they brought many of their sick after the Sabbath had ended (Mark 1:32–34). Jesus was a generous guest. When He entered Peter and Andrew's home, He saw Peter's mother-in-law, who was sick, and healed her. Her appropriate response was to rise and serve them (Mark 1:29–31). Many other healings and miracles happened in and around Peter's home. We will learn about these together as we continue through this study.

How Peter Lived

The Gospels tell us Peter was casting, mending, or washing nets. How could all three Gospels give differing stories? First of all, Matthew, Luke, and John do not seem to be far apart from one another. It seems perfectly acceptable that washing and mending could be done at the same time. Mark's Gospel, however, said Peter and Andrew were casting their net into the sea. What is important here is not what is different, but what is the same. The point each author was making was Peter's occupation as a fisherman.

As noted in the introduction, fishing was a lucrative business. James and John left their father in the boat with the hired servants to go and follow Jesus. We see two things here: First, fishing was a family business. Second, it allowed for the hiring of servants. James and John's business seems quite lucrative. This helps us understand the gravity for them and the other fishermen, forsaking all to follow Jesus. It was an impressive move. They left certain security and the ability to provide for their families, not to mention leaving the family business and the expectation of their father, to follow a Teacher who could not promise financial security, as far as they knew.

Peter had three partners in business. Peter's first partner was his brother Andrew (Matthew 4:18; Mark 1:16). They most likely received their fishing business from their father. Peter's father had most likely passed away by this time, as he was not mentioned in relation to fishing, and the house was referred to as Simon (Peter) and Andrew's. Peter's other two business partners were James and John, the sons of Zebedee. We know this because when Peter's catch was too large, he called them over to help him. Luke 5:7 tells us they were his business partners. Their fathers may have known each other and worked together for many years.

THE CALL AND THE DISCIPLE

Day One: A Man Called

Read: John 1:35–42.

1. How did Peter hear of Jesus and/or hear Jesus at first?

Read: Luke 5:4–11.

2. How long did Peter say they had fished and caught nothing?

3. When and where did Jesus tell them to fish?

4. How did Peter respond to Jesus' command to fish? What characteristic does this show about Peter?

5. What resulted from Peter's obedience to Jesus?

6. Who did they call for help?

7. How did Peter respond to Jesus after the great catch of fish? What character traits are shown in Peter's response?

Personal Reflection

8. Describe a time you had a similar experience with Jesus?

How Peter Met Jesus

According to John's Gospel, Andrew had been a follower of John the Baptist and heard him say, "Behold the Lamb of God!" referring to Jesus (John 1:36). Upon hearing this, Andrew and another disciple sought to know where Jesus was staying, and Jesus invited them to see. John mentioned it was about the tenth hour, which would be late afternoon. Jesus most likely was being hospitable in inviting them to stay until evening (or even overnight before going on their way in the morning). It would have been a customary invitation in New Testament Israel. This helps make sense of how Andrew could have gone to bring Peter to Jesus to hear Him, and how Peter and Andrew could have been washing nets together when Jesus came upon them.

It is possible to conclude from the four Gospels that Andrew left Jesus after their first meeting to go and inform his family (Peter) of the man John the Baptist called the Lamb of God. It is also plausible Peter had gone with Andrew and heard Jesus speak at some point before Jesus came walking by the Sea of Galilee (Matthew 4:18). However, we *know* Jesus came walking along the Sea of Galilee. He met His disciples where they were. Jesus did not wait for them to come to Him in a synagogue or elsewhere. He came to where they lived and worked, and met them in their element. Jesus even spoke to them from their own sphere of understanding: "Follow Me, and I will make you fishers of men" (Matthew 4:19; Mark 1:18).

The Catch

Luke's Gospel recounts Jesus telling Peter to put out into the deep and cast his net for a catch of fish. Peter, the seasoned fisherman, grumbled about the request. Peter let Jesus know they had already worked all night and caught nothing. Yet he gave the responsibility to Jesus by saying, "At your word I will let down my net" (Luke 5:4, 5). Peter knew one fished in the deep at night and in the shallow waters during the day on the Sea of Galilee. Peter probably felt the Teacher should stick to His area of expertise and let Peter worry about the fishing: his area of expertise. He let down his net, and to his utter surprise, there were too many fish for him to haul into his boat. He had to call his business partners to help bring in the load.

The boastful, experienced fisherman who'd set out to prove the Teacher wrong (in front of a crowd) "fell down at Jesus' knees, saying, 'Depart from me, for I am a sinful man, O Lord!'" (Luke 5:8). Why did Peter react this way? Because, in his pride, he'd set out to prove a man wrong, and in his failing to do so, he was humbled and recognized Jesus *was* special. He may not have fully understood Him as the Messiah, but he most likely recognized Him as a great prophet due to the miracle he had just experienced. This shows Peter, though a boastful man, could also be humble, repentant, and teachable.

This is what Jesus is looking for in all His disciples: people who are able to humble themselves, admit when they are wrong, repent of their sins, and be teachable. Is there anything weighing on your heart as you work through this lesson? Will you take a moment to humble yourself before the Lord and admit you were wrong, repent of the wrong, and ask Jesus to teach you a better way, to be more like Him?

Day Two: A Man Called

Read: Matthew 4:18–20; Mark 1:16–18; Luke 5:10, 11;

1. What was Peter's response to Jesus' invitation?

2. How do you reconcile the variations in the gospel accounts?

Personal Reflection

3. Have you responded to Jesus' invitation to follow Him? If yes, how was your response similar to or different from Peter's response?

How Peter Responded to Jesus

People so often marvel at the disciples when they read the Gospels. We are amazed by how Jesus could walk up to a guy and say, "Follow Me," and he just drops what he's doing and follows Him in almost robotic submission. However, with a closer look at the Gospel records, we see Peter was told of Jesus by his brother Andrew, who said he had found the Messiah. John also tells us that Andrew took Peter to Jesus, so Peter had an opportunity to hear Jesus speak (John 1:41).

John's Gospel tells us Jesus changed Simon's name to Peter the first time they met, while Matthew 16:18 records Jesus changing Peter's name after his divinely revealed confession that Jesus was the Christ. The difference is easily explained in John's Gospel account, giving Peter in a future tense, pointing to the Matthew 16:18 moment. It is possible John did this at the beginning, because his audience knew Simon as Peter, which would allay any confusion.

Peter had met Jesus before the invitation came. He had time to know of Jesus and even hear Jesus speak. He had time to ponder what he heard during those late-night fishing trips. He had time to think about the teachings of Jesus and consider the Man. When Jesus came and said to Peter and Andrew, "Follow Me, and I will make you become fishers of men," Peter and Andrew were ready; they left all and followed Jesus. They had already had enough time to think about the Man and were willing to leave all to follow Him. The same can be said for James and John.

There is a time when we know about Jesus; there is a time when we might hear some of Jesus' teachings; and there is a time when Jesus calls us to leave all and follow Him. Have you answered the call to follow Jesus as one of His disciples? If not, why not? If yes, have you truly forsaken all to follow Him? This doesn't mean you should leave your family or the family business, as Peter did. To forsake all and follow Jesus is to love Jesus above all else in your life. Jesus must become more important to you than your parents, spouse, children, family, friends, job, and yourself. He must come first in all things in your life. You do not have to love them less to place Jesus first.

Did you feel conviction in your spirit over any of these things? If you felt the Holy Spirit convicting you in any of these areas, would you stop and repent of making any of the above an idol in your life? Anything placed above Jesus in importance in your life is an idol. Apologize to the Lord, ask Him to forgive you, and then put things in proper order in your heart and mind.

Many New Testament Jews believed to honor one's parents was the greatest commandment. Taking care of one's aging family members was of high priority in Peter's day. We already mentioned businesses were often handed down from father to son, so to abandon one's job was to abandon one's family's finances as well as their expectations. Therefore, for Peter, Andrew, James, and John to leave their families and family businesses was not just an enormous sacrifice on their part; it also went contrary to their culture. Their families would not be the only ones to frown upon their actions; so would their community. However, this shows even greater the sacrifice they were willing to make to follow Jesus.

What sacrifices are you (or have you been) willing to make to follow Jesus? Have you left your hometown? Have you left friends, family, or a job? Have you gone against the grain of your culture's ideals? Is there a sacrifice Jesus is asking you to make that you struggle to yield to? Ask Him to strengthen your faith so you can walk in the fullness of abundance He has promised you. There is no greater freedom than being centered in the perfect will of God.

Another cultural negative could have arisen in New Testament Capernaum in Jesus' calling His disciples to follow Him. It was not the cultural norm for a rabbi to enlist followers. Rather, disciples found teachers they desired to follow and joined them. It was a cultural *faux pas* for Jesus to call His disciples to follow Him, and yet how impressive it was when they cast off the cares of their culture and the traditions of men to follow when He called.

Read: John 21:1–7; Romans 3:23, 8:1.

4. After Jesus' resurrection, He showed Himself to the disciples several times. Where did He meet them, specifically Peter, this time? Why do you think Jesus met Peter in this context?

5. Had they caught any fish after fishing all night this time?

6. What did Jesus tell them to do? Did they yet recognize who He was? Had they recognized who He was the first time this happened?

7. How many fish did they catch this time?

8. Who figured out who was on shore, and how did Peter respond to the news?

9. What does this story teach about failing the Lord in your walk with Him?

A Man Restored

Jesus called Peter, the fisherman, to become a fisher of men. Peter spent the rest of Jesus' earthly ministry trying to find his place in this calling. At the end of Jesus' earthly ministry, Peter failed his commitment to Jesus, and his despair went deep.

Peter again boasted when he said, "If I have to die with You, I will not deny You" (Matthew 26:35). This boast was in response to Jesus' telling Peter he would deny Him three times before the rooster crowed (Matthew 26:34). Peter, once again, discovered Jesus was right. Just as Jesus was right about lowering his nets the first time, He was right again, knowing Peter would deny Him. When Peter's final denial escaped his lips and his eyes met Jesus' across the courtyard, it was more than he could bear. He went out and wept bitterly (Luke 22:60, 61).

When Jesus appeared again to the disciples, Peter was still without direction following his failure. He went to Tiberias, and other disciples followed him there. Not knowing what else to do with himself, Peter announced he was going fishing. He returned to the last thing he knew before he left all to follow Jesus. This was one venue Jesus chose to show Himself again to the disciples, those fishermen He had called to be fishers of men, after an entire night of fishing in which they had caught nothing (John 21:1–7).

According to John 21:4, the disciples did not recognize Jesus physically when He called from the shore to inquire about their catch. Jesus, as at first, suggested they cast their net one more time, but this time He said, "and you will find some" (John 21:6). Peter's new response to this request was to do it. He had no arrogant pride, causing him to call back to shore and say they had fished all night and caught nothing. We see a changed man. He was a man who had learned some humility; a man who had been broken by arrogance; a man who could now be used for kingdom purposes.

When the fishermen cast their nets on the right side, they caught a multitude of fish. It was John, Peter's former business partner called to help him out the first time, who first made the connection. When he saw the net full of fish, he may have flashed back to their first calling to be fishers of men. He looked toward Peter and said, "It is the Lord" (John 21:7).

Peter's jubilee came when he, too, made the connection to the first miraculous catch and this one. The first catch brought an invitation for him to follow Jesus. This miraculous catch offered hope of restoration to the first call. Peter had been feeling his failure, but again, Jesus was there blessing his work. Peter could do nothing more than jump from the boat and run to Jesus. As we learned earlier, men fished in the deep at night and the shallows during the day. Jesus did not tell them to go out to the deep this time, but instead to cast their net where they were. They were most likely already in the shallow water when Jesus called out to them. This explains why Peter could jump from the boat and run to the Lord.

We will learn more in future lessons about the time Jesus spent with Peter on the shore. In short, Peter learned two things through the experience: First, he learned "all have sinned and fallen short of the glory of God" (Romans 3:23). Peter was a proud and boastful fisherman when he met Jesus. In the end, he claimed he would not fail the Lord, but he did. He learned he was capable of falling short of the Lord's glory. The second lesson Peter learned was when we fall short, Jesus makes up the difference: "There is therefore now no condemnation to those who are in Christ Jesus, who do not walk according to the flesh, but according to the Spirit" (Romans 8:1). Peter learned at this meeting with Jesus there was forgiveness and restoration available to all who would ask. Through repentance, restoration is made possible by the shed blood of Jesus. He restored Peter to his calling to be a fisher of men, and it was Peter's great jubilee.

"Jubilee" refers to a Jewish festival in which lands were restored to their original owners and debts were cancelled every fiftieth year in Israel. Peter had surely been restored to his original calling, and his debt was cancelled when Jesus died upon the Cross. He was free to be all Jesus had created and called him to be.

What about you? Are you walking in your jubilee? Are you set free from your debts by accepting Jesus' death on your behalf to pay for those debts? Have you thanked Him for carrying your debt to the Cross and paying your penalty? Have you asked Him to rule and reign in your heart? If you have walked with the Lord but feel as though you've lost your way, will you seek His forgiveness to restore to you your jubilee? If you need help with this, reach out to a spiritual leader in your study group or church to pray with and help you walk through these things. However, this is something you can do on your own, as well. Have an honest conversation with Jesus (pray) and ask His forgiveness and restoration. Then find someone in your study, a Christian mentor or a leader in your church, and tell them about the commitment you just made so they can celebrate with you.

Day Three: The Disciple

Read: Matthew 8:23–27; Mark 4:35–41; Luke 8:22–25; Acts 12:3–6.

1. Where was Jesus in the midst of the storm, and what was He doing?

2. How severe was the storm?

3. What do you think the disciples were doing amid the storm?

4. Why did they call on Jesus? Who was more experienced at handling a boat?

5. Why did Jesus say they were of little faith?

6. What did Jesus do to help? How did the disciples respond?

7. What did Peter learn about storms? (See Acts 12:3–6.)

Personal Reflection

8. How have you weathered the storms in your life? What do you most need to do if you are experiencing a storm in your life right now?

Jesus Calms the Storm

Jesus was at the end of a full day of ministering, and He wanted to head to the other side of the sea. The disciples were immediately obedient to get into the boat with Him. They expected no trouble. At least four skilled fishermen were on board, whose custom it was to fish at night. They even took Jesus "as He was," making no preparations for emergencies (Mark 4:36).

Capernaum and Gennesaret are on the northwest shores of Galilee. The distance by boat was about five miles. The vessel would most likely have been a small fishing boat common to the area. It was low to the water, with a large main sail to propel it. A raised bench was found in the stern, which would have either a leather cover or a pillow upon it. It would be the only place where a person could sleep undisturbed in a boat taking on water.

Jesus found His first moment's peace after a full day of ministry as He got into the boat. It was His first moment of peace in a few days. He was tired. He went to rest on the bench in the stern. We see a picture of Jesus' humanity as He, too, became tired after a full day and needed to sleep. He was in good hands with the experienced sailors, so He could drift off to sleep and allow them to transport them to the next destination for ministry. However, as they made their way, the wind rushed down upon the lake and violently disturbed the waters. The wind would have been loud, and the boat would have been rocking violently. The disciple-sailors were probably hollering back and forth over the wind, working together to survive the storm while Jesus slept peacefully.

According to Matthew, just before Jesus and the disciples entered the boat, a scribe approached Jesus and claimed he would follow Him anywhere He went. Jesus answered, "Foxes have holes and birds of the air have nests, but the Son of Man has nowhere to lay His head" (Matthew 8:20). Here we see Jesus with no home but lying in the stern of a fishing boat, on the water, in a storm, with His head resting tranquilly upon a pillow. We see divine provision for one walking in the will of God. We also see the rest of One who lives a sinless life. A clear conscience sleeps deeply.

While Jesus enjoyed His much-needed rest, the disciples embarked on what they expected to be a smooth trip to Gennesaret. They may have felt good to be able to serve Jesus in this way, to provide travel so the teacher could rest. They had most likely seen miracles of physical healing and demonic deliverance by then. They must have been proud to have been handpicked by Him to be His disciples. Maybe they were even looking forward with anticipation to see what would come of their time in Gennesaret.

As we stated earlier, the winds could suddenly pick up from the east, causing the Sea of Galilee to become very rough. These seasoned fishermen knew what they were up against the moment the storm began to pick up. They had embarked without preparations and knew they had a fight on their hands. They also knew and held the pressure of transporting Jesus; whether He was a great prophet or the Messiah, He was in their care. They must have felt the tremendous weight of responsibility.

Reading this section of scripture, it is easy to remember how Peter did not want any help from Jesus regarding fishing. Peter, after all, was the experienced fisherman, and Jesus a mere teacher. He knew there would be no fish in the deep during the day. Then the miracle happened: a great catch of fish. Here he is again: Peter, the experienced fisherman, with at least three other experienced seafaring men, battling a familiar storm on a familiar sea in a familiar boat. The difference was being on a five-mile trek with a very important passenger on board.

The disciples mustered all of their strength and experience to fight the storm. They managed their sail and fought the water coming into the boat, but they soon realized their efforts would not save them. They knew very well the danger they were in and turned to see Jesus, sleeping while they struggled to save their very lives *and* His.

The disciples did all they could do. When they could do no more but succumb to the storm and perish, they cried out to Jesus for help. Mark's Gospel reads as though they were somewhat angry with Jesus: "Teacher, do You not care that we are perishing?" (Mark 4:38). Do you see the comedy in this statement? Think of Peter, the all-knowing fisherman, who initially did not want Jesus' help because He was simply a teacher, not a fisherman. Now Peter and the other disciples questioned whether or not Jesus cared whether they were perishing, as if to say, "Why are You not helping us?" Yet it is entirely possible Jesus was waiting for them to reach the end of their strength before He could display His saving strength.

How many times have you been in the midst of a storm of life and felt like Jesus must be asleep in the stern? Have you ever cried out something similar to, "Lord, do You not care?" If you have not cried it out, have you ever just felt this way or wondered where Jesus was amid your terrible ordeal? Yes, maybe He is asleep in the stern. Perhaps He is waiting for you to get to the end of yourself, your strength, your understanding, and your own need for control, to the place where you can throw your hands up in surrender and cry out to Him for help. He can move in power, because you have gotten out of the way by yielding yourself to Him and His will and power. It is a humbling moment. It teaches us we must rely on Him alone in all things. Are you in a place right now where you struggle to control a situation you need to give up to the Lord and trust Him with? If you are afraid to give Him control, ask Him to strengthen your faith.

Matthew and Luke's Gospels agree: The disciples cried out to Jesus either "Lord" or "Master," which was a respectful title (such as "mister" or "sir"), "We are perishing!" (Matthew 8:25; Luke 8:24). However, Matthew's Gospel adds one sentence of interest: "Lord save us!" (Matthew 8:25). It was an almost-prophetic utterance. Later, when Jesus entered Jerusalem, the crowd cried out, "Hosanna (Oh, save)," to Jesus. It was an exclamation of adoration. Peter later said of Jesus, "Nor is there salvation in any other, for there is no other name under heaven given among men by which we must be saved" (Acts 4:12).

In this moment upon the sea, their boat filling with water, they were literally crying out to Jesus, the Teacher, to save them from perishing upon the water. The experienced fishermen were crying out to the Teacher, whose help was not initially appreciated, to save them. What did they think He was going to do? Did they actually expect Him to do anything, or were they crying out in desperation?

Jesus stood up in the boat. Try to visualize it. He spoke to the wind and the waves, "Peace, be still" (Mark 4:39). The wind and waves were immediately and intensely calm. Did He yell into the wind? Did He simply speak with authority? Mark's Gospel reports Jesus "said," suggesting He merely spoke the words of authority over the elements, and they obeyed His voice.

Greek mythology, commonly known in Bible times, ascribed power over nature to gods alone. Jewish history acknowledged humanity's ability to pray for changes in nature, such as Elijah's ability to pray for rain, but ascribes authority over nature to no man. Jewish history ascribes power over nature solely to the One True God (Psalms 107:23–30).

Jesus questioned His disciples. The question to determine was whether He was rebuking their lack of faith or encouraging them to greater faith? The miracles they had seen up to this point had not pointed to Jesus as having power over nature. Jewish record had never noted a man of flesh and bone ever having such power. Would it have been fair to expect the disciples to assume this power in Jesus, even with the miracles they had already experienced? Jesus first revealed He had power over sickness; so did other prophets. Jesus showed power over demons, to cast out and to silence them. No one else had done this. Yet, how far could a disciple's mind be stretched at this point in history? It is easy to look back and see what was obvious, but the disciples expected an earthly Messiah to rule and reign on the earth. They had no idea the breadth of Jesus' Messianic calling and ability. Each step was a step of revelation, building their faith.

Jesus asked, "Why are you fearful, O you of little faith?" (Matthew 8:26). This does not appear to be a rebuke. He acknowledged they had a *little* faith. Yet, Het intended to use this opportunity to grow their faith and expand their minds to possibilities not yet fathomed. These seasoned fishermen misplaced their little faith when they began to believe more in the storm than in the Savior. While they did not understand the breadth of the Messiah's reign and power, they should have believed the

Messiah would be protected at all costs (Psalms 91). If God were the God they believed in, they should have had faith in the protection available to them because they were in the boat with the Messiah. The Messiah must live and rule and reign. Yet they allowed their panic and fear to silence their faith. They relied on their expert, earthly experience. Jesus was releasing spiritual awareness through supernatural experiences.

When Jesus calls and you obey, you are in His will and under His divine protection. He doesn't promise there will be no storms along the way, but getting out of the boat (out of the will of God) will place you in the storm unprotected. There is no greater, safer, or better place to be than the center of God's will. Anyone can weather a storm in obedience and, with faith intact, experience a deep calm in their spirit and soul to carry them through. Are you in a storm right now? Is it a storm God has called you to walk through? Then have the peace of knowing He is in the stern, able and available to see you through it. If you are in a storm you caused, you can still cry out for Him to save you. He will pull you back into the boat if you are ready to let go of whatever you are hanging on to and give your trust fully to Him. He is able.

Jesus' followers must take this journey with this knowledge: "Sometimes God saves us from trouble; sometimes He saves us in trouble; sometimes He saves us from death; and sometimes He uses our death to glorify His name" (Carson, et al. 1994). What is most important is being in His will. Regardless of His chosen outcome, His will is the only place for a disciple to be found. Peter later wrote of trials and faith, "In this you greatly rejoice, though now for a little while, if need be, you have been grieved by various trials, that the genuineness of your faith, being much more precious than gold that perishes, though it is tested by fire, may be found to praise, honor, and glory at the revelation of Jesus Christ, whom having not seen you love. Though now you do not see Him, yet believing, you rejoice with joy inexpressible and full of glory, receiving the end of your faith—the salvation of your souls" (1 Peter 1:6–9). Jesus asked this question as He displayed His power over nature. We see the disciples' faith grow in their reaction to the surreal miracle they had just witnessed. They knew God was the only ascribed power over nature. They went from raging storm to deep calm in an instant, and they asked the all-important question, a question every person must be confronted with: "Who can this be?" (Luke 8:25).

Was the storm a surprise to Jesus or a tool He used to bring the disciples to this question? Was it a tool He used to broaden their minds and strengthen their faith? We need to view trials in a completely different way. The way of faith will view a storm as a momentary tool the Lord is using to grow us to be more like Him, as well as to broaden our minds to understand more about who He is, and to build our faith. With this knowledge, we can meet our next storm with faith to make it to the other side, knowing (believing) we will be better once we arrive. When you find yourself in a storm, train your focus on the finish line; it will give you the strength to weather the storm in His care. For He said in Isaiah 41:10, "Fear not, for I am with you; be not dismayed, for I am your God. I will strengthen you, yes, I will help you, I will uphold you with My righteous right hand."

Days Four and Five: The Disciple

Read: Matthew 9:9–13; Luke 5:27–32; 1 Corinthians 5:9–11.

1. Whose house was Jesus dining at? Have you seen Him do something like this before?

2. Who else did the host invite to dinner? Why do you think he invited them?

3. Who complained about Jesus dining with this group? To whom did they complain?

4. Who answered them, and what was the reply?

5. Why did Jesus come?

6. (Challenge) What was wrong with Jesus dining with this group in the eyes of those who grumbled against Him? Why was it right for Him to dine with them?

7. When is it right to dine with sinners? When is it not right?

8. What do you think Peter took away from this experience?

9. What lesson might you apply from this week's lesson?

Jesus Dines with Sinners

Matthew, being a tax collector, worked for the state. He was a Roman government employee. Tax collectors received their salaries by increasing taxes on their people and keeping the difference. Much like today, the tax collector was unpopular. However, in Matthew's day, they were not just disliked because people didn't like paying taxes, but because they were viewed as extortionists and collaborators with an enemy government. Pious Jews considered tax collectors ceremonially unclean, because they were in close contact with Gentiles so much of the time.

Jews were God's chosen people. The land they were in was given to Abraham and his descendants (the Jews) by God. They were to be a sovereign nation, and they were not to cohabitate with non-Jewish peoples. This was their state, being occupied by the enemy Roman government, and it was offensive to a pious Jew to see any Jew willing to work for their oppressors.

Matthew was sitting at his tax office, probably in Capernaum, when Jesus walked by and said, "Follow Me." Scripture tells us Matthew left all and followed Jesus. Matthew was not just leaving a job but a very lucrative career and a way of life. What would cause a person to leave what they knew to follow a Man they did not know very well? Was he disillusioned in his job and looking for something new? Or had he heard Jesus speak recently and realized He had something he was looking for and had not found with riches? We cannot know the answers to these questions concerning Matthew. We do know he left all to follow Jesus when He invited him, just like the other disciples.

Proper custom was for the disciples to provide the meals for their teacher. Matthew, in kind, invited Jesus to dine in his home, and he gave a banquet for all of his friends to meet his Teacher. Matthew must have been very excited about Jesus and the message He brought. We are told the banquet was full of tax collectors and sinners. This rings true, since pious Jews would not have joined a tax collector for an intimate meal of table fellowship. These were the only people who would have a tax collector as a friend.

The Pharisees were a religious and political party in Jesus' time. Their name meant "Separate Ones." They sought perfect interpretation and observation of their scripture, as the scribes interpreted it. The issues were in interpreting scripture through a lens of tradition and social customs long held by Jewish thought. However, the Pharisees' motives were to serve their God the best way they knew how. Unfortunately, they became too sure of themselves and began to admire themselves for their piety in following God's laws and for their tithing practices. They became legalistic and prideful, which caused them to take issue with those who did not do as they did or who challenged them, as Jesus' actions did on this day.

Inviting a religious teacher to dine in their home was commendable, but not for a religious leader to dine with sinners. Table fellowship implied a certain level of intimacy. Pious Jews would stay far away from tax collectors, sinners, and Gentiles, especially for table fellowship. This was where the Pharisees openly opposed Jesus for the first time. Jesus' action of dining with tax collectors and sinners would have upset their religious understanding. They would consider this to be a ceremonially unclean thing to do, because a Pharisee or pious Jew would never engage in or approve of table fellowship with such a group of people.

The problem was in how the Pharisees, in their pursuit of religious piety, had created such rules of self-protection from sin, they ostracized sinners. They would not take the message to a sinner, because they did not want to become ceremonially unclean. Therefore, in their attempts to please God, they were leaving God's children condemned, with no way of escape.

By the time this event occurred, Jesus had been in Capernaum and around Galilee for a while. He had taught in their synagogues as one having authority, healed on the Sabbath, cast out demons, and healed all kinds of sickness and disease. His ministry was public, and His fame had spread even to Syria. These pious Pharisees, being leaders in the community and feeling protective in their position, were watching Jesus very closely.

Jesus did not fear them or their legalistic rules; He challenged their understanding of God. In the synagogue in Capernaum, when Jesus cast out the demon, they even asked, "What new doctrine is this?" (Mark 1:27). It is possible the Pharisees wanted to be sure the fruit of Jesus' life matched what they esteemed to be pious, since He was gathering such a following. They came across as wanting Jesus to come under their authority as religious and political leaders, and their frustration built as He continued to outwit and expose their shortcomings from this point forward.

Notice how the Pharisees did not confront Jesus; they instead turned to His disciples. "Why does your teacher eat with such people?" (Mark 9:11). If their trouble was with Jesus' actions, they should have confronted Jesus with this challenging question. Yet they did not go to Jesus. They were not seeking to straighten out a misguided brother; they were seeking to discredit Him to His disciples, to cause them to question Him. What spirit might be behind such an act? Peter later wrote in his first letter, "Be sober, be vigilant; because your adversary the devil walks about like a roaring lion, seeking whom he may devour" (1 Peter 5:8). Does not Satan today roam around, seeking to cause Jesus' disciples to question Him? What did Satan do in the Garden with Eve? He caused her to question why God would want to keep her from knowledge. Once she questioned God with her finite understanding, she chose to sin against Him (Genesis 3). It is the first trick of Satan recorded in scripture, and it is the same trick he uses today to fool believers into sinful actions. Surely, he was using the Pharisees' pride and arrogance to encourage them along this route.

Jesus Teaches the Teachers

Jesus heard the question posed to His disciples and responded with a simple but earth-shattering truth: "People who are well do not need a doctor, but only those who are sick" (Matthew 9:12). What a profound and challenging statement for the Pharisees to hear. This was completely backwards from their beliefs and actions, yet it was profoundly true. They had been denying healing to the spiritually sick in pursuit of their piety. The truth had to hit like a slap in the face. What were they to say to this?

Jesus, God incarnate, born in a manger to a poor family, sat in intimate fellowship with the outcasts of Jewish religious society. He went to the people who knew their need and to challenge the religious leaders of the day to see their own need, as well: "A healer must get his hands dirty; and a mission of salvation cannot be achieved by staying in respectable company" (New Bible Commentary, p. 916).

Jesus knew the Pharisees prided themselves on knowledge and implementation of scripture, so He offered them a scripture to study for themselves: "But go and learn what this means: 'I desire mercy and not sacrifice'" (Matthew 9:13). This would hit to the core of the Pharisees' doctrine. They were intent on keeping religious ritual and esteeming themselves as nearly perfect in their obedience to the law. However, this is what God had been saying to them over and over throughout the centuries: Love God first, then love fellow man.

Jesus took this statement from Hosea. It describes what Jesus meant when He said it to the Pharisees. God is a relational God. He desires humankind to have a right relationship with Him first and then with each other. People cannot have a good relationship with each other unless their relationship with God is right first. The Pharisees had watered God's law down to a series of rules and rituals to appease God. In this, they were treating Him more like an idol than the living God. Jesus offered them a doorway to correct their error.

Hosea 6:6 says, "For I desire mercy and not sacrifice, and the knowledge of God more than burnt offerings." God's laws are instituted for our protection. God, who created us, knows best what we need to function at our highest level. God's laws reveal God's heart for humankind while teaching us how to cohabitate in the best possible way. At the core, God's law is relational; it teaches the right relationship with God and the right relationship with one's neighbor. When relationship is taken out of the mix, it becomes nothing more than idol worship and pointless ritual. Jesus guided His disciples back to relationship and challenged the Pharisees to change their doctrine from ritual to relationship.

Day Six: The Call and The Disciple

1. Review this week's lessons and highlight your big takeaways. Be prepared to share these if you are meeting with a group.

2. Did you learn something about Peter this week? Share your thoughts.

3. How do you see your big takeaway(s) relating to the world around you today? To the Church in the broader sense, or the local church?

4. How might you apply one of these takeaways this week?

WITNESS AND APOSTLE OF HEALING MIRACLES

Day One: Witness to Healing Miracles

Read: Matthew 9:18–19, 28; Mark 5:21–24; Luke 8:40–42.

1. (Challenge) When Jesus crossed again by boat to the other side, where was He?

2. (Challenge) Matthew 9:28 says, "When He had come into the house." Whose house? Why is this significant?

3. Who came and asked Jesus to lay hands on his daughter? What was his profession?

4. What was Jesus' response to the man?

5. What happened as they were on the way?

The Desperate Act of a Jewish Leader

Jesus returned to Capernaum, where He had spoken in the synagogue and healed many times. It was also where He stayed, at Peter's house, where many brought the sick for Him to heal. Peter's home would become a center for Jesus' ministry. He and His disciples once again travelled to their destination in a small fishing boat.

When He arrived on the shore, He was met by a great multitude. Mark 5:21 tells us it was not just a multitude, but a great multitude. Jesus had already amassed a considerable following, as He prioritized spending time with outcasts. He drew them by loving, by lifestyle, and by healing. Jesus had shown kindness to the broken-hearted. They had received a love they had never known from someone they knew was very special. They may not have fully understood who He was, but they must have been awed by the powerful Man of God who chose to dine with them rather than with church or city leaders. He was bringing hope to the hopeless.

Jesus was met by the multitude on the shore. Jairus also met Him there. Scripture tells us Jairus was a ruler of the synagogue. As an official in the synagogue, he would have been a prominent community member. His job was to administrate and arrange services and other dealings in the synagogue; however, the work was done by others. This was most likely the synagogue in Capernaum where Jesus astonished the crowd by teaching with authority and casting out a demon (Luke 4:31–36).

Due to Jairus' position, he could have sent a servant to seek Jesus' help, but he went personally. This prominent man came to Jesus in his desperation, not caring about the great multitude of outcasts, his colleagues, or his reputation in the community. All hope was gone for Jairus, so he traveled to Jesus and humbled himself in His presence. For Jairus to fall at Jesus' feet was an act of humility and a position of worship (Matthew 9:18; Mark 5:22). Jairus had most likely seen Jesus heal others; now he needed to know if He would do the same for his daughter.

The beauty is seen in Jesus' willingness to be interrupted by Jairus' humble pleading while faced with a multitude of needs. He stopped what He was doing and followed him. There is a point in every person's life when they have to decide who Jesus is to them and where He stands in the priorities of one's life. This was such an occasion for Jairus. There he was, ruler of the synagogue (of the One True God), a well-known figure in the community, and he had been brought to a point where he was desperate enough to fall to his knees publicly and confess his need for Jesus. He also displayed a certain amount of faith in Jesus to heal his daughter.

Every person has to come to Jesus of their own accord. Have you decided, with firm resolve, who Jesus is to you? Have you been experiencing your relationship with Jesus, or do you vicariously experience this relationship through others? If you do not have a personal relationship with Jesus, you do not have to wait until a desperate situation arises. Stop right now and tell Him you believe you are a sinner in need of a savior, and you believe He is the Savior. Ask Him to come in and be Lord of your life today, and begin an eternal and personal relationship with Jesus.

Matthew's Gospel says Jairus' daughter was already dead, while Mark and Luke say she was ill. Matthew's account is condensed, as he does not give as much detail to the story as the other two writers. Matthew was writing to Jews to show Jesus as the long-awaited Messiah. Maybe he was trying not to offend his reader at this point and merely wanted to make the point of restoring the dead to life. We will return to this on day three, as we first traverse another interruption in the flow of events.

Day Two: Witness to Healing Miracles

> According to Brown, Driver, & Briggs, the word used for "wing" can also
> be translated as "tassel" or "garment" (Brown, Driver, and Briggs 2003, 489).

Read: Matthew 9:20–22; Mark 5:25–34; Luke 8:43–48; Malachi 4:2; Leviticus 15:19–27.

1. Where did the woman touch Jesus?

2. What did the Jews expect the Messiah to have in His wings or tassels? (See Malachi 4:2.)

3. What do you think this woman believed about Jesus?

4. What was wrong with what this woman did? Why did she fear and tremble?

5. What was unique in Jesus' response to her? What do you think this taught Peter and the other disciples? How might this have challenged them?

The Desperate Faith of an Unclean Woman

Jesus and Jairus walked toward his home to minister to his dying daughter; the great multitude followed them. Whether they had been waiting for Jesus to return because they needed healing, wanted to hear His teachings, or wanted to see a miracle, they were not going to let Him out of their sight. Maybe they were curious to witness if He would heal Jairus' daughter. For whatever reason, the crowd followed, and Mark 5:24 tells us the crowd thronged Jesus. This means they were pressing in on every side of Him. The crowd touched him from all sides; this was the scene as a woman, desperate for healing, reached out and touched the hem of His garment.

  The woman had a flow of blood for twelve years. This flow of blood was a menstrual flow. According to Leviticus 12:2, a woman with a flow of blood was unclean during the time of her flow and for seven days after her flow stopped. During this time, the woman would be set apart from everyone else: family, husband, children, and society. It was a time of complete isolation. Here, we have a woman whose flow had not stopped for twelve years. A woman with this issue for twelve years would not only have physical problems, but also religious and social complications, as well. Her social value would diminish, and her marriage prospects would be non-existent. She would have no friends or socialization, a religious and social outcast. Many teachers avoided touching women at all, lest they be made ceremonially unclean by accident. When made unclean, a person must bathe, wash their clothes, and remain unclean until evening (Leviticus 15:11–19).

  Mark's Gospel also tells us this woman spent all she had going to doctors, and suffered many things at their hands (Mark 5:26). At this time, Jewish and Gentile doctors used superstitious remedies rather than scientific knowledge to treat patients. This was a woman desperate for help, desperate for a life, who saw a ray of hope in Jesus. She was possibly one of the great multitude who waited for Jesus upon the shore. If this were the case, she took a significant risk of being found out by the crowd, as well as taking the risk of causing others to become unclean.

The woman's condition should have rendered her fearful of approaching Jesus, yet her faith in who He was produced a faith act of near-heroic proportions. She risked public disgrace and further exile by just entering the crowd. Yet in her desperation, she chose to act on faith. What sort of faith would cause her to act? She believed a simple touch to the hem of His garment would heal her (Matthew 9:21). She would be spared public humiliation and rejection. She could sneak up behind Him and merely touch the hem of his garment. No one would have to know.

Why did this woman believe merely touching the hem of Jesus' garment would bring healing to her body? The edge of the robe may refer to the tassels worn at the four corners of the outer garment. The tassels and weaving around the hem of the garment were to remind the people of God's commandments (Numbers 15:37–41; Deuteronomy 12:12). The word for "tassel" can also be translated as "wing." Malachi 4:2 says, "But to you who fear My name, The Sun of Righteousness shall arise with healing in His wings."

Many Jews expected the Messiah would have healing in the tassels of His garment. This woman believed she could be healed by touching the hem of Jesus' garment – the tassel. This speaks to who she believed Him to be: the long-awaited Messiah. Her faith in the healing power in His tassels gave her the courage to reach out for her healing. She did not have to confront Jesus and expose herself to the crowd. Instead, she just had to come from behind by faith and grasp a tassel. No one would even have to know, and then she could have a normal life.

The woman did not expect Jesus' ability to feel the power-surge of healing flow out of Him (Mark 5:30). Jesus knew who touched Him, but he gave her the chance to come forward rather than be called out. He responded to her faith but was not satisfied with a covert healing. He desired a personal relationship. He would make her know she was fully accepted and confirm her healing before the great multitude, including Jairus, a synagogue ruler. In one sentence, Jesus restored her social and religious life to her. The personal relationship with Jesus healed more than her body. She must have been overwhelmed by Jesus' loving acceptance of her after she performed an act which, if she had not been healed, would have made Him unclean. However, Jesus was never worried about being made unclean by a soul who needed His touch. Just as He reached out and touched the leper and said, "I am willing; be cleansed," He was also moved to respond to the woman's faith (Matthew 8:3). This is why faith moves mountains, because it moves the heart of God.

Day Three: Witness to Healing Miracles

Read: Matthew 9:23–26; Mark 5:35–43; Luke 8:49–56.

1. What turned Jesus' attention back to the sick girl?

2. What two things did Jesus tell the father to do or not do?

> It was customary for mourners to come and weep, wail, and make a big noise over the death of someone. This is who Jesus met as He came to and entered the house.

3. What did Jesus say to the mourners?

4. Why did they laugh at Him?

5. Who did Jesus take into the house with Him? Why do you think He did it this way?

6. How was the girl healed? What did Jesus say? How fast was she healed, and how healed was she?

7. Considering who the man and his wife were, why would Jesus command them to tell no one?

8. Put yourself in Peter's sandals; what lessons were made available to him through these healings?

The Desperate Faith of a Jewish Leader

While Jesus was speaking with the woman who had interrupted His travel to Jairus' house, one of Jairus' servants interrupted with news of his twelve-year-old daughter's death. Jesus was on the way to a very important man's house to heal the very important man's daughter when He stopped to heal a very socially unimportant woman. How many teachers of the time would set aside a man for a woman, let alone an important man such as Jairus for an insignificant, unclean woman? Jesus was different, and He calls His people to be different. Jesus looked toward Jairus and told him to have faith. His daughter was dead. He could believe for healing; could he believe for a life restored? What about you? Where does your faith need to increase today?

The twelve-year-old girl had been a minor until her twelfth birthday. In contrast to her father's importance, she was socially insignificant. Due to age and gender, the girl actually would have had no social status. However, everyone has status in Jesus' eyes. Everyone should have status in your eyes, as well. Look around the next time you travel somewhere. See the people you usually disregard and realize Jesus would be looking to spend time with them, to meet their needs, and to invite them into His kingdom. Ask the Lord how you can participate in this ministry.

The girl's importance is in direct contrast to her father's in this story, but her status is similar to that of the woman with the issue of blood. The girl died short of marriage, while the woman was most likely never married due to her condition. Both were unable to bear children. Both were of low social status and regarded with little value. Both were unclean: The woman's issue of blood and the girl's dead body were both taboos, especially for a teacher (Leviticus 15:19–33; Numbers 19:11–22). If the teacher became unclean ceremonially, he would have to separate from his pupils, wash his clothes, bathe, and remain separated until evening.

When Jesus, Jairus, and the great multitude arrived at the house, they found mourners assembled and wailing. It seems strange to our Western culture to find mourners already at a home, even before the entire family is there. However, in Bible times, professional mourners were required at the death of any person, regardless of wealth or social status. Due to the climate's decomposition rate, mourners would come together quickly. As an important figure, Jairus would have had many mourners at his home. These mourners were astonished and mocked Jesus when He suggested the girl was only sleeping. After all, these were professional mourners, and He was just a teacher (nearly the same response Peter gave Him when told to go out into the deep and lower his net). These folks were not interested in Jesus' opinion of a situation in which they were experts. Therefore, they were put out and missed seeing the miracle.

Faith can reach out and grab a miracle in desperation, as the woman with the issue of blood did. Faith can bring Jesus' attention, as Jairus' did. However, a lack of faith also inspires a response. Lack of faith accepts the current situation and mourns and wails it, but it does not consider reaching for a miracle. What miracle have you given up hope for? What situation are you simply accepting in your life, which a little faith might change? Sometimes, the miracle is your changed opinion, and sometimes, the situation changes. Yet neither will happen if you do not have the faith to approach Jesus and ask for the miracle (Matthew 21:21, 22).

Jesus allowed only the girl's parents, Peter, James, and John, to enter the room with Him. Jesus kept the mourners out because of their lack of faith, but also because He was not ready for them to proclaim Him as the Messiah. Jesus brought in the girl's parents because, first, they were her parents, and second, to build and strengthen their faith. He brought Peter, James, and John because they would emerge as leaders in His church after His ascension. Moments like these were faith-building lessons and training opportunities for the three disciples.

Jesus, with great affection, took the girl by the hand and told her to arise. The word translated as "little girl" can also be translated as "little lamb." The Shepherd came to restore one of His little lambs. It is a beautiful picture. He also reached out and touched her hand while she was yet dead: an unclean act. Two times he was touched by the unclean and had not been contaminated, because His love covered it.

Jesus used two unclean women of low status to display several truths about Himself and the kingdom of God. Jesus is "the resurrection and the life. He who believes in [Him], though he may die, he shall live" (John 11:25). Jesus has resurrection power in Him. He resurrected two situations. First, He restored life to a dead womb, resurrecting hopes of marriage, children, and a life. Second, He restored life to a dead body, resurrecting a hope for life, marriage, and children: the chance to be somebody.

Jesus, in both healings, displayed His authority over death. In restoring the girl, Jairus, a ruler of the synagogue, could not deny Jesus' authority over death. His faith in Jesus as the Messiah must have been strengthened through the act. While scripture speaks of Jewish leaders opposing Jesus, it also speaks of those who supported Him, although quietly. This was Jesus' home base of operations; it was good for Him to have the faith of the ruler of the synagogue.

Jairus came at first believing for a miracle of healing for his daughter's sickness. Jesus had already been seen healing many sicknesses in the community. It was not a far stretch for Jairus to believe Jesus could heal his daughter. Yet Jesus had a better plan for Jairus. Jesus challenged his faith beyond its bounds when the girl died. He may have intended to challenge Jairus' view of the unclean and those lacking social status in stopping to heal the woman with the issue of blood. He demonstrated the importance of the needs of all people. Social status meant nothing to Jesus, but *need* did. He challenged Jairus to move beyond anger with Him for allowing his daughter to die, while He allowed for an interruption along the way to heal her sickness. He encouraged him to let his faith grow from believing for the difficult to believing for the impossible.

The healing in this section of scripture came, for the woman, through a faith in who Jesus was: the Messiah. Through faith, she believed for the impossible. Do you honestly, from the core of your being, know who Jesus is? Have you acknowledged Him as the Savior of your life? If you believe in Him, are you keeping Him in a box of your understanding and expectation, or are you exploring the possibilities of who He is by allowing yourself to believe for the impossible? What problem do you have in your life now that desperately needs a touch of resurrection power? Are you taking it to Jesus and leaving it at His feet in trust? Do you believe He cares for you like He cares for others? If you have difficulty with any of these questions, first take them to Jesus in prayer. If you still need understanding or support after prayer, seek a leader in your church to help you.

This is a study on Peter, so why look at scripture where He is hardly mentioned? We are looking at these scriptures because Peter was present with the disciples for these teaching moments. Through watching the growth of the disciples, we also see Peter's growth in understanding who Jesus is. We also watch Peter transform from a confident, even arrogant, business-owning fisherman into a humble follower of Christ. At this time in scripture, we see Peter, like Jairus, learn how an unclean woman with a twelve-year-old issue of blood was important to Jesus. Peter saw Jesus respond to her faith, claim her to be well, and restore her to religious and social life. He also heard Jesus call her daughter in front of Jairus as He was on the way to heal Jairus' daughter, signifying her value to Him. He not only desired to see her restored to health but also wanted her restored to life.

Peter then saw Jesus continue on the journey to heal a sick girl who had already died. He probably heard Jesus tell Jairus to believe. Peter watched as Jesus dismissed the mourners, who would not believe the girl was only sleeping. Peter knew the mourners knew the difference between a dead girl and a sleeping girl; they were professionals. He then watched as Jesus performed an unclean act by taking the dead girl by the hand. He heard Jesus call the girl a little lamb and tell her to arise, and then he watched as the girl did what she was told.

Peter had seen Jesus do many miracles of healing. He had seen Him calm the wind and the sea with a gentle command, heal a woman's flow of blood without a word, and raise a dead girl to life. His faith in Jesus' ability was growing daily. He must have pondered daily who He was. He believed Jesus to be the Messiah, but for Peter, He was a Messiah in a box. Peter and most Jews expected the Messiah to come and restore Israel to the Jews and have an earthly reign. They were not expecting the Messiah they got. Jesus was in the process of gently expanding their belief in Him, until they threw the box away and believed for the impossible, so they could believe in a Messiah who was all-powerful and completely able to do all things. How about you? What has Jesus challenged you to believe for today? Are you ready to let Him out of the box you have built for Him? Write down in what way you will do this today.

Day Four: Sent Out as an Apostle

Read: Matthew 10:1–8, 11:1; Mark 3:13–19; Luke 6:12–16.

1. Who were the twelve disciples?

2. When were they referred to as apostles, and who referred to them as such?

3. (Challenge) Were they referred to as disciples again? Explain your answer.

4. Who were the apostles sent to? Why them?

5. What were the apostles to proclaim? Why this message?

6. What were the apostles to do? Why do you think this was added?

7. Why do you think Peter and the other disciples/apostles were given this opportunity?

8. What do you think they got out of it?

Personal Reflection

9. How are you freely giving what you have freely received?

10. How are you taking advantage of the opportunities God has given you to serve in the kingdom? What have you gotten out of opportunities to serve Jesus?

Jesus Sends out Twelve Apostles

Luke tells us Jesus went up on a mountain and prayed all night before choosing the twelve disciples He would send out as apostles (Luke 6:12). Mountains have often been depicted in scripture as a meeting place with God. Men such as Moses and Elijah met God upon the mountain. Why would Jesus have to pray all night long to choose His twelve disciples? If Jesus was fully God and fully man, He surely would not have wrestled with Father God over who should be sent. According to Ephesians 3:9, Jesus was at Creation and an integral part of Creation. Psalms 139:16 tells us we were each known before the foundations of the world, and our life stories were already written down before we were born. What might Jesus have prayed about all night if these things are true?

Jesus was about to pick His twelve closest disciples to teach and train for ministry after He was gone. He understood the perils they would face in the present and much more after His resurrection and ascension. In Matthew 10:16, Jesus said He was sending them out as "sheep amongst wolves." John recorded Jesus' prayer for His present and future disciples, which may give insight into how Jesus might have been praying through the night. Jesus prayed for them to have His joy, for protection from the evil one, and for them to be sanctified by the truth. Jesus' prayer also revealed His giving them the glory the Father had given Him (John 17:9–22). Later, at Gethsemane, Jesus told the disciples to wait and pray so they would not fall into temptation. He went further and prayed until He was strengthened to bear the Cross. Finally, Hebrews 7:25 tells us, "He always lives to make intercession for [us]." The evidence in scripture points to Jesus' shepherd's heart for His disciples. It reveals He most likely spent the night praying for their apostolic journeys. He most likely prayed they would hold to the message given, they would be protected from the wiles of Satan, and their preaching would be attested to by miracles of physical healings and casting out of demons.

Jesus always lives to make intercession for His disciples. If you are a disciple of Jesus Christ, you must know He intercedes for you. You are never alone, and when you feel alone and like no one cares, or you feel alone in your walk, you can rest assured Jesus Himself covers you with the perfect prayer for you in your situation. He has also prepared you to succeed in every way in the ministry you find yourself in. He does not call and send you out on your own. He prays over every situation before it arises and equips you to handle it. Now this is good news.

Jesus called them "apostles" at the point He sent them out. Mark calls them "apostles" only this one time, and it is also the only place Matthew uses the term. "Apostle" means "sent ones." They were sent as representatives, given full authority of the One who sent them. When the Gospels were written, the apostles were already commonly called apostles, so the term "apostle" in the Gospels would be understandable.

As apostles, in this part of the Gospel stories, the disciples were given a commission to do precisely as Jesus had been doing. The twelve men Jesus called were four fishermen, one a tax collector, and seven, about whom we do not know much except they were regular people. There are a few lists of the twelve, and they are most often spoken of as disciples, not as individuals. We also see the disciples were normal, fallible human beings. Yet we also see God's ability to use them.

Jesus gave the twelve men authority over sickness and evil spirits, and power to raise the dead. Displaying power over sickness and disease was a sign of the coming of the kingdom of God. Jesus shared His power with fallible human beings. How could these people become worthy of such an honor? They had to spend time with Jesus, hearing His message, seeing His ways, and modeling their lives after His own. They had time to get to know Him and His heart for those He sent them to. Jesus shared His message, mission, and power and authority with them. He sent them to the lost sheep of Israel. It was not yet time to send them to the ends of the earth. It was time to awaken Israel to the coming of the Messiah.

You cannot minister for Jesus in your power. You cannot force your calling to come. Jesus first has to prepare the way for you. He prepares the hearts of the people you minister to, just as He did for the disciples. He was preaching the kingdom, healing the sick, and raising the dead before He sent the disciples to go out and do the same. The people's hearts were being prepared. Jesus is also your intercessor. He will not send you out until He has prayed for you to succeed in the ministry, He called you to. Your job is to be in His Word daily, to know Him more and more, to learn His ways and heart for those He will send you to, and then to wait on Him. Jesus will not let your calling pass you by.

Day Five: Power and Authority

Today's lesson jumps forward in history to discuss how the apostles' experience then is similar to what Christ followers can experience today.

Read: Matthew 10:1; Mark 3:14, 15; Luke 9:1; Ephesians 1:20–2:6; Luke 11:5–13; Acts 1:8.

1. What were the twelve disciples given, and who gave it to them?

2. (Challenge) Use a Bible app to look up both words in their original languages. What do you learn?

Read: Ephesians 1:20–2:6; Luke 11:5–13; Acts 1:8.

3. Where is Jesus seated now?

4. What does it mean to be in Christ?

5. What power and authority is available to those in Christ? When does this power come?

6. Are you in Christ today? If you are not sure, take a moment and ask Jesus into your heart to be Lord over your life. If you want help, ask your study leader or pastor to help you.

Personal Reflection

7. Have you received the baptism of the Holy Spirit? How do the Luke verses help you understand how to receive the gift of the Holy Spirit?

According to Luke, all you have to do is ask. Like asking for salvation, you must believe He will give you what you seek. Ask now, by faith, for God to send you the Holy Spirit in power in the name of Jesus.

Jesus Sends out All Christians

According to Ephesians 2:6, Jesus is seated in heavenly places, and we are seated there together with Him. What does it mean for Him to be seated there? The answer is found in Ephesians 1:20–21: "Which He worked in Christ when He raised Him from the dead and seated Him at His right hand in the heavenly places, far above all principality and power and might and dominion, and every name that is named, not only in this age but also in that which is to come." Jesus is seated at the right hand of God the Father, which signifies He has attained to all the power of the Godhead. He is seated over all things and has power over all things. There is nothing alone or in mass more powerful than Jesus.

What does it mean to us if we are also seated with Christ? The Ephesians verse states the seating in the past tense. It has already been done. We have been seated with Christ in the heavenly places. Therefore, we can also claim the same position of power over principalities, powers, might, dominion, and everything under heaven. Yet we can only claim this verse— these truths—if we are found in Him.

If you want victory in your life, you must be found in Christ Jesus. This means doing more than attending church occasionally or calling yourself a Christian. It does mean you become a person who pursues a relationship with Jesus, the living God, through Bible reading, prayer, worship, Christian fellowship, and obedience. It means you cast off self and yield to His way of doing things. You are no longer in control; you give up the right to control your life to follow Jesus, where you will find a much better life.

Scripture tells us we are "made alive together with Christ" (Ephesians 2:5). When Jesus rose from the dead, He also raised us up with Him. When the disciples went out as apostles, they were given a taste of the future they would experience after Jesus' resurrection and ascension, the same taste we experience today because of Jesus' work on the Cross. Jesus' resurrection power lives in everyone who calls upon His name in the fullness of power. All Jesus is accessible to those who lay down their lives for Him.

How do Christians tap into the power of Jesus? Jesus told His disciples just before He ascended into heaven that power would come on them when they received the Holy Spirit. He said it would be a power to witness (Acts 1:8). Considering this lesson, when Jesus sent the twelve out as apostles, He sent them out to witness to the lost sheep of Israel. Within the power to witness, He gave them power over demonic spirits, sickness, and disease. We still have the same commission today, so how do we tap into the power to witness? We do it today the same way they did it then: by receiving the Holy Spirit.

Luke explains very well how one receives the Holy Spirit. It is as easy as receiving Jesus as Savior (John 3:16). Luke brings this truth to life through a parable. The most important thing when studying parables is remembering they are not allegories; everything in the story does not represent something else. Parables must be studied to get the story's point, not sift through their intricacies.

Luke's parable speaks of a man who went to his neighbor's house to beg for bread. He had company come unexpectedly and did not have bread to offer his friend. Hospitality was a way of life, and for him to not offer his guest something to eat would have been a greater shame than begging his neighbor for bread. During this period, the homes would likely be one-room. Everyone would sleep on the floor, which would probably have been crowded. They would have been locked behind a heavy door, which would make a lot of noise if opened. The man in bed would have considered the inconvenience of finding his way around in the dark and would have been concerned with waking the children. Someone reading this parable during Luke's time would have understood this part of the story.

The point of this parable is found in the neighbor's persistence. It caused the man to get up, make his way to the bread, and then to the heavy door to give the man what he had been asking for. The spiritual point of the parable is that if a human will respond to the persistence of a neighbor, how much more will God respond to the persistence of the child He loves? "Persistence" means "shamelessness." The neighbor came boldly and asked for what he wanted, and he shamelessly did not give up until he got what he desired.

At this time in history, people believed one of three things about the Holy Spirit: They thought the Holy Spirit was reserved for a few of the most holy people, the Holy Spirit had departed, or the Holy Spirit belonged to the community. It would be too much to think the Holy Spirit might be available to anyone who asked. Today, people believe the Holy Spirit has passed away or is of the devil. Some think He only appears during the Church's major events or spiritual and historic transitions. The question we need to ask today is, why would God allow this account of how to receive the Holy Spirit and accounts of people receiving the Holy Spirit into canonized scripture (the Bible) if it was not for His people today? If the Holy Spirit gives power to witness—preach the good news, heal the sick, and cast out demons—why would God not provide the Holy Spirit to us today? The only one who would not want Christians to believe the Holy Spirit is available and accessible today is the one whom the Holy Spirit grants Christians power over: Satan.

"How much more will your heavenly Father give the Holy Spirit to those who ask Him?" (Luke 11:13b). If you have never received the baptism of the Holy Spirit, which is a separate act from salvation, all you have to do is ask God to baptize you with the Holy Spirit and believe you have received it. It is stated above: He will give the Holy Spirit to those who ask Him. One scriptural example of how this is a separate act is the twelve disciples themselves. They believed Jesus was the Messiah before He had risen again. They were Christian believers before Jesus ascended to heaven, yet the Holy Spirit did not fall on them until the day of Pentecost, fifty days later. They believed in Jesus as their Savior and, at a separate time, fifty days later, received the baptism of the Holy Spirit.

This is not meant to be a deep dive study on Holy Spirit baptism. Hopefully, if you have questions, you will take your questions to scripture and to Jesus in prayer. Ask Him to reveal His truth to you, and be willing to receive it in surrender. We studied earlier how the Pharisees missed spiritual truth and application because they studied through a lens of culture and tradition. Ask Him to remove any distorting lens you might have. Go to Him confident in His ability to protect you in and through your questions. I said, Jesus, if this is You, I want all of it and more (than I can imagine). If it is not you, protect me from it. I trusted Him to guard me from what I did not know or understand, and He proved Himself true and faithful to me. He will do the same for you.

Jesus chose twelve disciples to go out as apostles. Judas was among them, the man who would later betray Him. Peter and John were among them, men who would later lead the first Christian church. After being baptized with the Holy Spirit on the Day of Pentecost, Peter would preach his first public sermon, and the church would grow by three thousand souls in one day. He chose them to go out and practice preaching, healing, and casting out demons. He did it while He was with them to answer their questions and encourage them along the way. He did it so they could help spread the word, to call as many of the lost sheep of Israel as they could back to the fold to see their salvation.

Peter had matured by this time from a rough fisherman to a man obedient to his Lord, a man chosen to preach, heal, and cast out demons. He was being prepared for greater things, but it began with first answering the call and then being faithful to the call through surrendered obedience. He is not the only one who answered or obeyed, but he is the one we are studying. Just think of how far he had come already.

Day Six: Witness and Apostle of Healing Miracles

1. Review this week's lessons and highlight your big takeaways. Be prepared to share these if you are meeting with a group.

2. Did you learn something about Peter this week? Share your thoughts.

3. How do you see your big takeaway(s) relating to the world around you today? To the Church in the broader sense, or the local church?

4. How might you apply one of these takeaways this week?

FEAR, FAMILY, AND LOYALTY

Day One: A Perspective on Fear

Jesus, continuing His address to the twelve He called out as apostles, began to counsel them on priorities. Current Jewish thought believed the Messiah would come into power and bring peace with Him. Yet Jesus said, "Do not think that I came to bring peace on earth. I did not come to bring peace but a sword" (Matthew 10:34). They expected an earthly Messiah to restore earthly power to Israel and bring peace to the nation. Jesus brought peace, but not as they were expecting. John recorded Jesus as saying, "Peace I leave with you, My peace I give to you; not as the world gives do I give to you. Let not your heart be troubled, neither let it be afraid," and "These things I have spoken to you, that in Me you may have peace. In the world, you will have tribulation; but be of good cheer, I have overcome the world" (John 14:27, 14:17, 16:33). In this portion of scripture, Jesus was giving the disciples a kingdom perspective on fear.

Read: Matthew 10:25–31; Luke 12:1–4.

1. What is the meaning of Matthew 10:27?

2. What is the meaning of Luke 12:1–3? (See Matthew 10:25.)

3. Who are we not to fear? Why?

Disciples Are Instructed Not to Fear People

Jesus counseled the disciples against fear three times in the Matthew passage. He first instructed them not to fear man (verse 26), then not to fear those who can kill the body (verse 28), and finally not to fear whatever might happen (verse 31). Jesus referred to religious leaders of the Jewish religion and political leaders of both Jewish and secular nations.

Jesus promised His disciples that all secret plans would be made public. "Darkness of night" refers to secrets being shared under the cover of darkness. The nighttime was considered the best time to pass along secrets (Luke 12:3). Jesus referred to the hypocrisy of the Pharisees with these statements. They would make secret plans against Jesus to bring Him to the Cross, and they would make secret plans against His disciples, as well. Jesus referred to this in Matthew 10:24–25: "A disciple is not above his teacher, nor a servant above his master. It is enough for a disciple to be like his teacher, and a servant like his master. If they have called the master of the house Beelzebub, how much more will they call those of his household!" Jesus knew what awaited His disciples and taught them what to do amid the perils. Jesus instructed the disciples against fear of those who could kill the body (Matthew 10:28). Jesus said this knowing He would face the Cross and be subjected to torture and humiliation at the hands of humankind. However, He knew even though men could kill the body and silence one's witness, they could not kill the soul nor separate it from the love and presence of God. The Jewish leaders who conspired against Jesus could not experience the very real presence of God with them in Jesus because their hypocrisy so blinded them. Yet Jesus also spoke these words directly to the disciples, telling them whatever they spoke of in secret would be proclaimed upon the rooftops. It warns all of Jesus' disciples against falling into the practice of hypocrisy.

Hypocrisy is an easy sin to stumble into for those who compartmentalize their lives. There can be a work persona, a church persona, and a family persona, all different and all in the same person, according to where you are at a particular time. You may find it easy to cuss at work, get drunk at home, and behave like a holy saint in church. Yet Jesus warned all these things would be revealed in the last days, as though shouted from a rooftop. It will no longer be a secret sin between you and Jesus. It will become known to all. Either your hypocrisy or your depth of devotion and character will be revealed. Which do you prefer? What changes do you need to make today to overcome secret sin? James tells us to confess our sins, one to another (James 5:16). Do you have someone you trust who will be honest and straightforward with you about your sin? This could be a mentor or a peer who will speak truth in love. This person will love you through the ugly stages of your life and is a treasure. They will not make you feel good about your sin, but they will also not condemn you. The will value and help you in your transformation process. They will walk with you as you become the person God has called you to be until you live the abundant life (John 10:10). Jesus' message to the disciples was to avoid hypocrisy for any reason, but especially out of fear due to peer pressure or a need to impress authority figures, because God's authority is greater than all (Luke 12:4–7).

Day Two: A Perspective on Fear

Read: Matthew 10:29-33; Luke 12:5–9.

1. Who are we to fear? Why?

2. According to Matthew 25:29-46 and Revelation 1:17-18, who should we fear and who should we not fear? Why?

3. According to the sparrow verses, why should you not fear?

4. What is the worth of a sparrow? Who notices when one sparrow dies?

5. How much are you worth to God compared to a sparrow?

6. What happens to one who proclaims Jesus before men?

7. What happens to the one who does not proclaim Jesus before men?

8. How well does God know you and pay attention to you?

9. In what way are you to fear the One who can destroy body and soul and yet cares deeply for you?

Disciples Instructed to Fear God

True Christianity does not just seek to avoid Pharisaic hypocrisy. True Christianity proclaims, openly and unashamedly, Jesus as Lord. This was what Jesus was instructing His disciples about. While Luke's Gospel focuses on the secret plans of hypocritical Pharisees, Matthew's Gospel focuses on Jesus' telling the disciples to shout from the rooftops what they had heard from Him in private meetings. He was telling them that to be His disciples, they must expose themselves by sharing the good news of the kingdom openly. He did not mean to shout it from the rooftops literally. This saying commanded Jesus' disciples to prioritize preaching the gospel over fear of man.

One who walks in the will of God has nothing to fear. This is the greatest thing to remember about fear. Jesus did not stop at His command to His disciples to be loyal to Him, regardless of the outcome, and leave it there. He also offered them an insight into the Father's care for them. Jesus used a standard Jewish "how much more" argument to make His point to the disciples (Matthew 10:29–31; Luke 12:6–7). He compared the worth of a sparrow to a man's worth in God's eyes. Jesus explained even though the sparrow was the cheapest thing in the marketplace, "not one falls to the ground apart from [God's] will" (Matthew 10:29). The comparison of God counting the number of hairs upon one's head was an Old Testament way of saying nothing would happen to a person without God allowing it (1 Samuel 14:45; 2 Samuel 14:11; 1 Kings 1:52). It also shows God's intimate care for His children. Judaism and Christianity both reveal God as being intimately involved with His followers. Other religions keep their gods at a distance, detached from their followers. Therefore, Jesus' command to preach the gospel openly was meant to expose false religions as well as hypocrisy.

The only fear a disciple (Christian) should have is fear of God. A disciple will be more concerned with failing God than pleasing men (Matthew 10:26–27). It is a matter of loyalty. Amid religious conflict, or even merely fear of what might happen, loyalty to Jesus must always come first. What a disciple must fear the most is *not* being found on Jesus' side. As Matthew explained, it is better to fear the One who can kill both body and soul (Matthew 10:28). This One is Jesus (Revelation 1:18). He holds the keys; He has power and authority over "hell and death."

Ancient texts, including the Dead Sea Scrolls, agree. Jews believed all things would be revealed and a great judgment would take place in the last times. They expected the wicked would be revealed and the righteous would be saved and delivered from everything which came against them (Luke 12:2–3; Isaiah 29:15). Jesus presents Himself also as their adversary or advocate in the heavenly court in the final judgment (Luke 12:8–9). He will know who has served Him and who has served man, who has been a fearless advocate and who has been a silent witness, and He will speak for or against, accordingly.

In the Old Testament, Ezekiel prophesied, "Behold, I shall judge between sheep and sheep, between rams and goats" (Ezekiel 34:17). Jesus repaints this prophetic picture in Matthew 25:31–46. He will separate the sheep from the goats, the righteous from the unrighteous, and then pronounce their eternal reward or condemnation. In Bible times, sheep and goats were separated at night. The goats were kept inside because they needed warmth, while the sheep remained outside in the open air, with the shepherd guarding their gate against predators. Sheep were more valuable than goats. Pagans of the day interpreted dreams by attributing good with sheep and bad with goats. It was this understanding Jesus was speaking to when discussing the final judgment of humankind; the final judgment will determine whether His followers proclaimed the gospel unashamedly or held their peace for fear of man. What is it to fear Jesus? Do you cower, awaiting the mighty hand of God to come crashing down? Do you fear the Lord will cast you into eternal fire for a single mistake? Certainly not! Fearing Jesus is akin to respecting Him. However, this kind of respect comes from the depths of your soul. Respect for God is a higher, more powerful respect than how we understand it between men. It exalts God to the highest position, over all else held dear in your heart. All trials and persecutions are worth it when you realize the day will come when Jesus will acknowledge His followers before God in heaven. However, fearing the wrath of the One who can cast you into eternal hell is also healthy.

Day Three: A Perspective on Fear

Read: 1 Peter 5:4–7.

1. What reward do those who fear Jesus receive when He returns?

2. What will God do for those humble to His will?

3. What are Christians to do with their worry and anxiety? Why?

Personal Reflection

4. (Personal) Give an example of a time you were fearful of someone. What was the result?

5. Give an example of a time when you feared God more than any human. How did it work out?

Peter Instructs the Church to Cast Cares upon Jesus

After hearing these words of Jesus and after living a lifetime of ministering for Jesus and practicing what He was taught, Peter spoke the same message to Christians everywhere. When Peter told the church to "clothe [themselves] with humility," there was a literal picture for His readers of wrapping clothing upon themselves tightly and knotting them on (1 Peter 5:4–7). It was a picture of preparing for work or service, similar to a modern-day picture of rolling up your sleeves to get to work. However, Peter's picture went further, as if to speak to servants preparing to do their work of service for their master. They would dress to keep their clothing from interfering with their ability to do their job to the best of their ability. The picture Peter painted of humility was not self-deprecation but of actively seeking to serve others without thought or regard for self. It is a picture of one giving oneself completely over to the service of kingdom business. This kind of humility allows God to bring one to their full potential in Him, to be all He created and intended them to be. Humility of this kind is the road to living the abundant life Jesus came to give (John 10:10).

Peter's use of the phrase "God's mighty hand" clearly referred to the strength and power of God. However, to a Jew familiar with the Old Testament or Jewish belief, the phrase further meant God's ability to rescue you from peril. By this time in Peter's life, he understood this concept very well. He had been jailed and threatened with death a few times, and upon being delivered, he returned to preaching the gospel, just as Jesus called him to do. He knew the requirement to minister for God included a dependent and expectant faith in God's will and ability to deliver. Christians often fall short in their faith in God's ability to deliver when His timing does not match their own. So many times, Christians quit waiting upon the Lord because they grow weary. They lose their faith in who and how He is and give up on Him because they don't want to suffer anymore. This, however, cannot relieve suffering, because now those Christians find themselves continuing to suffer, as well as being outside of the will of the Lord. Peter said, "in due time." God's timing is always perfect, even when you cannot see the end; you must remember that God not only sees the end of a matter, but also beyond it. Rest in His perfect timing in all things.

"Casting" has the connotation of hurling or throwing quickly. It gives the picture of getting rid of something quickly. Peter understood that worrying about what might happen or mulling over and over what might come (or what is expected to come) will only distract you from kingdom destiny. It will quench your witness and consume you with thoughts of self rather than selfless service. He spoke of one's cares or anxieties (fears), yet the disciples of the Lord cannot fear what He has called them to. You must remember: if God has called you to a purpose, He will deliver you from anything coming against you in His perfect timing, according to His perfect will. Why? Because "He cares for you" (1 Peter 5:7).

There will be a final judgment. All truth will be revealed. The goats will be separated from the sheep. The sheep and the goats graze together during the day. They dwell together and dine together, but they will not rest together. How you serve the Lord in this life will determine what kind of judgment day you will experience.

Everyone who calls themselves a Christian is a disciple of Jesus. Each one is called by Jesus to openly proclaim what they hear in the secret places of their heart and their devotional times with Him. Christians cannot afford to let fear of man, peer pressure, or fear of the unknown keep them from proclaiming the good news of Jesus. People everywhere are serving dead passions, trying to fill a void only Jesus can fill. When Jesus' disciples remain silent, those voids remain empty, and false religions continue to proliferate.

Jesus' disciples must have faith in His ability to rescue them out of every situation. Fear is not an option for those of faith. God's care for His disciples is beyond their greatest hopes and dreams. Disciples need to live as if this is true. He has numbered every hair upon their head. This is how much He cares for His children. (How many parents have counted every hair on their child's head?) Yet God shows His care in intimate ways because He loves His children so much. There is nothing to fear for those who walk in the will of God.

Day Four: Instructions on Family and Loyalty

Jesus' life and ministry is a study in contrasts. In this study, we see Jesus came to bring peace, yet He also brings a sword, and even though He brings a sword, He also brings a new depth of familial intimacy (Isaiah 9:6; Matthew 10:34, 12:49–50). Peter and the other disciples learned how to balance familial responsibilities with loyalty to Jesus within this dichotomy. They were also taught about counting the cost of discipleship and the rewards for those who would count the cost and yet follow.

Read: Matthew 10:34–39; Mark 9:50; Luke 12:51–53, 14:26, 27; John 14:27; Isaiah 9:6, 26:3, 32:17, 52:7; Zechariah 9:9, 10.

1. How do you reconcile Jesus' statement, "I did not come to send peace, but a sword," in the Matthew verses with His being referred to as the Prince of Peace (Isaiah 9:6)?

2. Who does Jesus say He has come to set one against another?

3. What would make one unworthy of Jesus?

4. To whom was Jesus speaking at this point? Why would this be an important message for them at this time and for the years to come?

5. Why would this be a vital lesson for Peter specifically? Where has Jesus' ministry been based up to this point? What characteristics do you see in Peter through this?

6. What is the cross Jesus is referring to? What is His point?

7. What does it mean, "He who finds his life will lose it; and he who loses his life for My sake shall find it" (Matthew 10:39)?

Jesus Brings Peace

The Old Testament prophesied the Messiah as one who would bring peace to Israel. Israelites thought the Messiah would bring national peace. They believed He would restore the ancient boundaries of the nation and drive all their enemies out. They understood the Messiah to be an earthly savior with an earthly reign, much like the reigns of David and Solomon, except the Messiah's reign would be everlasting (Isaiah 9:6).

The difference between what the Israelites understood the prophets to say and what has really taken place is spiritual. Jesus came to die for the sins of all people, to bring reconciliation between humanity and God on an individual basis. Jesus was the perfect sacrifice because He died once for all, but also because He rose from the grave and conquered death (Romans 6:8–10). Jesus made the way for humankind to overcome sin and live eternally with Him. He also opened to us the realm of the kingdom of God through repentance (Mark 1:15). Jesus, the Messiah, did bring peace, but not in the way it was expected. He brought a better peace; a peace between God and man (reconciliation), a peace which settles a person's soul (Romans 5:11; 2 Corinthians 5:18, 19).

The peace Jesus brings is also promised to be a sustained peace. First of all, peace is promised to those who keep their focus upon the Lord. Jesus' disciples are promised perfect peace when their eyes remain focused upon Him (Isaiah 26:3). When disciples consider who and how Jesus is, they will not be so easily distracted by difficult circumstances or trials. Isaiah also tells us the way to peace is found in righteous living, a righteousness lived out in quietness and hope (Isaiah 32:17). The good news is, Jesus' disciples no longer have to attain to righteousness through perfect living, but rather by accepting Jesus' work on the Cross and living in the victory He won for them (1 Peter 2:24). Jesus' peace is perfect peace and eternal peace for anyone who chooses it and walks in it (Romans 8:3, 4).

Jesus' disciples are commanded to have peace between them (Mark 9:50). Jesus used the example of salt to relay this message. Salt is a seasoning that brings out the flavor of foods, but it is also a preservative. A disciple who has peace with other disciples seeks to bring out the best in others while preserving peaceful relations with them. Why would Jesus have to command His disciples to have peace between them? Indeed, it is not humankind's natural tendency to have peace amongst them. History gives many examples of this, even church history. Jesus said to His disciples, "Peace I leave with you, My peace I give to you. Not as the world gives do I give to you. Let not your heart be troubled, neither let it be afraid" (John 14:27). The peace Jesus leaves overcomes worry and fear; therefore, He commands His disciples to be at peace in their hearts as well as amongst one another.

Day Five: Instructions on Family and Loyalty

Read: Matthew 12:46–50; Mark 3:31–35; Luke 8:19–21.

1. Who came seeking Jesus?

2. Did He run out to see them?

3. Whom did Jesus point to and say, "Behold My mother and brothers"?

4. What qualities must you possess to be Jesus' mother or brother?

Read: Matthew 19:27–29.

5. What shall be received by those who forsake all and follow Jesus?

6. What shall be the inheritance of those who forsake all and follow Jesus?

7. Who asked this question? What does this tell us about him?

8. Has this study challenged you in any way? Have you made your family an idol in competition with Jesus? Is He truly first in your life?

Jesus Brings a Sword

Jesus' statement of how He did not come to bring peace but a sword is better understood in light of the above. Jesus, the Messiah, came to bring peace, but not peace between nations. He brings the peace of reconciliation, the peace of heart, and the confidence of hope. He also promises to sustain peace eternally and commands His disciples to remain at peace with one another. The sword Jesus brings is a sword of division between individuals based on how they respond to Jesus and His work on the Cross.

Jesus depicts this sword of separation as being between intimate family members: father and son, mother and daughter, and a woman and her mother-in-law. He goes on to say people of a household will be enemies of one another (Matthew 10:35, 36; Luke 12:52, 53). In reading these verses, you must remember to whom Jesus was speaking. He was addressing a Jewish population. They had ideas of what their Messiah would be like, what He would do, and how He would do it. Jesus knew He was going to challenge Jewish traditions, which in some cases became more important to families than the written commandments of God (Matthew 10:37). He also knew He was going to challenge them socially as well as religiously. Jesus knew His ways would challenge theirs, and His disciples' families would reject them for their beliefs.

Jesus went as far as to say those who call themselves disciples of His must either hate their families or not love them more than Him, depending on whether you are reading Matthew or Luke (Matthew 10:37; Luke 14:26). Jesus knew the hypocrisy of many Jews, and He knew for them to merely *believe* He was the Messiah would not be enough. His disciples must prioritize Jesus over their need for approval from their families. Many people even today believe Jesus is the promised Messiah, but they will not give Him priority in their lives, causing them to fall short of a saving relationship with Him. There is a difference between believing He is the Savior and accepting Him as your personal Savior. Accepting Jesus as personal Savior often requires breaking from family expectations and some traditions. It is a willing sacrifice when you receive the revelation of the Savior.

The cost of following God in the Old Testament required separating from the other nations and obeying God. For your sins to be forgiven, you had to sacrifice an animal you owned. You had to sacrifice your personal property, which was often a source of income. You had to confess your sins over the animal and then kill it for the forgiveness of those sins. You would then have to sacrifice another animal next time you sinned and repeat the cycle every time you sinned for the rest of your life (Leviticus 4:27, 28). Jesus was now telling His disciples the cost of following Him had been raised (Matthew 10:38). He was now asking His disciples to count the cost of losing a way of life (Jewish traditions) and very likely immediate family members, as they disagreed about who Jesus was. Jesus even went as far as to call His disciples to give up their own lives for Him. The cost they were counting was their own hopes and dreams, what they thought life would be like, what they thought they would do for work, and so on. Jesus asked His disciples to lay it all down and pick up a cross, their cross, and follow Him.

Why would Jesus use a cross as an example at this point? He had not yet taken up His Cross. It may have been a visual of how separated one must be from their ideals and expectations. The cross was a picture the disciples would understand because crucifixions happened regularly in Roman-ruled Israel. The cross symbolized utter helplessness at the hands of an army, pain, suffering, and loss of life. Those who bore a cross were also treated as the dregs of society. Those who bore the Roman cross were compelled to do so; Jesus asked His disciples to weigh the cost of following Him and choose to take up their cross. Using the example of the cross would get Jesus' point across before His crucifixion and drive His point home after His ascension, when the Holy Spirit reminded them what He had said.

The Holy Spirit would also remind Jesus' disciples of the blessings for those who counted the cost and yet followed (Matthew 10:39). Those disciples who choose to let go of their dreams and expectations and pick up the cross of following Jesus will receive better rewards than they could ever dream for themselves.

Jesus Brings Intimacy

The peace Jesus brings to those who follow Him goes far beyond family ties and traditions. It reaches significantly further into an intimacy known only through a Holy Spirit connection. Those committed disciples of Jesus bear within them the Holy Spirit, who confirms them as children of God (Romans 8:15). This new familial relationship connects believers to God as His adopted children. It makes all disciples brothers and sisters in Christ. While Jesus becomes the priority in every believer's life, so does God's family.

While Jesus was teaching, His mother and His brothers were outside wanting to speak to Him (Matthew 12:46). His mother, Mary, and His half-brothers (His immediate family) were outside. Notice they were not there to seek His teachings. If they were there as followers, they would not have sought to interrupt Him while He was teaching His disciples. They displayed an expectation of Jesus' preference. They assumed because they were His immediate family, He would set aside His ministry time for them; after all, one of the Ten Commandments tells Him to honor His mother and Father (Exodus 20:12) Mary had a scriptural expectation Jesus would honor her more highly than the people who were following Him around. It being improper to interrupt Jesus' teaching did not occur to them.

Mary and Jesus' brothers were not the only ones who displayed this expectation. Even Jesus' disciples expected Him to interrupt His teaching to meet with His immediate family. The disciples interrupted while Jesus was teaching about the enemy of their souls to tell Him His family was outside (Matthew 12:47; Mark 3:32). The disciples were ready to set themselves aside to put Jesus' relatives first, not realizing the time with Jesus was short. They also expected Jesus to honor His mother and brothers before them. Yet Jesus came from the Father in heaven, and He would honor Him first. However, those He spoke to did not have an understanding of this. Mary, His mother, would be the only one with this possible understanding, yet she too did not fully understand (Luke 2:19, 49).

Jesus amazed everyone with His following statement. The statement and teaching amaze people still today. While Mary and His brothers, the woman who raised Him and the brothers He grew up with, were standing outside, Jesus said those inside were His mother and His brothers (Matthew 12:49). He appeared to reject His relatives completely. This was another example of Jesus going against the grain of His culture. He continued, "Whoever does the will of My Father in heaven is My brother and sister and mother." It is not enough to believe Jesus is the Son of God and He died for sins; to be a true disciple, one must also obey God's will. It is a lesson in priorities for His disciples.

So far this week, the study has focused on relationships. First, it shows us that Jesus, the Messiah prophesied to bring peace, does in fact bring peace, just not the peace expected. The peace Jesus brings is the peace between God and humanity. Jesus' work on the Cross released humanity to choose to have a personal and intimate relationship with God through the forgiveness of sins. Then we see Jesus also brings a sword, a sword that cuts familial loyalty and gives preference to loyalty to Jesus. This sword does not destroy family relations, but it is a natural occurrence when one person in a family becomes a disciple and the others do not. Finally, Jesus taught that spiritual brotherhood becomes more intimate and is preferred to blood relationships. When familial relations distract you from doing God's will, they are no longer a good relationship, and preference must be given to God's family. Those who do the will of God are truly Jesus' immediate family.

Think of Peter. Jesus' ministry revolved around Peter's home, where Peter could be close to his immediate family while still following Jesus. Yet there came a time in Peter's life when he was called away from his immediate family to follow Jesus. Peter appeared to have close intimacy with his family; he had to rearrange his priorities to fulfill what God had planned for him. Just think how things would have gone for Peter and the church if he had not gotten his priorities ordered of the Lord. Now think of the tremendous impact his life has had on the entire church from the beginning, because he did get his life aligned with the plan and purpose of God.

Are you giving preference to your earthly family? Do you allow them to keep you from attending church or distract you from serving Jesus in areas you know you are called to? Have you made your family an idol by putting them before the Lord? Ask Jesus now to show you if there is an area where you need the peace of forgiveness in your life. Ask Him if there is a sword of separation that needs to slice through your allegiances to align them aright. Then ask Him if there is an intimacy with the family of God you have been robbing yourself of, because you have ordered your priorities incorrectly. You may be afraid of asking Him these questions. This may indicate that there is an idol in your life. Remember, there is no better place than the middle of God's will for you. Changes may be difficult initially, but the results will be worth it, beyond what you can think or imagine.

Day Six: Fear. Family. and Loyalty

1. Review this week's lessons and highlight your big takeaways. Be prepared to share these if you are meeting with a group.

2. Did you learn something about Peter this week? Share your thoughts.

3. How do you see your big takeaway(s) relating to the world around you today? To the Church in the broader sense, or the local church?

4. How might you apply one of these takeaways this week?

BREAD AND WATER

Days One & Two: The Bread of Life

Read: Matthew 13:36, 15:15; Mark 4:10–12, 7:17–18, 9:11–12, 9:28, 10:10.

1. What were the disciples seeking?

2. Where were they when they sought this?

3. How did Jesus respond to them every time? Why did Jesus only give this in private?

4. Who is the only disciple named doing this? What character trait does this show? Is this a change in his character from what we've seen in the past?

Feeding Knowledge

The beginning of this lesson reveals Peter's growth in his ability to be taught by Jesus. Peter, who began as somewhat of a know-it-all, humbled himself to ask Jesus to explain things further (Matthew 15:15). Whenever the disciples did not understand what Jesus meant when speaking to the crowd, they did not ask Him for an explanation immediately. This was a benefit of being a disciple. They waited until they had a private audience with Jesus and then asked Him for further instruction (Matthew 13:36, 15:15; Mark 4:10–12, 7:17–18, 9:11–12, 9:28, 10:10).

Jesus explained to His disciples they had the privilege of gaining kingdom knowledge; this was why He explained things to them but not the crowd outside (Mark 4:11). The lesson to be taken from this is, Jesus is not going to share the mysteries of the kingdom of God with someone who is merely trying on Christianity to see how it fits. The mysteries of the kingdom of God belong to those who give their heart to Jesus with full commitment of faith, obedience, and hunger for truth.

Read: Deuteronomy 18:15; Matthew 14:13–22; Mark 6:30–44; Luke 9:10–17; John 6:1–14.

5. Where did Jesus and the disciples go? Why?

6. Why did the multitude go, and how did they get there?

7. Why did Jesus tell the disciples to feed the people?

8. (Challenge) Why do you think Jesus had the crowds sit down before blessing and breaking the bread?

9. How many baskets full did the disciples take up after the crowd had eaten and were satisfied? What is significant about this to you?

10. According to John 6:14, who did the men believe Jesus to be?

11. What did Moses and God say we should do in regard to this Man?

Bread from Heaven and a Prophet Like Me

Moses led the Israelites out of Egypt. All was going well until they began to get hungry while wandering in the desert. They began to look back on their captivity with longing because of the food they ate. They forgot their former plight and started complaining about Moses and Aaron, their leaders. However, their criticisms were not actually against Moses and Aaron, since the two men were merely following God's leading. Their complaints were really against God. When God heard the complaints of the Israelites, He rained manna down from heaven for them to gather, prepare, and eat daily (except on the Sabbath day). It was a miraculous, life-sustaining act (Exodus 16:1–8).

This is a good lesson to remember when we don't like the way things are being run at church or the direction things are going. We must not forget it is our leader's responsibility to follow God and lead us. Unless our leaders do something immoral, we must follow their lead. Even if you believe they are missing God momentarily, God will work it all out. Therefore, those not following God's leaders are the ones He will judge.

I will interject here with my advice for anyone in consistent disagreement with church leadership. The first response is prayer. We are called to pray for our leadership. We aren't praying for them to see our point of view; we are praying for them to hear from God and lead us with integrity. We pray they are protected from the enemy's wiles, for their health, and unity in the Body of Christ. Then we trust God beyond their human frailty (not sin). If you have been doing this and still find discomfort or discord, ask the Lord if He is releasing you from your church. Pray and ask Him if He is calling you to a new adventure in a different community of believers. You do not have to part with anger; you can hear His call to change and leave as friends, not remain as foes.

Moses told the Israelites, "The Lord your God will raise up for you a Prophet like me from your midst, from your brethren. Him you shall hear, according to all you desired of the Lord your God in Horeb in the day of the assembly, saying, 'Let me not hear again the voice of the Lord my God, nor let me see this great fire anymore, lest I die'" (Deuteronomy 18:15, 16). The Lord God had spoken the Ten Commandments to the Israelites at Horeb. Terrified by the voice of the Lord God, they asked not to hear it again. They said they would be fine hearing from Moses instead of God (Exodus 19, 20). This is when Moses told them One like him would come in the future, and they would hear Him.

Jesus was taken to be a great Prophet by the people of His day, and they did hear Him. He spoke directly to them through the voice of what appeared to be a mortal man. They recognized Him as such when He looked to heaven and gave thanks for the bread. They were in a desert, just as the Israelites were with Moses when manna rained down to feed them. This was a sign to the multitude and the disciples: Jesus *was* the Prophet spoken of by Moses. Jesus met the needs of the multitudes and taught the disciples valuable lessons. However, He was also teaching a truth about Himself. John recorded the revelation coming during the second miraculous feeding: "Then those men, when they had seen the sign that Jesus did, said, 'This is truly the Prophet who is to come into the world'" (John 6:14).

Day Three: The Bread of Life

Read: Exodus 16:1–5, 31; John 6:33–35, 47–59.

1. Compare and contrast the Exodus verses with the feeding of the five thousand.

2. What does Jesus call Himself?

3. What happened to the people who ate manna? What happens to those who eat the Bread of Life?

4. What religious ritual do you see in John 6:55–58?

5. Where did Jesus make these statements? What do you find significant about this?

Read: Matthew 15:32–39; Mark 8:1–9.

6. What similarities or contrasts do you see between the first miraculous feeding and the second?

7. Why do you think there was a second miraculous feeding of a multitude?

Feeding Multitudes

There are two instances in scripture where Jesus feeds a multitude. One is feeding five thousand, and the other is four thousand. The feeding of the five thousand took place because a great multitude followed Jesus to a deserted place. The disciples asked Jesus to send the crowd away so they could get something to eat. The feeding of the four thousand began with Jesus' compassion for the crowd and telling the disciples to feed them. The disciples were bewildered by both instances; they saw the impossible in both cases. Where could they get food in the desert to feed a multitude? Even if they could find a market in the wilderness, they would not have the money to purchase enough food for everyone.

Jesus used the first instance, when the disciples approached Him, as an opportunity to meet a need and teach a truth. In the second instance, Jesus sought to meet a need, but why did the disciples need a second lesson? The answer to this question can be seen in their response to Jesus' asking what they had. Both times, they saw the lack of supply to meet the needs of a hungry multitude. However, Jesus saw in them something He could bless to meet the need. This was one of the lessons He was trying to get across to them. Jesus showed grace in using His disciples where they were and with what they had. He blessed, increased, and then used the same disciples to minister.

Jesus took from them what they had. In the first case, it was five loaves and two fish; in the second, it was seven loaves of bread. In both cases, Jesus commanded the multitude to sit down before He blessed the offering. This may have been to organize them for distribution; however, Jesus likely wanted all to see what He was doing and with what supply. He did not want anyone to miss the miracle or the message. All saw the meager offering, and all saw Jesus lift it to heaven and bless it; then they all saw Him break the bread and distribute it through His disciples. Both feedings resulted in all being filled or satisfied with the meager offering blessed by Jesus. The five loaves and two fish were reported to have left twelve baskets of leftovers, and the seven loaves had seven left over. The first fed five thousand men plus women and children; the second fed four thousand men plus women and children. If these were families where each man had one wife and one child, the first would have fed fifteen thousand people, and the second twelve thousand people.

Do you feel ill-equipped to do something Jesus has asked you to do? Do you feel inadequate? Are you willing to offer Him what you have and trust Him with the rest? When faced with an insurmountable task, do you look at the lack or believe for the miracle? Did you notice Jesus prepared the crowd to receive from the disciples? He had them sit down, and then the disciples distributed to them. This is a beautiful picture of how He uses disciples, even today. Jesus draws the crowd, not the disciples: preacher, teacher, or prophet. Jesus prepares the crowd to receive and then uses the disciples to distribute what they have already received from Jesus. Then those who have received ought to turn around and share what Jesus has blessed in them to yet another multitude. While Jesus uses disciples to do the ministry, without His drawing, preparing, and blessing, there is no ministry; disciples are just doing things in their own power with no eternal benefit. Finally, the twelve disciples distributed and had more left than when they began. They went from loaves to baskets full. It is the same in ministry. When disciples give sacrificially, they are not simply filled again but increased. Praise the Lord.

Bread of Life

Soon after, Jesus proclaimed himself the Bread of Life in the synagogue in Capernaum. People had recognized Him as the Prophet to come, but they had not fully grasped the truth of His mission. This proclamation, witnessed by the disciples, would fully come to light for them after His death and resurrection.

Jesus began with whoever believed in Him would have everlasting life. He equated Himself to the Bread of Life and compared Himself to the manna the Israelites ate in the desert. Though His audience would clearly understand what He was referencing, they did not comprehend the point. Jesus said those who ate manna in the desert still died. The manna sustained them physically until physical death overtook them.

He also said He was the bread come down from heaven. The difference was in His being living bread. He shocked them by saying whoever ate of this bread would live forever. He continued, if they did not eat His flesh or drink His blood, they would have no life in them. Eating human flesh and drinking blood of any sort was against their law. He taught these things in Capernaum, where He had begun His ministry. People there had seen miracles of physical healing, healing of demonic possession, the dead raised to life, and they may also have heard how He calmed the wind and the waves. Suddenly, the great Prophet was asking them to eat His flesh and drink His blood!

Jesus said the one who does this abides in Him. He spoke this way at another time, which pulled together the feeding of the multitudes, the recognition of Him being the One to come, and His claiming to be the Bread of Life. Jesus, at the Last Supper, took and broke bread, distributed it to each disciple, and told them to take and eat it; it was His body. He did the same with the wine, claiming it to be His blood. His disciples still follow His directions today when partaking of communion.

Jesus is the Bread of Life. He gave His body to reconcile all who believe on Him. He restores humanity to the relationship with God intended at Creation. To receive the gift of salvation is to take of His body and to drink of His blood; it is accepting the work He did on the Cross as a perfect act, restoring us to God's kingdom. To live your life for Jesus through daily devotion and Christian living is to abide in Him.

Are you abiding in Him today, or are you feeling somewhat distant? Do you need to take a moment for communion with Him? You can do this at home with bread and juice. Take the bread and think of what Jesus did for you on the Cross. Confess your sins and accept His forgiveness. Take the cup, know His blood washes away your sins, and places you in a new covenant relationship with Him. Then abide in Him daily.

Day Four: Walking on Water

Read: Matthew 14:22–34; Mark 6:45–52; John 6:15–21; Job 9:8; Psalms 30:5, 46:1–5.

1. As this story begins, what were the disciples trying to do and why? Were they giving up?

2. Whose eyes were upon them as they struggled to obey?

3. When did Jesus come to the disciples? (Challenge) What time is it?

4. According to the Psalms verses, what comes at the turn of the morning?

5. How did the disciples respond to Jesus' coming?

6. How did Jesus let them know it was Him? (Challenge) What was He saying?

The Obedience

Jesus commanded His disciples to get into the boat and go to the other side of the lake after miraculously feeding five thousand men (plus women and children). They did not question why Jesus was staying behind, nor did they argue with His command. This was a significant change from their first calling. Remember Peter grumbling when asked to cast his net into the deep water in the first lesson? Peter had no words at Jesus' command this time, only obedience. Maybe Peter had been walking with Jesus long enough to know His voice always guided him in the right direction.

Jesus stayed behind to dismiss the crowd, which proclaimed Him to be the Prophet Moses spoke of, who was to come. Jesus was sending them on their way, but they were planning to take Jesus by force and set Him up as King. There is a vast contrast between the two sets of followers of Jesus: the disciples and the multitude. The disciples did not question Jesus' command to get into the boat without Him, while the multitude would not be sent away. They were unwilling to release Jesus from their grasp once they determined Him to be a deliverer of Israel. One group sought to serve Him, and the other sought to use Him to serve their own agenda.

Disciples today still treat Jesus the same way. There are those disciples who unquestioningly go where Jesus sends them. Their lives are given up to His will. In contrast, other disciples follow Jesus for what they can gain from their relationship with Him. They make their plans and ask Jesus to bless them. They are constantly out in front of Jesus, asking Him to catch up to their plan for their life. They are never satisfied. There is no contentment in a life trying to control Jesus, but there is great contentment in a life submitted to Jesus (1 Timothy 6:6).

Where are you today? Are you missing your contentment? Maybe you have run out ahead of the Lord. Prayerfully seek the answer to these questions: "Lord, am I following or leading You?" and "What do I need to do differently?" Then wait for His reply. He is a gentle Savior and will respond if you ask with an honest and humble heart.

Jesus retired to the mountain to pray, separating Himself from the crowd and the disciples' questions, to spend time with His Father in prayer. He looked up and saw the disciples struggling to row across the sea. He probably reminisced about their last crossing in a storm and their panic at the wind and waves. Yet, in this moment, He saw them faithfully rowing amid the storm, even while He was not in the boat. Maybe He smiled a little, enjoying how far their faith had come. They were not crying out for Him. They were not turning around and coming back. They were merely continuing to row in the direction they were commanded. Maybe He was also smiling about what He was about to do.

The Challenge

The disciples were doing all they could to reach the place Jesus assigned to them, even though the winds were against them (Mark 6:48). Scripture says Jesus went to them at about the fourth watch, between three and six o'clock in the morning. The disciples had toiled all night, and they looked up and saw a being on the waves, walking toward them. They cried out in fear. They had been in a storm before when the wind and the waves caused them to cry out. However, Jesus' salvation then caused their faith to grow. This time, we see the wind and the waves are not disturbing them, but a man walking toward them on the water is. It was a new opportunity to grow in faith, coming from an unexpected place. Jesus calmed them with His voice.

Psalms 30:5 says, "For His anger is but for a moment, His favor is for life; Weeping may endure for a night, but joy comes in the morning." Psalms 46:5 also states, God's help comes at the break of dawn. Storms were often seen in Bible times as the wrath of a god. This scripture may have crossed the disciples' minds, either at this time or later, as they reflected on it. They fought the storm all night, but Jesus came in the morning, and what was revealed to them through the experience brought them great joy.

Day Five: Walking on Water

Read: Matthew 14:22–34; Mark 6:45–52; John 6:15–21; Job 9:8; Psalms 30:5, 46:1–5.

1. What was Peter's response? Why do you think this was his response?

2. Why do you think He asked Jesus to command him to come to Him? Does this tell you anything about Peter's understanding of who Jesus is?

3. What happened when Peter tried to walk on water? Why?

4. What insight does Job 9:8 offer about this?

5. What happened when Jesus got into the boat?

6. Between Jesus' announcement of who He was and the Job verse, what would the disciples have to conclude about Jesus? Do you think they fully understood who He was at this point?

Personal Reflection

7. What have you learned about Peter through this week's study?

8. Are you in a storm right now? Will you share it with someone?

9. How does it comfort you to know Jesus' eyes are on you in the storm, and you are never alone?

10. Do you find comfort knowing His help comes right on time? In what way?

11. Are you ready to let Jesus command you to get out of the boat and walk on the water of a ministry He has called you to, without fear or doubt? If yes, what is it, and what has been holding you back from it?

The Request

Peter's sanguine personality shines through as he blurts out, "Lord, if it is You, command me to come to You on the water." Why would he say this? On one hand, he possibly thought it was the most fascinating thing he had ever seen and wanted to do it too. The text shows he did not think about it before he spoke, except to ask Jesus to command him to come to Him. This is interesting. Peter seemed to know he could not walk on water as Jesus did, unless Jesus commanded him. Yet what would have caused Peter to come to this conclusion, and in such a spontaneous moment?

Peter and the other disciples had recently been sent on a mission as apostles. They were given power to heal sickness and cast out demons. However, they were only given this power at Jesus' command (Mark 6:7–13). Peter must have understood how all power and authority over sickness, disease, and nature belonged to Jesus. He had been allowed to heal and preach as Jesus had done. Now he wanted to try walking on water like Jesus.

Jesus acquiesced to Peter's request. One has to wonder why. What was the point of Jesus agreeing to this request? Was it simply to be recorded in scripture for future generations to talk about faith in storms? Was it to send a message to Peter and the disciples in the moment? Nothing Jesus did then or does now is by accident. There can be something gained for all who witness. The disciples witnessed Jesus' command over not only the wind and the waves but also the natural laws of the universe. They all knew people sink in water, but Jesus defied gravity, and by His command, gravity was defied for Peter. However, the lesson of faith is not to be missed, either. Scripture is clear: As long as Peter had his eyes on Jesus, he stood or walked upon the water. Nevertheless, his faith waned when his eyes were removed from Jesus, and he focused on what he feared most. When he allowed the fear to set in, he began to sink. Yet even when he was sinking, Peter knew where to turn. He cried out for Jesus to save him, and He did.

Jesus' own words tell what happened to Peter when He asked why he doubted. When disciples take their eyes off Jesus, doubt easily sets in. Doubting robs disciples of blessings. The book of John gives one example: The disciple, Thomas, doubted Jesus had risen from the dead. He said he would only believe when he saw with his own eyes and touched with his own hands the nail piercings and the puncture in His side. When allowed to do this, Thomas proclaimed Jesus as Lord and Savior. Jesus responded, "Thomas, because you have seen Me, you have believed. Blessed are those who have not seen and yet have believed." Those who walk by faith—even upon the water—are blessed. Those who doubt or need proof lack blessing.

While Peter had an incredible experience, he also had a humbling one. He stepped out in faith, but his faith could not sustain him. While he was again humbled in the sight of his peers, he should not have been seen as a fool, for at least he stepped out in faith. Peter cried out for Jesus to save them from the first storm. In the second storm, he asked Jesus to command him to walk through the storm. When we move from "save me" to "teach me," it is spiritual growth. Peter should celebrate his growth, not be humiliated by the stumble.

What has the Lord asked you to step out in, which feels like He is asking you to walk on water? Will you step out in faith, without doubting? Will you follow Him, keeping your eyes upon Him? Your faith will be rewarded with great blessings.

The Proclamation

The wind and waves ceased once Peter and Jesus were safely in the boat. According to John's Gospel, they were immediately at their destination when they entered the boat. After all these events, everyone in the boat proclaimed Jesus to be the Son of God. Why would these events turn their hearts so assuredly to this proclamation? They had already seen Jesus calm the wind and waves, proving His authority over nature. They had been sent on a missionary journey and experienced preaching and healing, as Jesus gave them power to do. Why would His walking on water make a difference? Job 9:8 may help explain why this was so moving for the disciples. Scripture clearly states, "[God] alone … treads on the waves of the sea." The disciples came from an area of pious Jews. They most likely knew their scriptures well. Who else could Jesus be but the Son of God, the Messiah to come, worthy of their worship?

How will you apply this to your life this week? Peter stepped out in faith, stumbled, got back into the boat with Jesus, marveled, and was immediately at his destination. You must step out of the boat to grow in your revelation of Jesus. Peter may have stumbled, but his eyes were opened to see Jesus more clearly than he had seen Him before. Peter's stumbling and bumbling did not keep him from reaching his destination, for they arrived immediately. What if transforming our thinking to know our stumbling (failures) can move us closer to our destination? Jesus can use all things to grow us into His image. So take courage, step out of the boat this week, and see what God will do for you.

Day Six: Bread and Water

1. Review this week's lessons and highlight your big takeaways. Be prepared to share these if you are meeting with a group.

2. Did you learn something about Peter this week? Share your thoughts.

3. How do you see your big takeaway(s) relating to the world around you today? To the Church in the broader sense, or the local church?

4. How might you apply one of these takeaways this week?

LEAVEN, CONFESSION, AND CROSS TALK

Day One: Lessons on Leaven

Read: Matthew 16:5–12; Mark 8:14–21; Colossians 2:8.

1. What did Jesus tell the disciples to beware of?

2. How did the disciples respond to Jesus' statement?

3. What did they determine Jesus meant? Why were they focused on this?

4. What did Jesus call them, and what did He say kept them from understanding?

3

5. What miracle had they forgotten? Had it happened long ago?

6. What did they finally understand Jesus to be warning them about?

7. Use a Bible dictionary and look up "doctrine." What does it mean?

8. What was wrong with the doctrine of the Pharisees and Sadducees?

Disciples Beware of Leaven

Jesus began this lesson for the disciples with a simple warning: He told them to "beware of the leaven of the Pharisees and Sadducees" (Matthew 16:6). It was a simple statement, but what did Jesus mean by "leaven"? He began this discourse after the Pharisees and Sadducees had come to test Him by seeking a sign from heaven (Matthew 16:1). These mortal men, who studied the scriptures to gain the best understanding of God's will, basically asked Jesus to prove He was the Messiah to them. They believed their position in the temple as well as in Judah gave them the right to condescend to the Savior and seek proof of His station when He was not even promoting Himself as the Savior. He was known by His works.

The religious leaders of the day could not see what was right in front of them because they had so indoctrinated themselves. If they had heard the words of Jesus as students (disciples), they might have seen Him as the Savior: their Savior. Instead, they listened for one of two things. First, they listened to see if He lined up with their understanding of the Messiah from scripture. Second, they listened for things they could refute. Paul said in Romans 10:17, "Faith comes by hearing, and hearing by the word of God." If this is true, the Pharisees and Sadducees were not listening to hear, but to judge. Their arrogant approach kept them from hearing, seeing, and believing. Scripture has taught us, "faith is the substance of things hoped for, the evidence of things not seen" (Hebrews 11:1).

In Mark 8:15, Jesus says the disciples ought to beware of the leaven of Herod, as well. What could He mean by the leaven of Herod? Herod was half-Jewish and half-Gentile, and he managed a Hellenistic kingdom. Hellenists not only accepted all religions, but they also desired the inhabitants to practice all religions together. Herod also wanted to see Jesus perform a miracle (Luke 23:8). While being half-Jewish and half-Gentile is not a sin, it is a sin to live in both worlds. You could not call yourself a Jew and live a Hellenistic life. Jews were called to be set apart from the world and other religions. The same is true for Christians. One cannot claim to be a Christian while practicing other religions; one cannot claim to be a Christian and lead a worldly life.

Don't Forget the Bread?

When the disciples heard this warning from Jesus, they did not understand what He was talking about. Scripture has already shown them to be teachable by asking Jesus questions about the parables He spoke. However, they didn't ask Jesus what He meant this time. Instead, they discussed it among themselves, trying to figure it out. What was different this time? Before, they had asked Jesus what He meant when He spoke in parables to the people. The difference was in Jesus speaking directly to them, and they appear unwilling to admit they did not understand Him. Their focus turned toward themselves rather than their Teacher and the current lesson. The disciples seemed to be taking a position of defense rather than humility and teachableness.

Jesus was not just talking to the multitude. He was speaking to His students. They did not want to admit they did not have the answer. Pride had snuck in and was in the way. Sometimes, Christians are teachable until they are called to a position, and then suddenly, they think they are supposed to have all the answers. The lie says they will look spiritually lacking if they don't know everything associated with what they are doing. What they need to do more than anything is show their humility to admit what they do not know and seek the Lord for understanding, or ask questions of those who lead them in the church.

The disciples had just recently witnessed two miraculous feedings of multitudes. They had one loaf with them, according to the Mark verses. Jesus seemed surprised they still did not understand the message given through the feeding of the multitude. They had not yet understood Jesus was the Bread of Life. How could they conclude Jesus was hinting they had forgotten to bring bread with them? Scripture answers this question: Jesus said they were of little faith, and their hearts were hardened (Mark 8:17). These hardened hearts could not see the deity of Jesus.

Jesus spelled it out for them. He was not speaking of bread but of the leaven of the Pharisees and Sadducees. When the disciples heard He was not speaking of bread, they realized Jesus was speaking of doctrine. Doctrine is what a faith group holds true and authoritative on spiritual matters, including God, Jesus, the church, humanity, and so on. Comparing the doctrine of the Pharisees and Sadducees to yeast is to say it penetrates every area. As yeast works its way through dough and causes air bubbles to make the dough rise, so does the Pharisees and Sadducees' doctrine infiltrate every aspect of the church and puff it up. Theirs was a doctrine of hypocrisy and legalism. They had allowed their traditions to become more important than the God they thought they were serving, and they laid burdens on God's people He had not called for. Their hypocrisy turned people away from God.

Jesus was preparing His disciples to lead the church after His ascension. Jesus desired the disciples not to copy how the Pharisees and Sadducees had done things. They sought honor and authority. Jesus taught humility and service. Too many Christians think their happiness will come from their getting to do a particular ministry. Yet they do not realize the cost of ministry. Ministry means service. Once called to a position, such as the disciples were, an anointing of responsibility descends like a cloak, bringing the expectation of service. While accepting your calling brings more sacrifice of yourself, it also brings abundant blessings.

Day Two: The Confession

Read: Matthew 16:13–18; Mark 8:27–30; Luke 9:18–20.

1. Where did the disciples and Jesus come to? Locate it in the map section of your Bible or look it up in a Bible dictionary and share what you learn.

2. Why do you think Jesus began by asking who men said He was? How did the disciples answer?

3. Who spoke up when Jesus asked who the disciples thought He was? What did he say?

4. Why did Jesus say Peter was blessed?

5. In what way did Jesus change Simon, son of Jonah's name, and what did He say about it?

6. Upon what rock would Jesus build His church?

Who Am I?

Jesus brought His disciples to the region of Caesarea Philippi. It is located about twenty-five miles north of Capernaum near the easternmost headwaters of the Jordan River. The Source of Life brought His disciples to the source of the life-sustaining Jordan. There, Jesus opened the door to a conversation with His disciples about who He was. He began benignly by asking the twelve who others said He was. This allowed them to voice what they were wrestling with themselves. Some people thought He was John the Baptist come alive, but the disciples knew Jesus and John were alive at the same time. Other people said Jesus might be Elijah, Jeremiah, or one of the other prophets come back to life. Jesus listened, allowing them to work through their considerations, and then He asked them pointedly, "Who do you say that I am?"

Peter spoke first, "You are the Christ, the Son of the living God" (Matthew 16:15, 16). This is the most important question every person has to answer. Who do you say Jesus is? It is very different when discussing what others say and deciding who Jesus is to you personally.

Jesus called Peter blessed and told him he had not figured it out on his own. Jesus said only Father God could have revealed this to Peter. Belief in Jesus does not come through intellectual pursuit. Salvation comes by faith (2 Timothy 3:15). "Faith comes by hearing, and hearing by the word of God" (Romans 10:17). Peter made his claim by a divine revelation from God the Father, and Jesus had called him blessed and changed his name.

Matthew used the name Peter throughout his book to allay any confusion on the reader's part. Peter was well known throughout the Christian world, and calling him "Simon" may have been confusing for the reader, since the name "Peter" brings with it so much more. Here, we are at the historical point of Jesus changing his name from Simon (hearing or obeying) to Peter (rock or stone). Jesus stated, "On this rock I will build My church and the gates of Hades shall not prevail against it" (Matthew 16:18).

What is the rock Jesus was referring to? Was He speaking of Peter, the rock, or of something different? If Jesus were speaking of Peter specifically, He would most likely have said, "on you I will build." He didn't say "you." He said "this." So what is "this rock"? If Jesus was not speaking of Peter, then He must have been speaking of Peter's actions. Peter had just confessed Jesus as the Messiah (Savior) by revelation from God the Father. The rock upon which Jesus would build His church is the revelation knowledge of Jesus being the Christ, Messiah, Savior. This revelation comes only from God the Father and must be confessed before others for salvation. The apostle Paul stated, "If you confess with your mouth the Lord Jesus and believe in your heart that God has raised Him from the dead, you will be saved" (Romans 10:9).

Day Three: The Confession

Read: Matthew 16:18–20.

1. What does "the gates of Hades shall not prevail against it" mean?

2. What keys did Jesus give to Peter? What would Peter be able to do with these keys? What does this mean? Consider the conversation begun in Matthew earlier in the chapter and at the beginning of this study.

3. What would Peter be binding or loosing on earth?

4. Why would Jesus warn His disciples not to tell people He was the Christ?

The Gates of Hell

Jesus said the "gates of hell shall not prevail against it." Gates are the doors in and out of a walled city. While Satan has power in this world, the gates of his realm will not be able to hold anyone God chooses to bring out, nor will they keep out the gospel message or the revelation of God. In the simplest of terms, the gospel message and revelation knowledge of Jesus will meet anyone God the Father chooses. Nothing can stop Him from revealing Jesus to a lost soul. Conversely, the gates of hell cannot rob anyone of their salvation revelation. No one's salvation can be taken from them. They can give it away by turning back and committing to a life of sin, but no one can take it (2 Timothy 2:12; Hebrews 5:9, 9:28; Revelation 12:10, 11).

Keys of the Kingdom

After proclaiming Peter's new name, Jesus also said He was giving him "the keys of the kingdom of heaven." We know Jesus spoke only to Peter because the "you" in the sentence is singular. He was addressing Peter, then used the singular "you," which indicates He was still speaking to Peter. Jesus also bestowed upon Peter the rights to use the keys to the kingdom to bind and loose on earth and in heaven. This seems like a lot of power to give a mortal man. What would Peter be binding and what would he be loosing?

There was a room in the temple where scrolls of the Law were kept. The scribes and priests who studied and interpreted the Law had keys to this room. They were charged with the proper study of God's Law to teach about God and doctrine. They bound sin by the Law and loosed guilt by the Law. Jesus gave Peter the keys to the kingdom. In short, Jesus gave Peter the final authority on the new Christian doctrine after His ascension.

For example, in a good marriage, someone must have the final word (Ephesians 5:23, 24). Jesus places the husband over the wife, like He is head of the church. This means he lives a life of sacrifice for her sake, but he was also given the final word on matters to bind arguments. God has placed the responsibility on the husband's shoulders to care for his wife and family. Similarly, Jesus had placed upon Peter the responsibility to care for His church as He does. He would be expected to sacrifice for the church, to be a servant leader, and to have a final say when doctrinal questions arose.

Peter seems an unlikely candidate for this job. He was a speak-before-thinking kind of guy. This is not the personality one would think Jesus would give this job to. However, God created the personality types. Peter was outgoing and confident in what he believed, whether it was fishing or his faith in Jesus. He may speak before thinking, but when speaking for Jesus, sometimes it is deemed a skill rather than a hindrance. He had the courage to speak his mind when confident in his beliefs. His personality type would not be bullied by anyone, and his faith in Jesus the Messiah humbled him to seek His will. Peter would not have to do this alone; this is the best news. The Holy Spirit would help him when it was time (John 14:13–17; Acts 1:8).

Jesus finished this proclamation with a command for disciples to tell no one He was the Messiah (Christ). His time was not yet. Jesus knew many people, even the disciples, misunderstood what He was to do upon the earth. Many believed He would restore an earthly kingdom to Israel, drive out the Romans, and restore the kingdom of David and Solomon. However, their expectations of the Messiah were much too low at this time. Jesus had already had a group seek to make Him king forcibly, but He did not come to be an earthly king (John 6:15). He is the King of Kings and Lord of Lords. He came to be King of the entire realm of God, which includes all things on earth and in heaven. He came to die on a Cross to conquer sin and death and to release His children into eternal salvation (Ephesians 2:16; Philippians 2:8). The disciples would not understand this until after Jesus' ascension and the infilling of the Holy Spirit.

Peter had come a long way, yet had a long way to go. His humanity was apparent when he discussed with the disciples what Jesus meant about the leaven of the Pharisees and Sadducees. His hardness of heart was seen in his agreeing with the other eleven. The dullness of his mind was seen in his forgetting about the miraculous feeding of the five thousand and the feeding of the four thousand. However, his spirit man was apparent in his ability to receive God's revelation and proclaim Jesus was the Christ, the Son of God, before his peers.

Peter's humanity is an example of every person. Each one begins spiritually dull. Each tries to figure things out independently, such as when the disciples discussed the bread amongst themselves instead of asking Jesus. Each person's heart can be hardened enough to experience and later forget a miracle. Each person has the potential to receive divine revelation from God the Father, which reveals to their heart of hearts Jesus the Messiah, *their* Savior. Each one has a calling in this life, which seems to them to be something they are not worthy of. Yet in Christ and through Christ, all things are possible (Matthew 19:26; Mark 9:23). He calls us to things too high to do on our own, so we continue to rely on Him.

Peter is an excellent example of a disciple's journey from salvation to sacrificial service. He was not made perfect by his calling, but through his calling, he was being perfected. Take a note from Peter's lesson book here for your own life. Stop striving for perfection; you cannot attain it. Seek excellence in all you do, and do it as unto the Lord. Remember: He has already chosen you; you don't have to strive for His approval. You only have to remain humble, yielded, and willing to learn and serve. Let Peter's example encourage you in your walk with Jesus today.

Day Four: Cross Talk

Read: Matthew 16:21–23; Mark 8:31–33; Luke 9:21–22.

1. What did Jesus begin to show His disciples?

2. (Challenge) Why would Jesus begin to show them now? (See Luke 9:18–20.)

3. From whom was Jesus to suffer many things? Why might the disciples have a difficult time believing this?

4. What did Peter do with the information Jesus shared? Why might he think it was okay to do this? (See Matthew 16:19.)

5. Did the disciples understand what Jesus came to do? What were they expecting in their Messiah?

6. How did Jesus respond to Peter? Why was He so harsh?

7. What do you think Jesus meant by saying Peter was an offense to Him?

8. What did Jesus say was wrong with Peter's focus?

Jesus Looks to the Cross

Jesus acknowledged Himself as Christ to His twelve disciples. Once Peter confessed Jesus as the Christ, the door was opened for Him to teach His disciples what His Messianic purpose truly was. Jesus had to help them overcome what they expected so they would be able to follow His plan. Their expectation of an earthly Messiah brought with it hopes of grandeur on their parts. They might have envisioned a palace greater than Solomon's, seats of honor in the kingdom, and riches beyond comprehension. Jesus needed to bring them down to earth to help them understand His role in delivering Israel (and the world) and their place within His kingdom plan.

     After Peter's great confession, Jesus began to show the disciples how He *must* go to Jerusalem. Jesus was a Messiah with a mission. He had to set His face unwaveringly toward Jerusalem, knowing what would come. He explained to them how Judaism's governing and priestly authorities would reject Him. They would neither accept nor believe Jesus was the Messiah. He revealed the leaders of

Israel, those who should have recognized and exalted Him, would be the very ones to inflict suffering and death upon Him. However, He added, He would rise again on the third day (Mark 8:31).

The disciples had a lot to take in. They had been hoping for an earthly victory, but Jesus began speaking of something very different from their expectations. Undoubtedly, the disciples expected the national leaders to get behind the Messiah. Jesus was making no sense to them. Peter found His story so far off he took Jesus aside and rebuked Him. Jesus had just given him the keys of the kingdom and told him whatever he bound or loosed on earth would be bound or loosed in heaven. Perhaps Peter was trying to exercise his newfound authority in the kingdom. Yet he found out quickly he had no idea what to do with the keys entrusted to him. He also discovered they did not place him on equal ground with the One Who gave them to him. This is an excellent example of why Jesus had to begin teaching about Jerusalem and His crucifixion, to give them time to come around from their way of thinking to His.

Jesus Adjusts Peter's Focus

Jesus quickly restored order in the kingdom when He rebuked Peter quite harshly. Jesus called Peter Satan and told him to get behind Him. First, for Peter to have keys to the kingdom did not give him authority over Jesus nor make him equal to Him. The keys to a household were given to a trusted servant to oversee the house's affairs, but they did not give him command over the master. Peter needed this experience to understand his role with the keys. Thus, Jesus reminded Peter to get behind Him. Peter was to follow Jesus wherever He led him; getting out in front of Jesus would only lead in the wrong direction and at the wrong time.

Jesus also called Peter two things: Satan and an offense. Jesus was not calling names; He was making a point. Satan has been against Jesus from the beginning. Satan had offered Jesus the world and tempted Him in every way (Luke 4:1–13). Surely, He would be tempted not to go to Jerusalem. To be an offense, one is a literal stumbling block. Jesus was tempted, just as we are (Hebrews 4:15). There is no question any human would be tempted not to go to Jerusalem if they knew their fate was crucifixion. Jesus did not need any of His disciples to sway Him away from His purpose. He needed His disciples to get on board with His plan and find out what their roles would be in the plan. The twelve needed to seek how to serve Jesus in every situation, even the unexpected ones.

Jesus told Peter his problem was one of focus. Peter was focused on earthly things. As discussed before, Peter expected an earthly Messiah with an earthly reign. He was hoping for a prominent position in this Messiah's earthly kingdom and believed he had just been given the position with the receiving of the metaphorical keys. However, Jesus told him his focus needed to be heavenward. Peter was selling himself short by focusing on the earthly. God had so much more for him than earthly riches and honor, but he would only find it by following Jesus, even when he did not understand or things didn't make sense.

Day Five: Cross Talk

Read: Matthew 16:24–28; Mark 8:34–38; Luke 9:23–26; John 14:6.

1. What teaching did Jesus begin immediately after rebuking Peter?

2. What was Jesus asking His disciples to deny? What do you think this meant?

3. How do you think Peter took this lesson on denying oneself? What was his lesson to learn?

4. What did Jesus mean by "take up his cross"? What do you think the disciples thought He meant? Remember, Jesus hadn't gone to the Cross yet, so the reference is not in light of the crucifixion.

5. What is the promise to the one who would save his own life?

6. What is the promise for the one who would lose his life for Jesus?

7. How can you save your soul?

8. What does it mean to be ashamed of Jesus? What is the promise to one who is ashamed of Him? What is the promise to one who is not ashamed of Him?

9. What generation does the one ashamed of Jesus belong to?

10. What was Jesus referring to when He said some would not pass away until they saw Him coming in His kingdom?

11. What lessons do you think Peter took from these statements?

Jesus Teaches on the Cost of Discipleship

Jesus also took the opportunity to begin to teach the disciples what their roles would be in His coming kingdom. Jesus was working toward changing not only their expectations of their Messiah, but also their expectations for their roles in His kingdom. Jesus ministered with humility. He made Himself low to lift humanity up (Philippians 2:6, 7). He expected His followers to do the same. Jesus began to teach the twelve the cost of discipleship.

Jesus started by addressing self-denial. The word "deny" has the connotation of disowning oneself. To become a follower of Jesus, you must give up ownership of self along with hopes, dreams, and desires, giving them all to Jesus and for Jesus. Jesus had plans for the twelve far better than they could have imagined (Jeremiah 29:11; Ephesians 3:20). This was where Peter was; he thought royal honor was more attractive than self-sacrifice. However, in the kingdom of God, there is nothing better than self-sacrifice to bring about a close, personal relationship with Jesus and a deep feeling of soul satisfaction. Giving up dreams and trading them for Jesus' plan is always far better than the plans disciples have for themselves. Jesus made a statement about taking up a cross and following Him. Jesus had just said He would die and be raised again. He would die on a cross, but the disciples did not realize it. There was, of course, the idea of a metaphorical cross, but there was a further understanding here: the visual of one who is accurately picking up his cross and carrying it to his death by choice.

The Roman Empire had been in power long enough for the disciples to understand what Jesus meant. Taking up one's cross meant they were carrying the cross beam on their backs towards the place where they would die a slow death. The one who takes up a cross has been deemed unworthy of life in the community, and the community lines up to spit, jeer, and reject this person from society. It is a time when you feel the world's hatred upon your shoulders. Just as the Jewish leaders would reject Jesus, so would His disciples be rejected, shamed, and even martyred. There is no room for self-seeking or pride in a disciple of Jesus. Humility is key in the kingdom (James 4:10).

Jesus knew the suffering His disciples would endure at the hands of those who denied Him. He knew some would be martyred for their faith, as well as be consistently rejected and abused by the Jewish authorities. He was teaching them to trust Him through it all. Walking in one's calling is the only way to have life satisfaction, even if it causes divisions with the world (2 Corinthians 2:16). Jesus warned, under kingdom principles, the one who tries to save his life will lose it, and vice versa. The one who tries to save his own life lacks faith in Jesus. The one who loses his life for Jesus' sake will find the one He planned for him and rejoice in it (Isaiah 55:8, 9).

Jesus, knowing what His disciples would suffer, gave them a warning and a promise regarding whether or not they acknowledged Him publicly. He said those who hide their love for Him are ashamed of Him. His promise to them was His silence about them before God the Father. Those who hide their relationship and love for Jesus withhold blessings from themselves during their life and find judgment in the end times. He said the one who is ashamed of Him belongs to a sinful and adulterous generation. This generation is not saved in the judgment. Those who will be saved unashamedly confess Jesus as Christ (John 14:6; Romans 10:9).

Jesus promised some of His disciples would still be alive when He came in His kingdom. Jesus' three years of ministry centered on one message: "The kingdom of God is at hand" (Matthew 4:17). Jesus won the victory upon His resurrection. Some commentators believe He was come in His glory then. Eleven of the disciples saw this (Judas Iscariot did not). Others believe He was come in His glory when he transfigured on the mountain. If you believe either of these, you are in good company.

Peter went from confessing Jesus as the Christ to rebuking Him for speaking of His death. The Lord lauded Peter and then harshly rebuked him. He'd been given the keys to the kingdom, but he was in training for how to use them. Jesus had called Peter out to be a leader in His kingdom, which would later be the church, but Peter didn't understand all this then. Disciples find it very much the same today. A direction of ministry is given, but the Lord never gives us all the information. He first wants His disciples to agree with and surrender to His plan, then He molds them for service. This was where Peter went wrong at first and where so many Christians fall apart today.

Jesus gave His disciples a glimpse of the future to set them in the right direction. Psalms 37:4 says, "Delight yourself in the Lord, and He shall give you the desires of your heart." Christians often take this to mean Jesus will give them everything they want. However, many times, what Christians *think* they want will not fulfill them, and the plans Jesus has for them will bless them to overflowing. The word "desire" can be used in two ways in Hebrew. The first form is translated as "wish." He will give you your heart's wishes: your hopes, dreams, and desires. The second way "desire" can be translated is "petitions," which means requests. He will give you a longing in your heart, and then He will also fulfill it better than you can think or imagine. However, the most critical part of this verse is "Delight yourself in the Lord." This is where many Christians become frustrated.

The impatience of waiting upon the Lord can cause us to stop delighting in Him. There is a passion-fire burning within to serve kingdom purposes. Yet, when the training becomes difficult or uncomfortable, too many people give up shy of fulfillment. Just like Peter wanted a position in the kingdom, Jesus also wanted to give him a position there. However, Peter's ideals fell far short of Jesus' plans for him. He pointed Peter in the right direction and then began to mold him to fit his calling: a calling he would not have thought of on his own, but a calling he was created for. Peter was severely rebuked before his peers as part of his leadership training. Christians must continue to delight themselves in the Lord, even in tough times. Having peace with God (salvation) is one profound thing to delight in during a life storm. Yet there are many promises to hold on to during those storms to encourage a disciple's ability to delight in Him. Here are just a few:

"And we know that all things work together for good to those who love God, to those who are called according to His purpose" (Romans 8:28).

"Yet in all these things we are more than conquerors through Him who loved us. For I am persuaded that neither death nor life, nor angels nor principalities nor powers, nor things present nor things to come, nor height nor depth, nor any other created thing, shall be able to separate us from the love of God which is in Christ Jesus our Lord" (Romans 8:37–39).

"Being confident of this very thing, that He who has begun a good work in you will complete it until the day of Jesus Christ" (Philippians 1:6).

Peter would learn through these lessons (and more to come) how a disciple of Jesus must place God's kingdom and plan first before his own aspirations and even before his understanding. When disciples set their agendas aside, they truly become the clay He can mold into the person they were created to be in and for the kingdom.

Day Six: Leaven, the Confession, and Cross Talk

1. Review this week's lessons and highlight your big takeaways. Be prepared to share these if you are meeting with a group.

2. Did you learn something about Peter this week? Share your thoughts.

3. How do you see your big takeaway(s) relating to the world around you today? To the Church in the broader sense, or the local church?

4. How might you apply one of these takeaways this week?

THE TRANSFIGURATION AND CHARACTER LESSONS

Days One and Two: Witnesses Jesus' Transfiguration

Read: Matthew 5:17, 17:1–4; Mark 9:1–5; Luke 9:27–33.

1. Who did Jesus take with Him up the mountain?

2. (Challenge) Why these three?

3. What happened to Jesus on the mountain when He began to pray?

4. Who did Jesus speak with on the mountain? Why them, and what did they talk about?

5. What was Peter's response? Why?

Jesus' Inner Circle

Jesus invited three disciples to witness a glorious miracle on the mountain. He invited Peter, James, and John. There were a few occasions in which Jesus permitted only these three men to witness what He did (Matthew 17:1; Mark 5:37, 9:2, 14:33; Luke 8:51). Why He did not invite the others, we are not told.

We know Peter became head of the church, and John was often mentioned alongside Peter in ministry after Jesus' ascension. James would also become a church leader in Jerusalem. John wrote five books of the New Testament and Peter contributed two. Jesus was preparing these three men for specific purposes in ministry, which most likely were not necessary for the other disciples. They would not all be heads of the church at Jerusalem. The three were not treated special because Jesus liked them best. They received the blessed revelation because of their purposes and callings.

Read: Exodus 16:10, 19:1–3, 24:15–18, 40:34; 2 Chronicles 5:13–14; Matthew 3:17, 17:5–9; Mark 1:9–11, 9:6–13; Luke 9:33–36.

6. What overshadowed the group while they spoke? What was it, or what did it represent?

7. Who spoke from the cloud, and what did He say?

8. When did this happen before? What was different this time?

9. Why would the disciples be so afraid?

10. How were the disciples comforted?

11. What was Jesus' command to the disciples concerning what had happened? Why?

Read: 2 Peter 1:16–18.

12. What was Peter's recollection of this event, and what was its significance, according to Peter?

13. What does Peter tell us Jesus received from God the Father?

14. Review Peter's life up until this point; review where he came from and what he had come through and experienced up to this point.

Jesus' Transfiguration Circle

Jesus brought His three disciples with Him up a high mountain. Only the Gospel of Luke tells us the purpose of the trip was to pray (Luke 9:28). Luke's Gospel reveals the transfiguration happened as Jesus prayed (Luke 9:29). The Synoptic Gospels all describe the Transfiguration of Jesus. Matthew said, "His face shone as the sun, and His clothing was white as the light." Mark said, "His clothes became shining, exceedingly white, like snow, such as no launderer on earth can whiten them," and Luke described it as, "the appearance of His face was altered, and His robe became white and glistening" (Matthew 17:2; Mark 9:3; Luke 9:29).

When Jesus transfigured, two men, Moses and Elijah, appeared and spoke with Him. Moses was the greatest leader Israel ever had. He spoke face to face with God and introduced God's Law to the Israelites (Exodus 24:12, 33:11). He represented the Law. Elijah was the greatest known prophet in Israel. His boldness and courage to stand up to one of Israel's most corrupt and dangerous kings were well documented. Elijah represented the prophets (1 Kings 17–21).

The Gospels give a fuller understanding in light of Moses and Elijah representing the Law and the Prophets. Jesus said, "Do not think that I came to destroy the Law or the Prophets. I did not come to destroy but to fulfill" (Matthew 5:17). Luke 16:16 says, "The law and the prophets were until John. Since then, the kingdom of God has been preached, and everyone is pressing into it." A final example is found at John 1:45: "Philip found Nathanael and said to him, 'We have found Him of whom Moses in the law, and also the prophets, wrote—Jesus of Nazareth, the son of Joseph.'" Jesus came to fulfill the Law of Moses and the promises of the prophets, which Elijah was representative of. The witness for the disciples was in having seen Jesus with the Law and the Prophets; He was the fulfillment of what they had been waiting for: the Messiah.

In perfect sanguine style, Peter, excited about what he saw, blurted out words, not really realizing what he was saying or why. Most likely, he just needed to participate in what was happening. He volunteered himself, James, and John to build three tabernacles: one for Moses, one for Elijah, and one for Jesus. He seemed to be looking for why Jesus brought the three of them. Interestingly, Peter knew who Jesus was speaking to. They would never have seen a photograph of Moses or Elijah, yet they knew who they were. Did they hear Jesus speak their names or know by revelation? Scripture does not answer this question. Nor does scripture record any response to Peter's suggestion. Instead, while Peter spoke, a cloud overshadowed them and caused the disciples to fear.

All the Gospels report the cloud as a bright cloud coming over them. Luke said it "overshadowed them," and they also entered it. The cloud was the presence of the glory of the Lord God. God's presence was seen as a bright cloud throughout the Old Testament. When God spoke to Moses, His presence appeared in the cloud (Exodus 16:10, 19:1–3, 24:16). The glory of the Lord expressed in the cloud appeared to show God's approval of the first Tabernacle as well as Solomon's Temple (Exodus 40:33–35; 2 Chronicles 5:14). God appeared in the cloud to tell Moses to lead Israel. He also appeared to show His approval.

When this cloud appeared over and encompassed Jesus, Moses, Elijah, and the disciples, a voice came from within. God's voice spoke from the cloud to lead His people (the disciples and all who come after them) to the truth of Who Jesus is: God's Son. God's voice also came from the cloud to express His approval of Jesus and tell the disciples to hear or listen to Him. There could be no more questions for these disciples after this encounter. Jesus was the Messiah, well pleasing to God, and they needed to begin to really listen to Him. No more preconceived ideas; they needed to hear what He was saying and get on board with His plan.

The last time God spoke audibly from the cloud, He addressed the whole congregation of Israel (Exodus 19:9, 20:1–22). God spoke the Ten Commandments to the entire congregation of Israel in the wilderness. The Israelites asked not to hear God's audible voice again because they feared it. They said they were okay with Moses speaking to God and relaying His messages to them, but they did not want to hear God's voice again, because they feared they would die. This time, God spoke to a few chosen men and commanded them to hear Jesus. They, too, were afraid, but Jesus' touch comforted them.

Jesus' Silent Circle

The three disciples had just witnessed not only a miracle, but the very presence and voice of God the Father. They heard God say Jesus was His Son, He was well pleased with Him, and they should listen to Jesus. Anyone with this experience would want to share it with everyone they meet. The disciples may have already thought they had witnessed this event to begin spreading the good news of Jesus, the long-awaited Messiah. Yet Jesus commanded them to be silent about what they had seen and heard.

The foursome was not even off the mountain before Jesus commanded Peter, James, and John to hold their information until after He had risen again. While it seemed like an odd request, it was still not yet Jesus' time. Jesus came for a specific purpose; it had to come about according to God's plan. If the disciples had begun telling their story right away, Jesus would have had a much more difficult time preaching, teaching, and preparing His people for what was to come. They would all the more try to make Him king of the Jews on earth and would be devastated by His death on the Cross. Even worse, more people may have stood to fight the mob when it came to get Him in the Garden of Gethsemane. His plan would still have been carried out, but possibly at the cost of many lives.

Peter wrote about this experience in his second epistle later in his life (2 Peter 1:16–18). He recalled the transfiguration as the majesty of Jesus Christ, to which he and the other disciples were eyewitnesses. He continued, the voice of God came from the cloud of magnificent glory, giving honor and glory to Jesus, proclaiming Him to be His Beloved Son, the One in Whom He delights (Psalms 2:7; Isaiah 42:1; Matthew 17:5).

Peter made decisions for his life to allow him to experience intimacy with Jesus. While Peter was created for a purpose and a calling, he still had to participate in the training exercises. He could have said no at any point along the way. Yet scripture shows, in Peter, a discipleship journey many Christians can relate to. He left the life he knew and was comfortable with. He had many character flaws or weaknesses when Jesus met him. It was a long road to the famed name of Apostle Peter.

Peter was a grumpy, know-it-all fisherman who received an abundance of fish and gave up his work to follow Jesus. He opened his home as a center for ministry, showing hospitality. He was often gone from his family when traveling with Jesus, yet he was blessed to be taught by Jesus daily. He saw storms calmed; he walked on water and then nearly drowned, only to be saved again. He healed the sick, was given the keys of the kingdom, was harshly rebuked, and then was privileged to see Jesus' glory, honor, and majesty on earth. What an incredible discipleship journey he has had thus far.

Peter was not unlike disciples today. New believers come with character flaws and worldly behaviors. As disciples grow in Christ, they find ways to serve the kingdom. Sometimes, it is as simple as hosting a missionary in their home. While following Jesus, disciples experience storms and learn the difference between fighting the battle themselves and relying on Jesus for help. Soon, the disciple has gained enough faith to begin to walk as Jesus walked—on water—doing what once seemed impossible. Often, when you step out in faith, fear takes over, and you begin to fail until you cry out to Jesus for help. This is a journey of being molded from a worldly sinner to a Christlike servant of others. There are many mistakes and failures along the way, but a disciple cannot get caught up in feelings of failure or self-doubt. Every bump in the road of the discipleship journey is the touch of the Master's hand, molding His children into what they were created to be and do (Isaiah 64:8; Romans 8:28; Philippians 1:6).

Simply knowing Peter, the great apostle, had a discipleship walk full of imperfections ought to give every disciple hope for their walk with Jesus. They must continue with Jesus' lessons, tailored to them, and learn from their mistakes, while not letting failures cast them down. Embrace the journey where you are molded into Christ-likeness and the person you were created to be.

Day Three: Offense, Pride, and Forgiveness

Read: Matthew 17:24–27.

1. What town had they come to? Why is this significant?

2. Who came to Peter to ask about the temple tax? Why didn't they go to Jesus?

3. Did Peter lie?

4. What house did Peter come into?

5. What is Jesus' point in verses 25 and 26?

6. Why did Jesus say they should pay the temple tax?

7. How can you apply this principle in your life right now?

8. How did Jesus have Peter retrieve the money?

9. Peter usually fished with a net. What was different here?

10. How do we know this event took place?

Personal Reflection

11. What application(s) can you draw from this story for your own life?

Peter Fishes for Temple Tax

Jesus and the disciples had returned to Capernaum, their base of operations and Peter's home (Matthew 17:24). This was where Jesus first spoke in the synagogue after calling Peter, Andrew, James, and John to be His disciples. He amazed the assembly by speaking with authority and casting a demon out of a man (Mark 1:21–27). The people, priests included, were amazed by Him. However, the priests had not been too fascinated to keep from challenging Him.

Capernaum was where Jesus ate with tax collectors and sinners, and the Pharisees confronted His disciples rather than Him about it (Matthew 9:11). Capernaum was where Jairus came in desperation to ask Him to heal his daughter's sickness. She died before Jesus could get there, but He raised her from the dead, before her mother and father and before Peter, James, and John. While on the way to Jairus' house, a woman with an issue of blood was healed of her affliction (Mark 5:23–43). Jesus' base of operation was in Capernaum, and many brought the sick and afflicted to Peter's home for healing; many came to hear Jesus teach (Matthew 8:14–16).

The location of the temple tax collectors confronting Peter is significant. Capernaum's spiritual leaders had seen an abundance of miracles, which witnessed to the authority of Jesus' teachings, and yet, they were still challenging Him. They were testing Him. They were seeking to find fault in Him. This was most likely why Jesus said, "And you, Capernaum, who are exalted to heaven, will be brought down to Hades; for if the mighty works which were done in you had been done in Sodom, it would have remained until this day" (Matthew 11:23).

Those who collected the temple tax approached Peter to question him about his Teacher (Exodus 30:11–16). The Pharisees did the same thing when Jesus ate with tax collectors and sinners (Matthew 9:11). They were not bold enough to confront Jesus face to face. Rather, they sought to cause His disciples to question Him. Putting doubt into the minds of Jesus' disciples would be a much more effective tool in undermining Jesus' work than confronting Him directly. This is the oldest tactic in the book. This is the first tactic Satan used against God's children in the Garden of Eden. Satan caused Eve to question God's only rule for humans, and she and Adam ate of the forbidden fruit, bringing down a curse on all humanity (Genesis 3). Jesus' entire purpose is to come and redeem us from this curse, and God's ministers are actively working against it (1 Corinthians 15:45–58).

The tax collectors asked Peter, "Does your Teacher not pay the temple tax?" Peter said, "Yes" (Matthew 17:24–25). Is this a lie? The way Matthew has written this brief exchange does not make it clear if Peter was saying, "Yes, He does not pay," or "Yes, He does pay." The question is, "Does [He] not pay?" Therefore, a yes answer could affirm His not paying. However, it could also mean He does pay. Peter may have been giving a vague one-word, take-it-as-you-will answer to protect Jesus' reputation, the thing he must have been sure they were trying to fault. Scripture is unclear on this; however, the lack of continued dialogue lends to this explanation.

Jesus already knew what was on Peter's mind when he arrived home. He graciously dealt with Peter's question before he had to find the words to pose it to Him. Jesus brought Peter to understand that because He was God's Son, and because He was the Messiah, He did not owe a temple tax (Matthew 14:25, 26). The temple tax supports His kingdom. However, Jesus did not assert His position on this matter. Instead, with humility and meekness, He paid the temple tax to avoid offending the priests. He didn't have to pay, but it was more important to Him to have grace toward their ignorance rather than cause them to be His enemies (2 Peter 3:9).

Jesus sent Peter, the fisherman, out fishing to collect the money to pay the tax. This is a beautiful example of how Jesus blesses the skills and abilities of His children. Like a magician, he could have just pulled the coin from behind Peter's ear. He could have made it appear any way He desired. Yet He required Peter to make an effort to participate before he could experience the miraculous blessing. One beautiful part of the miracle was Peter's immediate obedience to what would have sounded like nonsense to anyone else. Peter had come a long way in his faith walk with Jesus. He believed what Jesus had said and obeyed to catch the first fish and look inside its mouth. Because of his obedience, he found a coin to cover Jesus and himself. Jesus could have provided just enough for Himself, but He is never just about Himself. He provided sufficient for His willing disciple, as well.

Days Four and Five: Offense, Pride, and Forgiveness

Read: Matthew 18:1–5; Mark 9:33–37; Luke 9:46–48.

1. Why do you think the disciples were having this discussion?

2. (Challenge) Why might Peter think it would be himself? Why might James or John?

3. What did Jesus use as the object of His lesson?

4. How does one become great in God's kingdom?

Peter Learns about Greatness

Jesus had been teaching the disciples about His rejection, death, and resurrection since they proclaimed Him the Messiah. Yet they still did not understand at this point. They had been disputing over who would be greatest in the kingdom. They were still posturing for position. Matthew's Gospel says the disciples came to Jesus and asked who was the greatest in the kingdom. Mark and Luke's Gospels say they were disputing which of them was greatest, and Jesus later brought it up. Either way, their focus was in the wrong place. They were looking for a political, earthly kingdom.

Peter may have leaned on his being given the keys of the kingdom, being named the rock, and Jesus saying He would build His church upon this rock. John and Andrew might have argued their following Jesus the longest. They were together and heard Jesus speak before the others had. Andrew came home and told Peter they had found the Messiah (John 1:41). James also had a claim, as he was one of the first to be called to follow Jesus. Peter, James, and John, being called to Jesus' inner circle, was also a good point to argue. They had been allowed to witness the raising of Jairus' daughter as well as His transfiguration on the mountain (Mark 5:37, 9:2). Whatever their reasoning, they were standing on finite human understanding. They were not standing on a calling of God; in their pride, they sought the best seat in the kingdom (Luke 14:8–10). Jesus was about to teach them one of the greatest kingdom lessons every disciple of Jesus needs to come to understand.

Jesus chose for the object of His lesson a boy young enough to be referred to as a child. Jesus replied, "Assuredly, I say to you, unless you are converted and become as little children, you will by no means enter the kingdom of heaven. Therefore, whoever humbles himself as this little child is the greatest in the kingdom of heaven" (Matthew 18:3, 4). Jesus made a hard point. He began by not speaking of kingdom position but of salvation. He used the child to make a point. They were in jeopardy of not even entering the kingdom of heaven with the course they were on.

They must be "converted and become as little children" (Matthew 18:3). Children are under the authority of their parents. They hold no position in the household. They are lower than the servants (Galatians 4:1, 2). Children have no voice and no choice in family matters; it is merely for them to learn the ways of God and obey their parents (Genesis 18:19). So shall it be for the children of the kingdom of heaven. Jesus' disciples must humble themselves under His authority, giving up control and status, seeking to know Him and His ways, and walking in righteousness, justice, and humility. "Therefore, whoever humbles himself as this little child is the greatest in the kingdom of heaven" (Matthew 18:4).

Read: Matthew 18:21–35.

5. How many times did Peter say he should forgive? Why this number?

6. How many times did Jesus say one should forgive? What did He mean by the equation He gave?

7. How badly in debt was the servant?

8. Who is the king in this parable, and how much did he forgive His servant? Why?

9. Did this servant learn from his Master and treat others in kind?

10. What happened when the Master found out about it?

11. What is Jesus' answer to Peter about how often to forgive his brother who sins against him?

Peter Learns about Forgiveness

Peter asked Jesus how many times he should forgive offenses from his brother. He questioned whether seven times would be enough. Jewish custom was three times forgiven and then no more. The meaning of forgiveness is to hold no malice toward the offender. Peter probably thought he was being very generous with the offer of forgiving his brother seven times.

Jesus' response to Peter was to forgive "seven times seventy." While seven is a perfect number, multiplying it seventy times suggests an infinite number. Peter was to forgive his brother's sins against him infinitely (Matthew 6:5; Luke 6:37). Jesus continued with a parable to help Peter understand how it is with the kingdom of heaven. Peter would need to understand this as he would lead the church in its foundational period. However, all Jesus' present and future disciples need to understand the kingdom principle of forgiveness, as well.

Jesus described a servant who was ten thousand talents in debt. He represented Jesus' disciples. The king decided to settle accounts. The servant did not know when his account would come before the king. He had debts he could not pay, and he did not know when his loan's due date was, such as the bank suddenly calling in a loan to be paid in full. The mortgage holder would likely not have the funds to pay the bank. The king represented God, and He forgave all the servant's debts. The man sought mercy, and just as God forgives the debt of sin when sinners receive Jesus as their Savior, the servant was forgiven his debt (John 3:16; 1 John 1:9).

The lesson Jesus was teaching is seen in the actions of the servant. The king's good gesture should have moved the servant to turn and extend the same mercy to his fellow servant. It was then in his power to grant the same forgiveness of debt to his fellow man. Yet instead, the servant physically attacked his fellow servant and demanded he pay all owed to him, which was much less than he had just been forgiven himself. He was in a position of power to forgive another man's debt, as the man begged him not for forgiveness, but for more time. He refused, and his actions were made known to the king.

The lesson, most importantly, points to what happens if one does not forgive seventy times seven. The unforgiving servant's debts were all piled back upon him, and he was delivered to be tortured until he should pay. Clearly, he would not be able to pay. He would be tortured until he was dead. It is like this in the kingdom of heaven. When a debtor refuses to forgive debts when God has forgiven his debts, his debts will be restored to him, and he, too, will be delivered to the torturers. This is a picture of the end-of-times judgment. Therefore, Jesus' answer to Peter was to forgive his brother as God had forgiven him. Hold no malice toward a fellow servant. Remember the debts you have been forgiven before holding anyone else guilty. Forgiving others keeps your debts cleared.

Peter learned many lessons in this week's study. As a disciple of Jesus, he learned he must live so as not to cause offense, which would draw others away from Jesus. As ambassadors of Christ, disciples are responsible for not turning people away from Jesus. Being right isn't always the best method of ministry. Jesus did not have to pay the voluntary temple tax, but He did to avoid giving the priests any reason to doubt Him.

Peter also learned how the juxtaposition of being called to the highest positions in the kingdom of heaven is to be called to the lowest place of servitude. To attain a high calling, a disciple must be willing and joyful in the lowliest tasks. The key to godly living is the willingness to serve in any position, not thinking yourself too good for any purpose. Peter would need to become a servant of all to be the greatest. Servants don't look to their own needs but to the needs of others first.

Peter's final lesson in this chapter had to do with forgiveness. He was generously willing to forgive his brother seven times: more than double the Jewish standard. Yet Jesus taught no end to forgiveness for a disciple of Jesus. A disciple ought to desire others to experience the freedom from the debt of sins, just as God in Christ has forgiven them.

The lessons for Peter are relevant today. Offense, pride, and unforgiveness all repel people from Jesus. When we demand our rights rather than give them up for the sake of others, we turn them off to Christ. When we deem ourselves more highly than we ought to, crushing others under our feet for position, we turn them away from Christ. When we refuse to share the forgiveness, we have received with others, our hypocrisy turns them off to Christ.

Paul expressed this well: "Therefore, if anyone is in Christ, he is a new creation; old things have passed away; behold, all things have become new. Now all things are of God, who has reconciled us to Himself through Jesus Christ, and has given us the ministry of reconciliation, that is, that God was in Christ reconciling the world to Himself, not imputing their trespasses to them, and has committed to us the word of reconciliation. Now then, we are ambassadors for Christ, as though God were pleading through us: we implore you on Christ's behalf, be reconciled to God. For He made Him who knew no sin to be sin for us, that we might become the righteousness of God in Him" (2 Corinthians 5:17–21).

Day Six: The Transfiguration and Character Lessons

1. Review this week's lessons and highlight your big takeaways. Be prepared to share these if you are meeting with a group.

2. Did you learn something about Peter this week? Share your thoughts.

3. How do you see your big takeaway(s) relating to the world around you today? To the Church in the broader sense, or the local church?

4. How might you apply one of these takeaways this week?

KINGDOM PRINCIPLES AND THE TRIUMPHAL ENTRY

Day One: Children, Riches, and Rewards

Read: Matthew 19:13–15; Mark 9:36–37; Luke 18:15–17.

1. Why would Peter (or the disciples) rebuke the people for bringing their children to Jesus?

2. How did Jesus feel about what the disciples had done?

3. What did Jesus say about the kingdom of heaven, and how is this possible?

4. Then what did Jesus do with the children?

5. (Challenge) Why was this an important lesson, especially for Peter?

The Value of Children

Jesus' fame had spread far and wide in the region. He was nearing the end of His three-year ministry in which He healed many sick and demon-possessed people. Multitudes had followed Him and brought their sick to Him; they saw Him heal and heard Him speak. People were making their minds up about who He was. Now they began to bring their healthy children to Him so He could touch them with His miracle-working hands and pray over them. Ancient Hebrew people were accustomed to having a major prophet or spiritually important figure lay hands on and bless their children. This was an act of dedicating their children to God. Israel had not had a major prophet for around four hundred years. People acknowledged they believed Jesus was from God, even if they fell short of believing He was the Messiah they had been waiting for. They did, however, consider Him a prophet or the Messiah; otherwise, they would not have sought Him out to lay hands on and pray for their children.

The disciples saw them bringing their children, who had no real need, and rebuked the people for bringing them to Jesus for prayer. None of the Gospel accounts explain why they did this. They most likely thought the children were too young to be brought to Jesus. However, they may have felt they were protecting Jesus from overwork. The disciples were closest to Jesus. They knew His work schedule and all He had done up to the moment. Since the children were not sick, they may have thought the parents should not bother Jesus with them then.

Jesus' response to the disciples presents us with a clue regarding the disciples' thinking. Jesus commanded them to allow the "little children to come to [Him] … for such is the kingdom of heaven" (Matthew 19:14). The kingdom of heaven has a different value system from humanity. All are equal. All have a right to come to Jesus, regardless of age, gender, race, or social status. Nothing is blocking any person from coming to Jesus, especially not His disciples. Jesus taught a kingdom principle: children are equally valuable and should be given access to Him. Adults should never assume a child is too young to come to Jesus.

Mark and Luke both record further teaching in their Gospels. Jesus used this opportunity to teach His disciples to "receive the kingdom of God as a little child [or they would not] enter it" (Mark 10:15; Luke 18:17). A childlike faith encompasses complete trust and belief in what has been heard. Childlike faith is also saturated with innocence and purity. Jesus said entry to the kingdom of heaven requires one to be filled with innocence and purity, believe He is who He says He is, and will do what He said He would do. Only then can the kingdom of God come fully alive within His disciples.

Jesus did not say you had to have innocence and purity to ask Him to be your Savior. He is the Purifier and Sanctifier of souls. He is speaking to those who are already His disciples. They already believe in Him. Now they are required to walk in faith, innocence, and purity. Otherwise, the kingdom of God will escape them throughout their Christian walk. They will go through the motions of their Christianity, but they will fall far short of who they were created to be and the inexpressible joys of kingdom living.

Day Two: Children, Riches, and Rewards

Read: Matthew 19:23–30; Mark 10:23–31; Luke 18:24–30; Acts 4:10–12.

1. Why do you think it is hard for a rich person to enter the kingdom of God? (Give scripture to support your answer.)

2. What does this mean: "It is easier for a camel to go through the eye of a needle than for a rich man to enter the kingdom of God?"

3. What was the disciples' response to this information?

4. Is it wrong to be rich? (Based on what scripture?)

5. What encouraging words did Jesus offer them at this point?

6. What did Peter later say was the way to be saved? (See Acts 4:10–12.)

7. How does this support Jesus' statement from question 5?

The Difficulties of the Rich

Jesus asked a rich young man to give away all he had to follow Him. The young man did not follow. He was not able to give up his comfortable life. The unknown was too frightening. He could not trust in Jesus to provide for his needs, as he trusted in his finances.

Jesus used this opportunity to teach His disciples about the kingdom of God. He said, "It is easier for a camel to go through the eye of a needle than for a rich man to enter the kingdom of God" (Matthew 19:24). This is a strong statement. Obviously, a camel does not fit through the eye of a needle. The disciples clearly understood Jesus was speaking of salvation, and they wondered then, who could be saved? They realized everyone seeks financial success. So then, who could be saved?

Mark's Gospel provides a little clearer understanding about the relationship of money with salvation: "How hard it is for those who trust in riches to enter" (Mark 10:24). Mark's Gospel suggests riches were not the issue, but one's relationship to them. This was not a statement against having money but a warning against trusting in it. Paul wrote in his letter to Timothy, "The love of money is a root of all kinds of evil" (1 Timothy 6:10). Solomon wrote, "The sleep of a laboring man is sweet, whether he eats little or much; but the abundance of the rich will not permit him to sleep" (Ecclesiastes 5:12). He also wrote, "The blessing of the Lord makes one rich, and He adds no sorrow with it" (Proverbs 10:22), and "The rich and the poor have this in common, the Lord is maker of them all" (Proverbs 22:2). Therefore, it is not a sin to be rich but a sin to trust in riches. We cannot enter the kingdom of God unless our trust is utmost in Jesus. This means holding onto possessions and money loosely, trusting Jesus with abundance and the lack of it. The good news is Jesus said, "With men it is impossible, but with God all things are possible" (Matthew 10:26; Mark 10:27; Luke 18:27).

Peter would later teach the only way to be saved is through Jesus (Acts 4:12). Paul would write, "If you confess with your mouth the Lord Jesus and believe in your heart that God has raised Him from the dead, you will be saved" (Romans 10:9). Salvation is a miracle available to anyone regardless of financial status, gender, age, race, and so on. Salvation is the first step. Then comes a life journey of being molded into Christ-likeness, which means changing your value system and character through a lifelong process guided by the Lord. However, salvation is not something you can attain by yourself. You can use no amount of riches or breeding to buy your way into heaven. We all must take an active part in humbling ourselves under the authority of the Lord. However, Peter did not understand this at the time.

Day Three: Children, Riches, and Rewards

Read: Matthew 19:27–30; Mark 10:28–31; Luke 18:28–30.

1. What question did Peter pose to Jesus? What kind of answer do you think he was expecting? Ask yourself what kind of kingdom Peter was expecting.

2. When did Jesus say His followers would receive their reward?

3. When is the regeneration Jesus speaks of in Matthew 19:28?

4. Who will sit on the twelve thrones and judge the twelve tribes of Israel?

5. What rewards did Jesus promise to those who have left all to follow Him?

6. When will this reward be received?

7. Who will be first and who will be last? What does Jesus mean by this statement?

8. Will all who are first be last and vice versa?

The Rewards of Sacrifice

Peter posed a question following the desire to know who would be greatest in the kingdom. He wanted to know what he and the other disciples would get for leaving all to follow Jesus (Matthew 19:27). Jesus did not rebuke Peter for asking this question. Either he understood Peter was asking what the reward for such action was, or He was looking forward to another teaching opportunity. They would not receive riches and fame, but what they had given up would be restored to them a hundredfold.

Of course, Peter and the other disciples would not receive a hundred wives, children, or businesses. The promise was not literal in this aspect. However, in kingdom living, they would gain spirit relatives in place of blood relatives they lost for Jesus. The family of God is a beautiful, connected family. One can travel to other parts of the world and find familial relations with those from different cultures and countries who worship Jesus. Regarding finances (Peter had left his business and his livelihood), the blessings of God would supply all his needs. This is not to say every Christian is called to quit work and become a travelling evangelist. However, once saved, your relationship to the material changes; abundant blessings pour forth as believers give of themselves and their finances. Blessings come in different forms, such as in the context of someone giving you a car, God providing the funds when you need to buy a car, or keeping a vehicle running miraculously. My good friend went to a mechanic for something, and he found her car had no oil in it, yet it had been running fine. Abundant blessings may also come in the form of birthing contentment regardless of what you have. There is a change in your relationship to the temporal.

Jesus also said these blessings come with persecutions: "For we are to God the fragrance of Christ among those who are being saved and among those who are perishing. To the one we are the aroma of death leading to death, and to the other the aroma of life leading to life" (2 Corinthians 2:15, 16). Jesus promised blessings a hundredfold in this life, here on earth, in the temporal. Yet He also promised persecutions along with it. His answer to Peter, then, and to all disciples of all times, is simple. There will be blessings. Whatever you give up to follow Him will be restored to you with greater satisfaction, but there will also be persecutions. He did not promise an easy life on earth. However, He does promise, at the end of life, eternal salvation, which is the true goal of every believer.

Jesus said, "in the regeneration" (Matthew 19:28). Regeneration is the spiritual change in your sin nature, producing a faith so you can relate to God. Only Matthew's Gospel records this statement of Jesus. Looking at the context, Jesus spoke of the regeneration as coming when He would sit on His throne of glory. Then He spoke of the rewards of the twelve, then to everyone who has sacrificed for Him, and then eternal reward. This is somewhat confusing when determining Jesus' use of the word "regeneration." Was He speaking of the spiritual regeneration to come upon His ascension, or was He speaking of the end times when He returns and a new heaven and earth are born?

The definition of the word points to the regeneration of the soul. The writer of Hebrews explains, Jesus, "After He had offered one sacrifice for sins forever, [He] sat down at the right hand of God" (Hebrews 10:12). The sacrifice spoken of was His death. After His resurrection and ascension, He sat down at God's right hand on the throne of His glory. John's Gospel says, "The Holy Spirit was not yet given, because Jesus was not yet glorified" (John 7:39). According to the first two chapters in the book of Acts, the Holy Spirit came after Jesus ascended to heaven and sat at the right hand of God. All of this fits with the primary definition of "regeneration."

What is confusing for most is that He promises His disciples they would be judges over the twelve tribes. This causes many to think Jesus was speaking of the end times. However, Jesus had already given Peter the keys of the kingdom for binding and loosing. The twelve were included in this because, except for Judas, they would teach and witness to Israel regarding Jesus, the Christ. Paul was the only apostle not present in this group then, who was called to witness to the Gentiles. Jesus answered the disciples' question regarding who would be the greatest in the kingdom. They would be. However, in the kingdom of heaven on earth, these important positions would not look like the world's kingdoms. These are positions of high honor and celebrity; they will come at great sacrifice—even martyrdom. Jesus was still speaking of the rewards of following Him.

Jesus said everyone who sacrifices family or possessions to follow Him will receive a hundredfold back on what they sacrificed. This does not mean they will literally receive back a hundred wives, children, or houses. It does mean He will satisfy every need for family and possessions. The kingdom of heaven exists with the presence of Jesus—and Jesus came to give life abundantly (John 10:10). Jesus was speaking of life in the kingdom on earth up to this point (Matthew 19:28, 29; Mark 10:30; Luke 18:30). He finished His statement by obviously transitioning to the "age to come," the afterlife, when He promised eternal life to everyone who follows Him. There are rewards on earth, but there are also persecutions. However, for those who continue with Jesus, there is the promise of eternal salvation. These are the rewards of those who give up the old life to follow Jesus in a new and better life.

Jesus finished His comments by saying, "Many who are first will be last and the last first" (Matthew 19:30; Mark 10:31). He did not say "all," but "many." He was referring to the Jews and the Gentiles. The Jews (Israelites) were the first to have an intimate relationship with God. However, many had fallen away completely or from the proper implementation of His Law. But many Gentiles, through Jesus' sacrifice, would come into the kingdom. As Paul speaks in the eleventh chapter of Romans, the life change in the Gentiles would draw some of Israel back into a right relationship with God through Jesus.

The disciples learned three valuable lessons after pondering who was the greatest in the kingdom. Jesus used these opportunities to teach His disciples about kingdom ways. He taught them how God intends children to be valued in the kingdom, the difficulties of those who pursue riches, and the reward of sacrifice.

Peter learned God's value of children and their equality in the spirit realm. While they are still to remain under the authority of their parents, they are as welcome to seek Him as any adult. Children are capable of a spiritual relationship with Jesus. Disciples should always assume they are to lead children to God, not ignore them until they are older.

Peter also learned how riches can be a danger to your salvation. He and the other disciples had been posturing for a prominent role in Jesus' kingdom, thinking of riches and power. However, Jesus warns of the peril for those who trust in riches. They will not enter the kingdom of heaven. They learned the sin was not in owning possessions, but in their relationship to their possessions.

Finally, Peter and the disciples learned the rewards of leaving all to follow Jesus. Jesus promised abundant returns on whatever was sacrificed to follow Him for each disciple. He would not leave a disciple in want. He would fulfill them in their walk, and provide for their needs; they would soon not feel the pain of their sacrifice.

Jesus promised He came to give life more abundantly. Disciples who can cut ties with the past, leave whatever holds them back, and freely give themselves to the call and purpose of God in their life will have an abundant, extraordinary life. However, He also promised the blessings would come with persecutions. Only within the dynamic of the kingdom of God can you be fulfilled with an abundant life and experience persecution at the same time. Jesus did not promise freedom from troubles and trials. He promised an abundant life within them. This is amazing.

Day Four: Witness to the Triumphal Entry

Read: Zechariah 9:9; Matthew 21:1–9; Mark 11:1–10, Luke 19:29–38; John 12:1–2, 12–19.

1. Where did they turn in to stay when they came near Jerusalem? (Challenge) How far from Jerusalem were they?

2. What did Jesus tell two of His disciples to do? What were His specific instructions?

3. How did His disciples respond to this odd request?

4. What did they do when they found what they were looking for?

5. Who questioned them? How did the disciples respond? What happened?

6. Was this a miracle?

7. What did they do when they brought the colt to Jesus? Why do you think they did this?

8. When Jesus sat on the colt, never before ridden, did it buck? Was this a miracle?

9. What did the multitude of disciples lay on the road? Why?

10. What did the multitude cry out? What were they expecting Jesus to do?

A Colt to Fulfill Prophecy

Jesus and His disciples neared Bethany, where they would stay with Lazarus, Jesus' friend and the one He raised from the dead (John 12:1). Bethany is about two miles from Jerusalem. Jesus commanded two of His disciples to go to the village opposite them and retrieve a colt, the foal of a donkey. This is significant.

Jesus was specific about it being a donkey's foal, not a horse. The colt, the foal of a donkey, had a critical role in the coming of the King. According to Zechariah 9:9, the foal was to carry the Messiah into Jerusalem as a sign her King had come: "Behold, your King is coming to you; He is just and having salvation, lowly and riding on a donkey, a colt, the foal of a donkey." This was done to fulfill scripture and be a sign to the people; it should also have been a sign to the elders at Jerusalem. Only the Messiah could ride a colt never-before ridden without incident. Only the Creator and Master of the universe could miraculously sit upon a never-before-ridden colt and have him remain calm and submitted. All those who saw Him mount the colt would realize this.

Jesus was also specific about where the two disciples would find the colt, how they should take it, and what they should say should anyone confront them for stealing. What might this have done for their faith? Their just doing it is most interesting. They simply obeyed their Teacher. They had walked with Him long enough by this time. They did not question His odd request, nor were they embarrassed when confronted. They merely obeyed, and everything worked out for them to take the colt and his mother to their Master (Matthew 21:2–3; Mark 11:2–3; Luke 19:30–31).

The Crowd Cries, "Hosanna"

The disciples, as a sign of respect and acknowledgment of Jesus as King, laid their garments on the colt before Jesus sat on him (2 Kings 9:13). Likewise, the crowd around Him laid their clothes and palm branches upon the road, making a king's highway on which Jesus would travel into Jerusalem. They, too, acknowledged their belief in Jesus of Nazareth as their Messiah by their actions. It was an exciting time in and around Jerusalem, as they ushered their Messiah into Jerusalem just before the celebration of Passover. The correlation of the two events may have seemed obvious to them. Passover signifies when God delivered Israel from Egypt's rule. Now their Messiah was coming near Passover, and maybe would deliver Israel from under Rome's rule. They understood the concept, but not the complete reality, as they followed Him into Jerusalem.

"Hosanna to the Son of David," was what the crowd cried out as they journeyed with Jesus toward Jerusalem and the temple. While "Hosanna" is an exclamation of praise, it is also a cry for salvation. "The Son of David" directly refers to the Messiah, who was to come through David's line. David's line was the earthly line of the kings, so Jesus was coming as the King Who saves, and this was what the crowd was calling out. They were professing their faith in Him as the King Who saves. They expected Him to come and take them out from under Roman rule, to re-establish their kingdom and God-given boundaries on earth, and to make it an everlasting kingdom. They thought this was the final earthly and eternal salvation of their land and their freedom. How exciting for them to be alive and watch history unfold before them.

Day Five: Witness to the Triumphal Entry

Read: Isaiah 56:7–8; Matthew 21:10–17; Mark 11:15–19; Luke 19:38–48; John 12:16.

1. Who noticed Jesus' arrival in Jerusalem?

2. Who did Jesus' disciples tell the crowd He was?

3. What did some of the Pharisees want Jesus to do?

4. Jesus' actions fulfilled scripture, so why didn't the Pharisees recognize it?

5. Where did Jesus go first, and what did He do?

6. How was the temple supposed to be used?

7. Who came to Jesus after He cleansed the temple, and what did He do with them? How do you think Jesus, being fully God and fully man, felt about this?

8. Why were the chief priests and scribes indignant?

9. How did Jesus respond to them? What was He saying?

10. Think of Peter and his expectations of the day. What emotions and thoughts do you think he was having throughout the day?

The Pharisees Rebuke Jesus

Jesus and the multitude arrived at Jerusalem and caused quite a stir, as the entire city noticed their procession (Matthew 21:10). Those in the city asked those who were with Jesus who He was. They recognized the entry and the procession as pointing to Him as someone special. They wanted to know in whose presence they were. The multitude with Jesus responded He was Jesus, the Prophet from Nazareth. This was not to discount Him as the Messiah, but to say who they were proclaiming as the Messiah. This was made clear by the Pharisees' reaction.

The Pharisees who confronted Him called Him Teacher; they recognized Him as a rabbi, if for no other reason than He came with followers. They wanted Him to rebuke His followers for crying out after Him as the Messiah. Jesus came into Jerusalem, lowly and riding on a donkey, fulfilling prophecy. The Pharisees prided themselves on knowing their scriptures, yet they did not recognize Jesus' entry as anything more than a threat to their power and control over the Jewish population.

In his Gospel account, John said not even the disciples completely understood what was happening. As previously noted, they were still expecting a different outcome at the end of the week than they got. God did not open their understanding fully until after Jesus was glorified (John 12:16). Therefore, while the Pharisees may have thought they knew how the Messiah would come, and it did not coincide with how Jesus came, God also did not open their eyes to see Jesus as the Messiah. Jesus did not come to be set up in the temple at Jerusalem and be worshiped in a human frame. He came to die on the Cross, convicted by His people, and condemned to death to pay the penalty for their sins and ours. Had the Pharisees seen Jesus as the Messiah, God's plan for our salvation could not have been fulfilled. It was a combination of Pharisaical arrogance and of God's keeping the revelation from them, which caused them to rebuke the Lord then, and later cry out for His crucifixion.

Jesus' response to the Pharisees' rebuke must have infuriated and offended them to the highest degree. They were rebuking Him for the Messianic attributes of His followers, and He responded by telling them if the crowd wasn't saying it, then "the stones would immediately cry [it] out" (Luke 19:40). He was proclaiming Himself to the Pharisees as the Son of David. He revealed His agreement with the crowd's assessment of Him being the Messiah, and He did have the power to save them.

Jesus Rebukes Jerusalem's Leaders

Jesus reached His destination in Jerusalem: the temple. The temple represented God's presence in Israel; it was supposed to be a house of prayer (2 Chronicles 6:18–21; Isaiah 56:7; Jeremiah 7:11). Jesus entered the city with humility, but He entered the temple with all authority. He proclaimed it was supposed to be a house of prayer, but "[they had] made it a den of thieves" (Matthew 21:13; Mark 11:17). He referred to the priests and elders who had set up a marketplace within the walls of the temple. They would sell animals for sacrifice there to those who brought money to purchase them or for those whose offerings they did not approve. They had made it a common practice to disapprove of the sacrifices the people brought, find anything wrong with them, and then offer to sell them a replacement at a highly marked-up price. They were abusing the authority God had entrusted to them. Jesus drove them out and turned over their tables as His first act after being proclaimed the Messiah (Matthew 21:12; Mark 12:15; Luke 19:45).

The next thing Jesus did was stay in the temple. This is very interesting, since He had just caused a violent ruckus. What is more interesting is how the blind and the lame came to Him after His outburst against the money-changers, and He healed them (Matthew 21:14). What a beautiful picture of our Savior. He went into the place where all people were supposed to be able to meet with His presence and removed the most significant obstacles standing between them and God. He then turned to meet with the very same people and heal them of their infirmities. He desires to reconcile and heal. He is the same today. He wants to reconcile each person to a relationship with God and heal them.

The priests and scribes were incensed by Jesus' unwillingness to correct the children who were proclaiming Him to be the Messiah. In the same way, the Pharisees wanted Jesus to silence the crowds outside, the priests wanted Jesus to correct the children in the temple, all this while watching Him heal the blind and the lame. Unable to see the Messiah standing right in front of them, they insisted He come under their authority. Jesus healed the physical blindness of those who came to Him, but the blindness of the priests He did not heal. Instead, Jesus let them know the children's praise was perfect. This ended the conversation between Jesus and the priests.

What a day Peter had. He must have been thrilled about the prospect of the "colt, the foal of a donkey." He had already proclaimed Jesus to be the Messiah. He participated in removing his robe to lay it on the colt's back for Jesus to sit upon. He must have been amazed to think his own robe was used to support the Messiah as He triumphantly entered Jerusalem. His hopes and dreams were soon to be fulfilled.

How fervently the crowd cried out, "Hosanna to the Son of David! Blessed is He who comes in the name of the Lord! Hosanna in the highest" (Matthew 21:9). They cried out for salvation to the Messiah, the One upon whom their hopes had been set since Adam and Eve were ousted from the Garden, the One toward whom the Law and the Prophets pointed them since Moses. The overwhelming joy of the moment must have been exhilarating for Peter. Knowing he was not only alive for this moment in history, but he had been chosen to bear the keys of Jesus' kingdom. His hopes and dreams were about to be fulfilled (at least as far as he understood them).

He heard as the crowds asked who this was, and he heard the multitude proclaim the Messiah as they entered the city, with the temple in view. He was probably close enough to hear the rebuke of the Pharisees and Jesus' brilliant response about rocks crying out. However, he may have expected something different as they approached the temple. He may have expected the priests to recognize and welcome Him as the Messiah. Still, instead, he must have watched with a certain amount of amazed confusion as Jesus vandalized the money-changers' tables. Yet he may have felt a spark of joy at the rightness of His actions, too.

Peter was probably close behind the Lord as they entered the temple. Indeed, he ducked out of the way as Jesus cleaned house; however, he also would have witnessed Jesus' calm as the blind and the lame came anyway. Listening to the children sing perfect praise and watching Jesus heal the lame and the blind, knowing Him to be the Messiah, must have elicited praise within Peter as he worshiped his Messiah. Yet, how would Peter have responded in his heart and mind as the priests rebuked Jesus for not rebuking the children? How could they not see what Peter saw? This was not going the way he had expected. Then to hear the Lord say the children's praise was perfect toward Him, proclaiming Himself to be who they said He was, would restore Peter's confidence in and awe of his Master and his Messiah.

This was the beginning of a trying week for Peter. Everything he had been expecting would be turned upside-down in every possible way. He would be challenged to his breaking point, and this was just the beginning. These moments would open Peter's mind to allow the Lord to lead even his expectations in the kingdom.

Day Six: Kingdom Principles and the Triumphal Entry

1. Review this week's lessons and highlight your big takeaways. Be prepared to share these if you are meeting with a group.

2. Did you learn something about Peter this week? Share your thoughts.

3. How do you see your big takeaway(s) relating to the world around you today? To the Church in the broader sense, or the local church?

4. How might you apply one of these takeaways this week?

A FIG TREE AND THE END

Day One: Peter Marvels at a Withered Fig Tree

Read: Exodus 25:22; Leviticus 16:1–17; Matthew 23:37–39; Psalms 118:19–29; Isaiah 43:18–28.

1. According to Matthew 23:37–39, how was Jerusalem's house left? Why?

2. What was the house Jesus was referring to in Jerusalem?

3. Whose presence was to be found in the temple? Where was His presence found, and what was His purpose?

4. If Jesus was leaving the house desolate, what was He taking with Him as He left?

5. What did Jesus mean when He said, "You shall see Me no more till you say, 'Blessed is He who comes in the Name of the Lord!'"

A House Left Desolate

Jesus, speaking of Jerusalem, said her house would be left desolate (Matthew 23:38). He said it was due to Jerusalem's unwillingness to hear the prophets and those who confronted her wicked ways. Those who ruled Jerusalem through the centuries had become complacent in their worship of God. They made the temple and even the gold upon the temple of more worth than the presence of God within (Matthew 23:16, 17). Therefore, Jesus would leave the temple (her house) this last time, taking with Him the very presence of God.

God's presence was found above the mercy seat since Moses built the tabernacle in the desert. God gave clear instructions for the building of the tabernacle of the desert, as well as the temple at Jerusalem. Both places of worship contained the Holy of Holies, the central-most room of the worship center. This was where the Ark of the Covenant was kept, covered by the mercy seat, and where God's presence dwelt. This was why Israelites traveled to the temple with their sacrifices and prayers, to be in the presence of God. It was where God was said to hear and answer the prayers of His people (Exodus 25:22, 26:34; 2 Chronicles 6).

When Jesus left the temple, taking the presence of God with Him, He was removing the hearing ear of God and the help of His people. This is, until they would say, "Blessed is He who comes in the name of the LORD!" (Matthew 23:39; Psalms 118:26). According to Psalms 118, God's presence will return when Israelites as well as Gentiles acknowledge Jesus as the Messiah. However, this time He will not return to a temple with walls, but He will dwell in each person; the worshiper of God becomes His temple (1 Corinthians 3:17, 6:19; 2 Corinthians 6:16). Psalms 118 also refers to the chief cornerstone, which is Jesus (Matthew 21:42–44; Acts 4:11; Ephesians 2:20).

Peter explains well the concept of Jesus as the Chief Cornerstone: "Coming to Him as to a living stone, rejected indeed by men, but chosen by God and precious, you also, as living stones, are being built up a spiritual house, a holy priesthood, to offer up spiritual sacrifices acceptable to God through Jesus Christ. Therefore, it is also contained in the scripture, 'Behold I lay in Zion a Chief Cornerstone, elect, precious, and he who believes on Him will by no means be put to shame.' Therefore, to you who believe, He is precious; but to those who are disobedient, The Stone which the builders rejected has become the Chief Cornerstone, and a stone of stumbling and a rock of offense. They stumble, being disobedient to the word, to which they also were appointed. But you are a chosen generation, a royal priesthood, a holy nation, His own special people, that you may proclaim the praises of Him who called you out of darkness into His marvelous light; who once were not a people but are now the people of God, who had not obtained mercy but now have obtained mercy" (1 Peter 2:4–10).

Day Two: Peter Marvels at a Withered Fig Tree

Read: Matthew 21:18–22, 23:37–24:2; Mark 11:12–14, 20–24.

1. Why did Jesus go to the fig tree? What did He expect to find?

2. Why didn't Jesus find what He was looking for? Why curse the fig tree?

3. What curse did Jesus speak over the fig tree?

4. How soon did the fig tree wither after Jesus cursed it?

5. What was Peter so excited about when he saw the fig tree?

6. How did Jesus answer Peter?

7. Do Christians have this power in them today? How?

A Fig Tree Withered

Jesus went to the fig tree because He was hungry. Mark tells us He went to see if He would find anything upon it, because it was not the season for figs (Mark 11:13). Jesus found no fruit on the fig tree, which was not in season, and cursed it. He commanded no fruit to ever grow on the fig tree again (Matthew 21:19; Mark 11:14).

Why would Jesus curse a fig tree for not bearing fruit out of season? Was He angry at the fig tree? After all, Jesus had the power and ability to cause the fruit to grow on the fig tree, whether in or out of season. Therefore, there must have been a greater purpose in His actions.

The next morning, Jesus and His disciples walked by the same fig tree and found it withered from the roots. Peter was the one who pointed the fig tree out to the Lord, marveling over seeing its withered state (Matthew 21:20; Mark 11:21). Here was the object. Jesus explained the power of prayer His disciples would walk in after He was gone, and the Holy Spirit filled them. Jesus took the opportunity to teach Peter and His disciples that the prayer of faith would be answered. A prayer of faith trusts in God and believes what has been asked will also be received (Matthew 21:22; Mark 11:24).

Day Three: Peter Marvels at a Withered Fig Tree

Read: Matthew 21:18–20, 23:37–39; 24:2; Mark 11:12–14.

1. How is the lesson of the fig tree a metaphor for what was happening in Jerusalem and God's plan of salvation?

2. What should Jesus have found in Jerusalem? What did He find?

3. What did Jesus say of Jerusalem, which coincides with the curse on the fig tree?

4. (Challenge) Did the temple in Jerusalem wither like the fig tree? If yes, when?

5. Why do you think God allowed all of this to happen?

6. (Challenge) Why did Jesus give this object lesson to His disciples? What were they to understand from it, and why

A Living Metaphor

The fig tree example was a metaphor for Jerusalem and Israel's temple and worship system. The temple in Jerusalem had all the appearance of being a religious and holy worship center. However, when the Messiah, the God they worshiped, came near, they did not recognize Him. When Jesus went to the temple, He found the religious leaders working as money-changers rather than ministering to the Lord. No fruit was found in the activities within the temple walls or in the lives of its leaders.

Another aspect of the fig-tree metaphor reveals it was no longer the season for God to dwell in a temple built by hands. A new dispensation was coming in the form of the Holy Spirit. God would dwell within each person, Jew or Gentile, who called upon His name in faith, believing Jesus of Nazareth was the Messiah and believing in His atoning work. The fruit of the kingdom was no longer attached to a building or religious leaders, but by the indwelling Holy Spirit. Each person would have direct access to God and be empowered to bear fruit to God (Romans 7:4).

Jesus spoke to the fig tree and commanded it never to bear fruit again. The next day, it was withered from its roots (Matthew 21:20; Mark 11:21). Jesus said the temple in Jerusalem would be left desolate (Matthew 23:39). However, worship continued for years after Jesus' death upon the Cross. In AD 70, the Romans demolished the temple, even uprooting its foundation stones. Without God's presence in the temple, it withered long before it was destroyed. However, like the fig tree withered and eventually disappeared altogether, the temple was also utterly removed from the face of the earth.

Jesus used the fig tree to teach His disciples greater lessons. He began by stating the importance of having faith when they pray. He encouraged them to believe for the impossible when they prayed, because they had (and we have) a God who is able (Romans 4:21; Philippians 3:21; 2

Timothy 1:12; Hebrews 2:18, 7:25): "[He] is able to do exceedingly abundantly above all that we ask or think, according to the power that works in us" (Ephesians 3:20). The disciples would soon come against much opposition as they followed Jesus, building the church. The lesson of the fig tree was meant to expand their minds to the possibilities of life with the indwelling Holy Spirit and living in God's will.

Finally, the simplest and most straightforward teaching for Jesus' disciples regarding the fig tree is the need for every follower of Jesus to bear fruit. The fig tree was not ready, because it was not its season. The Bible teaches Christians to be ready in season and out (2 Timothy 4:2). It is not enough to "follow the rules." One must be engaged in a personal relationship with Jesus. Showing up at church and playing the role of Christian without heart, soul, mind, and strength attached is fruitless (Mark 12:30). The one who has all the appearances of a Christian but not the fruit of a Christian will wither and die. No one can sustain their own Christianity; only through the indwelling of the Holy Spirit and a close personal relationship with Jesus can one bear fruit.

"But the fruit of the Spirit is love, joy, peace, longsuffering, kindness, goodness, faithfulness, gentleness, self-control. Against such there is no law. And those who are Christ's have crucified the flesh with its passions and desires. If we live in the Spirit, let us also walk in the Spirit" (Galatians 5:22–25).

Are you walking in the fruit of the Spirit? Are you experiencing a relationship with Jesus regularly? Are you spending time in His Word and speaking with Him through prayer daily? Or are you simply going through the religious motions and feeling empty of love, joy, peace, long-suffering, kindness, goodness, faithfulness, gentleness, and self-control? If you are the latter, there is something you can do. You can confess your sin of hypocrisy and ask Jesus to come and dwell within and teach you His ways. He will honor the request of a sincere heart. Then the excitement of living a Christian life will dwell within and through you, in ways you could never imagine. What are you waiting for?

Day Four: Peter Learns about the End of the Age

Read: Matthew 24:1–14; Mark 13:1–13; Luke 21:5–19; 2 Peter 3:9–18.

1. Who asked Jesus about the end of the age?

2. What questions did they ask of Jesus?

3. What did Jesus say they should take heed of? What were they not to do in this instance?

4. What will they hear of? Does the end come with this?

5. What else will come before the end?

6. What does Jesus tell the disciples these are?

7. Do we see these things today? What does this mean to you?

8. Who will hate Jesus' disciples, and what will they do to them?

9. What is this an occasion for?

10. Why should they not worry about what they will say?

11. How will this affect their adversaries?

The Beginning of Sorrows

Jesus had been speaking to the disciples about His death and resurrection for some time. They had not fully understood what He meant, because His death was not a part of Jewish expectation for the Messiah. However, their curiosity was piqued. Peter, John, Andrew, and James sat with Jesus on a hill overlooking Jerusalem, and they asked Him what would be the sign of His coming and about the end of the age (Matthew 24:3; Mark 13:3).

Jesus, knowing His crucifixion neared, began to answer their questions about the end of the age and the signs of His coming. He warned them to be careful so no one would deceive them

(Matthew 24:5). Jesus warned the disciples how many would come claiming to be the Messiah. He warned them not to believe them nor be moved to go toward them (Luke 21:8).

Jesus continued and explained the disciples would "hear of wars and rumors of wars" (Matthew 24:6; Mark 13:7). Yet Jesus told them that not even at the onset of wars or even the rumors of them would the end come. The time would not yet be for the end of the age. This is a word to comfort disciples of all ages. There will be wars; Jesus said it. However, war will not end the age. Jesus said famines, pestilences, and earthquakes in various places are the beginning of sorrows (Matthew 24:8). "Sorrows," also translated as childbirth, gives the impression of great anguish. Yet, Jesus tells us this is only the beginning of sorrows.

The world has experienced many earthquakes in its history. Since the turn of this century, the Earth has suffered many significant earthquakes. A quick internet search reveals over twenty major earthquakes since the year 2000. The Indonesian quake and subsequent tidal wave come to mind. There have been various earthquakes of devastating proportions for centuries. There have been wars and rumors of wars, including two world wars, and yet the end has not come. However, the suffering has been great.

"Pestilence" refers to diseases such as the bubonic plague. However, we could refer more recently to the swine flu (H1N1) or COVID-19 pandemic and its subsequent variants. Many African, Eastern European, and South American countries suffer from famine. People in the wealthiest countries in the world are suffering from hunger. The signs of the beginning of sorrows have been with us for some time. What does this say about how Jesus' disciples must live today?

When Lawlessness Abounds

Jesus continued with Peter, John, James, and Andrew. He said all nations would hate His disciples. They should expect severe opposition in the world. They would be brought before councils and beaten in synagogues. Jesus was telling them that not only would the world hate them, but their people, the Jews, would, as well. They would be brought before rulers and kings. They would be arrested, betrayed, and even martyred for Jesus. The kingdom to come would be violently opposed. However, Jesus did not leave this message at this point. Rather, He gave hope and direction for perilous times. He told the disciples these things would provide an opportunity to share the gospel with councils, rulers, and kings (Matthew 24:9; Mark 13:9; Luke 21:10–13).

Amid the news of future suffering, Jesus gave a ray of hope. Jesus told His disciples they should not worry when they are being betrayed into the hands of those who despise the gospel. He promised to give them the words to speak and wisdom for their adversaries (Luke 21:15). No adversary will be able to answer the wisdom He will give them.

The disciples also learned it would not merely be strangers opposed to their message, but even their own families would deliver them up to councils. People in their own families would not accept Jesus as the Messiah and would violently oppose their message as blasphemous. Families' hearts might not be violently opposed to them personally; their intentions are more likely to be to straighten out their false beliefs. However well-intentioned the family members might be, they would come against the gospel of Christ. Therefore, it should not surprise a follower of Christ when family begins to pull away from them simply due to their beliefs. Jesus said it would happen. There are families around the world today who turn in family members and even attempt to murder those in their families who follow Jesus.

This should not come as a surprise. Yet by patient endurance, one possesses one's soul. Jesus was still speaking of the end and the signs of His coming. He said after these things have passed, "many false prophets will rise up" (Matthew 24:11). False prophets speak of the future on behalf of the Lord, but their prophecies do not come to fruition. Many have come through the centuries, proclaiming they know the world's end date. Yet it can be as simple as someone in the local church or community speaking of a future event that does not come to pass. However, we also know false prophets will arise and do signs and wonders, *and* their prophecies will come to pass. How do we know these are false prophets, then? Moses said they would not follow God's law; their words or their life would not line up with scripture, or they would entice followers away from Christ. Many have risen up and called people away to follow them. These are known in modern society as cults.

Jesus also said lawlessness would abound. He warned, "the love of many [would] grow cold" when this happened (Matthew 24:12). What do we see in the church today? Many are leaving the church. They go to various places. Some discontinue following altogether, others might remain in service performing nothing more than ritual, and still others corrupt and discredit the faith by their actions.

Where are you today? Are you zealous for the Lord? Are you seeking Him with all your heart, soul, mind, and strength? Or are you becoming a robotic Christian, simply going through the motions? Take time to pray and ask Jesus where you stand; ask Him to infuse you with a new love and fervor for Him. Ask Him to remind you of your first love for Him. Take time to recommit yourself, inviting Him to be Lord of your whole life, and commit to honor and please Him with the rest of your life. If you are unsure how to do this, ask your minister or a church leader to pray with you. They will be glad you asked.

Day Five: Peter Learns about the End of the Age

Read: Matthew 24:1–14; Mark 13:1–13; Luke 21:5–19; 2 Peter 3:9–18.

1. Who will betray Jesus' disciples?

2. Who will rise up after this?

3. What will happen when lawlessness abounds?

4. What must one do to be saved? What should it look like?

5. According to Matthew 24:13, Mark 13:13, and Luke 21:19, can one hold to the doctrine of "Once saved, always saved"? Explain your answer.

6. What did Peter and Paul teach on this subject?

7. What comes just before the end?

8. How close might the end be in light of all of this?

9. From the 2 Peter verses, what lessons did Peter leave us on the end times?

10. How are we to grow in our Christian experience?

Personal Reflection
11. Are there any changes you would like to make in your life after studying these verses?

A Steadfast Salvation

Jesus promised His disciples they would not lose one hair from their heads. Yet scripture as well as church history reveal disciples of Jesus were beaten, imprisoned, and martyred for their faith. How do these two things reconcile? Jesus used this expression to give them hope, knowing they would not suffer any essential injury to their person. Jesus spoke of divine protection for the one who is steadfast in perilous times. He said, "Do not fear those who kill the body but cannot kill the soul. But rather fear Him who would be able to destroy both soul and body in hell" (Matthew 10:28). There is nothing to be done to a disciple of Jesus to affect their salvation. No one can take it away.

Jesus continued this statement, saying His disciples would possess their souls by patience (Luke 21:18). This speaks to endurance, such as a hopeful waiting. While disciples of Christ suffer for their faith in Him, they continue to believe on Him and wait patiently for His deliverance to come. Not being swayed by challenging circumstances in the core of your faith is how you possess your soul. The final and most important outcome of a disciple's walk is to endure to the end. Whether this end is martyrdom, natural death, or being taken in the rapture, you must endure all things with a patient hopefulness to possess your soul in eternity (1 Corinthians 9:12; 2 Timothy 2:12).

Jesus spoke to His disciples about the requirements for them to be saved. He didn't want them to think believing He was the Messiah was enough to see them through to final salvation. Jesus said those who "endure to the end shall be saved" (Mark 13:13). There is no other reason Jesus would relay this message to His disciples throughout the centuries, unless your salvation could be lost. No one can take it away, but you can lose it by lacking hopeful endurance to the end.

Peter and Paul later taught on enduring to the end, following Jesus with righteousness and growing more and more into Christ-likeness (2 Peter 3:14–18). Paul wrote in his letter to the Philippians to "work out their own salvation with fear and trembling" (Philippians 2:12–15). He went on to exhort disciples to be found blameless in the end. In the same letter, Paul admitted he did not believe he had yet received his salvation, but he was working toward the goal (Philippians 3:13, 14). Paul, the apostle to the Gentiles, who evangelized much of the known world and planted churches everywhere he went, did not consider himself to be saved yet. He considered himself on the road to salvation.

The Philippians verses speak of reaching the goal; they refer to a race (Philippians 3:12– 21). It was a word picture for those in his time. They would have understood the word picture perfectly. If you ran in a race but did not run honorably, even if you reached the finish line first, you would not receive a crown, the award for running the race. The only runners who received a crown were the ones who ran a clean race and made it to the finish line. All who finished well received the prize. This is what Paul was referring to. He had not yet received the crown of salvation because he had not yet finished the race. Christians may say they are saved, but they truly mean they are on the road to salvation. Therefore, the doctrine of "Once saved, always saved" does not line up with scripture. If it did, Jesus, Paul, and Peter would not have encouraged disciples to endure to the end, nor would they tell them to work out their salvation with fear and trembling. Christians can be assured of their salvation process but must endure all things until the end, growing in grace.

Jesus had been speaking of end times events before His coming. He then revealed what would happen just before the end: the last thing to be set in place. Jesus said the gospel would be preached throughout the world (Matthew 24:14). There are still nations where preaching the gospel is illegal. However, radio and television signals are being sent into those countries, and there are underground missionaries. While we have not achieved total saturation of the gospel, we are closer than ever. Looking over what Jesus said would happen in the end times, it seems the end is very near. However, since no one knows the day or the hour, Jesus' disciples ought to live as though He is coming back in the next moment.

Peter's words on this subject are found at the end of his second letter, which he wrote shortly before being martyred for his faith and faithfulness. These are his final words to the church. He said the coming of the Lord would be sudden and unexpected. He said everything known would be destroyed and taken away; a new heaven and earth were to be expected. His exhortation was to let go of worldly things, live only for Jesus, and become more Christlike. Peter warned it was possible to lose one's steadfastness when allowing the wicked to influence them (2 Peter 3:9–18). James summed it up when he wrote that to be a friend of the world is to be an enemy of God (James 4:4).

There are two great lessons to gain from this week's study. First, we can discern the times by what is happening in the world. All Jesus mentioned regarding the end is currently happening in our world today. He said just before the end, the gospel would be preached in every nation in the world. We are increasingly close to this. Jesus' disciples today need to heed what is happening around them and measure their walk with Him by His Word. Now is the time to get right with scripture.

The second, Jesus requires His disciples to endure steadfastly to the end. He promised terrible times ahead for His disciples. However, Peter offers clues for how to be steadfast until the end. Disciples of Jesus must continue to grow in grace and the knowledge of Jesus. Disciples must continue to study the Word, relate with Him in and through prayer, make Him the center of their lives, and be transformed into His image.

Where are you in your walk today? Has the Holy Spirit convicted you in an area of your life as you've gone through this study? Take time right now for repentance and renewal. Seek God's forgiveness through Jesus' shed blood, and commit to walk with steadfast endurance to the end. Commit to be in His Word daily. This is the only thing to see you through to the end. May the Lord bless you and keep you as you pursue Him.

Day Six: A Withered Fig Tree and the End of the Age

1. Review this week's lessons and highlight your big takeaways. Be prepared to share these if you are meeting with a group.

2. Did you learn something about Peter this week? Share your thoughts.

3. How do you see your big takeaway(s) relating to the world around you today? To the Church in the broader sense, or the local church?

4. How might you apply one of these takeaways this week?

SERVICE AND DENIAL

Day One: Served by the Master

Read: Exodus 12:1–36; Matthew 26:17–19; Mark 14:12–16; Luke 22:7–13.

1. What Jewish holiday coincides with the first day of the Feast of Unleavened Bread?

2. What must be done on this day? (See Luke 22:7.)

3. Looking at the verses in Exodus, what do you learn about this Feast?

    a. What was the lamb to be like?

    b. How long does the lamb stay with the household? Why would this be necessary?

    c. When was the lamb to be killed, and how many people did it?

    d. What was to be done with the blood, and what was its purpose?

    e. For what purpose did Israel keep this feast annually?

    f. At what hour did the Lord strike?

    g. What was the result of the Passover for the children of Israel?

4. Who did Jesus send to prepare the Passover meal?

5. How did Jesus tell them to find the house they would celebrate in? Did it happen? Do you think the disciples might have been surprised by this?

Moses and the First Passover

God instituted the first Passover through Moses and Aaron while Israel was still enslaved by Egypt. Passover coincided with the final plague to come to Pharaoh's land. God said He would pass through the land in the night and strike all the firstborn, whether human or animal. This would be the final act, causing Pharaoh to let the Israelites go free (Exodus 12).

Four days before Passover, each family was to take one lamb (if a family were too small for one lamb, it would be one lamb for two households). The lamb was to be without blemish, a year old, and male. He could be taken from the sheep or the goats, and the lamb would be like a pet for four days. They would get to know this lamb more intimately as it stood out from the rest of the flock (Exodus 12:1–5).

The lamb was to be killed at twilight on the fourteenth day of the month, with some of its blood being spread upon the doorposts and the lintel (upper doorpost) of the house where the lamb would be eaten. The lamb was to be roasted on the fire with bitter herbs and eaten with unleavened bread. The whole assembly of Israelites was to do this at twilight, everyone at the same time in one accord. Those who chose obedience would experience the greatest deliverance from captivity the world had ever known (Exodus 12:6–11).

The most important part of the Passover meal was the blood of the lamb. Having been placed upon the doorposts and the lintel, the blood was a sign to the Lord. As He approached the house, He would see the blood and "pass over," not striking the firstborn whose lintel was covered by the blood. The Israelites were covered by the blood of the lamb for protection from the wrath of God (Exodus 12:13).

The Israelites were to eat the meal in haste and dress as if they were to leave in a hurry (Exodus 12:11). The Lord passed over at midnight, striking the firstborn in every place not covered by the blood of the lamb. This included Pharaoh's son. Scripture reveals Pharaoh called Moses and Aaron to him and asked them to take all they had and go serve the Lord, as they had requested (Exodus 12:29–34). They were set free of their bondage. God commanded Moses and Aaron to establish a feast for Israel to observe annually as a memorial of what God had done (Exodus 12:14).

Preparing for Passover

Jesus sent Peter and John to prepare for the Passover meal they would share (Luke 22:8). Jesus gave them elaborate directions for how they would find the house where they would have the meal. He told them they would find a man carrying a water pitcher as they entered the city. They were to follow the man to his home and ask the master of the house to use a room for the Passover meal. What is interesting to note in this study of Peter is the lack of argument recorded here. Peter's silent and immediate obedience shows a depth of spiritual growth. This is not the Peter Jesus first met, who argued about casting his nets again into the water. He had walked with Jesus long enough; his faith in Jesus' command and his humility to follow commands had grown abundantly.

Peter and John went to the city and found everything as Jesus had said. They found a man carrying a pitcher of water, and then they followed through with their directions and began to prepare the Passover meal. Were they surprised when everything worked out exactly as Jesus said? Scripture does not tell us they were surprised. Maybe they had seen enough by this time not to be surprised at all by it. However, it was a notable miracle. This would have bolstered their faith even more (Luke 22:7–13).

Day Two: Served by the Master

Read: Matthew 26:26–29; Mark 14:22–25; Luke 22:14–20; John 13:1–3.

1. How much had Jesus been looking forward to this meal? Why?

2. Jesus took the bread; what did he do with it? Who distributed it to the disciples? What did Jesus say about it? Why should they continue to do this?

3. Jesus took the cup of wine; what did He do with it? Who distributed it? What did Jesus say about it? When would He drink of it again?

4. Why do you think Jesus handed the bread to each one but gave His disciples the wine to distribute amongst themselves?

Jesus and the Passover

Later the same evening, when they gathered to celebrate the Passover meal, Jesus expressed the depth of His desire and anticipation to enjoy this particular meal with His twelve disciples (Luke 22:15). He was looking to the Cross. They did not understand what was to come in a few short hours. Yet Jesus expressed a great anticipation for this time with them. He was the Passover Lamb. In less than twenty-four hours, He would give His blood as a covering for them and for all who would call on His name. He was the only one who would go through the meal with this depth of understanding. This was the hour He instituted a new covenant with His disciples.

Jesus began with the bread. He took the unleavened bread, broke it, and handed it to each disciple personally. He commanded them to take and eat it, and said it was His body given for them. The bread was instituted to remind disciples of the work Jesus did on the Cross (Luke 22:19; Mark 14:22). The picture of Jesus personally handing the bread to each disciple and looking them in the eyes as He said it was His body given for them is an intensely intimate image. Displayed is the Savior's heart and the Father's plan. This is the picture of salvation being between humans and God through Jesus. There is no longer a need for the temple or the priest, because Jesus is now our High Priest who has made the final Passover sacrifice, once for all (Romans 6:10; Hebrews 7:24–28).

Jesus followed the bread with the wine. He had personally distributed the bread to each disciple, but the wine He commanded them to divide amongst themselves (Luke 22:17). They all drank from the same cup. Jesus said the wine represented the blood of the new covenant. He shed His blood upon the Cross for many for the remission of sins (Matthew 26:27–28). His blood covers us and protects us from the wrath of God. Today, we each come personally to the Cross and partake of the Bread of Life. This is a personal one-on-one relationship with Jesus. Yet we are also to share the gospel (the good news) with those who need to know God's saving grace through Jesus. This is dividing the wine between us. This is a continual act of evangelism, to share the shed blood of Jesus with those who need to experience the remission of sins. Salvation belongs to the individual on a very personal basis, but it is to be shared equally. We all drink from the same cup of salvation. Truly,

Jesus is the way, the truth, and the life, and no one comes to the Father except through Him (John 14:6).

Jesus Washes the Disciples' Feet

When the meal was finished, Jesus did something remarkable and unexpected. He put aside his garment, filled a basin with water, and then washed the disciples' feet (John 13:1–5). Wrapping a towel around His waist alone was an act of humility (or at least placing Himself in a humble position). However, the act of washing feet was a job reserved for the lowest servant in the house. Yet the guest of honor, the Lord and Savior, did not find it beneath Him to perform this service. It was an object lesson for the disciples.

When Jesus came to him, Peter was most uncomfortable with Jesus washing his feet. Peter knew it was backward. He should have been washing Jesus' feet (or one of the other disciples), not Jesus washing their feet. Peter refused to let Jesus wash his feet. He could not fathom such a thing. He was in a culture in which position was honored, and this made no sense to him. Peter was not too proud to have Jesus wash his feet; rather, just the opposite. Peter's honor for and humility before the Lord caused him to react as he did. Yet, after Jesus explained to Peter the importance of allowing Him to wash his feet, Peter submitted his head and hands to the Lord for washing too (John 13:6–9). We see Peter changed from a proud, boastful, and unteachable man to one who had become humble, teachable, and obedient to the Lord: a man who loved his Lord.

The entire point Jesus was making by washing the disciples' feet, in the form of the lowliest servant of the house, was to serve one another in like manner. Jesus displayed an example of service and humility for them to follow. By bowing down in humble service to His disciples, He gave them a benchmark for serving one another. He said they were not better than He was and therefore ought to serve as He served: with humility, seeking no honor (John 13:12–17).

When Adam and Eve sinned in the Garden, God sacrificed one animal per person to cover their nakedness. With the Passover, God provided one lamb per household. Moses' Passover released Israel from slavery in Egypt. Those who obeyed the directives and sacrificed their Passover lambs were spared. With the tabernacle, God gave a high priest to atone for the nation once yearly. In Jesus, God provided a Passover Lamb sacrificed once and for all of humanity, for all time. Through Jesus, we are set free from our bondage to sin. By His body, which was given for our sins, and by His shed blood, which covers us from God's wrath, we are made free indeed (John 8:36). Now this truly is good news.

Day Three: The Denial

Read: Matthew 26:31–35; Mark 14:27–31; Luke 22:31–38; John 13:31–38.

1. What did Jesus say would happen to all of His followers this night?

2. Why did He say it would happen?

3. Why did Jesus say He was going away?

4. What new commandment did He give His disciples?

5. Where did Jesus say He would go after He had risen? Do you think the disciples heard this with understanding?

6. Who answered Jesus, and what did he claim? What characteristic does this show of him?

7. What did Jesus tell Peter would happen this night?

8. What did Peter claim he would do before letting the Lord down?

Peter Proclaims His Loyalty

Jesus, knowing the hour of His arrest and crucifixion was near, began to prepare His disciples for what would come later in the evening. He announced all would stumble because of Him in the coming hours of the night (Matthew 26:31). Jesus' words came at the end of an intimate dinner, in which He spoke of a new covenant with His disciples. This was likely a shocking statement to them following the discourse of the evening.

Jesus continued to tell His disciples this would happen to fulfill scripture as well as God's plan (Isaiah 53:12). Zechariah 13:7 says, "I will strike the Shepherd and the sheep of the flock will be scattered." Jesus gave His disciples a new command in light of this. He told them they must love one another as He had loved them. He said to His disciples, this would be a sign to all to show they were His disciples (John 13:34, 35).

Jesus continued His final instructions to the disciples, telling them to go into Galilee to wait for Him there. He would appear to them there after He had risen. This statement had to be very confusing for the disciples. They were still expecting Jesus to reign in an earthly authority. They had no concept of Him dying literally and rising from the grave. They may have thought He was speaking in a parable, and He would explain later.

Peter spoke up and proclaimed his loyalty to the Lord. He claimed he alone would stand with Jesus and fight, even when all others had left Him (Matthew 26:33; Mark 14:29; John 13:37). Peter had come a long way to get to this place. To the core of his being, he was convinced Jesus was the Messiah sent from God to deliver His people. Many believed this was another example of Peter's prideful or boastful nature. However, considering the transforming progress Peter had made by this time, it seems in scripture he was ever devoted to Jesus. He was committing to the Man who had challenged, confronted, promoted, and taught him; the Man who had loved him well. Peter's character had transformed since his first meeting with Jesus upon the shores of Galilee. Peter was now a man ready to lay down his life for his Savior.

Peter's proclamation of loyalty, which the other disciples also owned, was met by opposition. Jesus had already said all would fall away. This was a time for Peter and the disciples to heed what the Lord was saying to them as well as find direction from Him. However, they could not fathom what would come in a few short hours. Jesus told Peter he would deny Him three times before morning (Matthew 26:34; Mark 14:30; Luke 22:31–34; John 13:38). Jesus revealed to Peter the source of what was to come: Satan had asked to sift Peter. Yet Jesus added He had prayed for Peter and intimated he would come back, and the direction He gave was to strengthen the brethren (Luke 22:31, 32). In short, Jesus had told Peter he would fall away in the worst way, but he would come back, he would be welcomed back, and then he should minister to Jesus' other followers. In a sense, He confirmed Peter's call and continued entrustment of the keys to the kingdom.

Peter could not fathom what Jesus had just said to him. Therefore, he repeated his commitment to the Lord, showing his heartfelt conviction. He pledged to die with Jesus before he would deny Him (Matthew 26:35; Luke 22:33; John 13:37), but the Lord's words were proven later in the garden.

Day Four: The Denial

Read: Matthew 26:36–46; Mark 14:32–42; Luke 22:39–47; John 18:1–4.

1. Where did Jesus and the disciples go after dinner? Look the name up in a Bible dictionary and find its meaning.

2. Who did Jesus take with Him out of the twelve? How far did He take them?

3. What did Jesus tell the three He was feeling? What sort of compassion did they show Him? Why do you think this is?

4. What did He tell them to do? How many times did He say to do it?

5. Why did they have to leave?

In the Garden

Jesus led the disciples to the Garden of Gethsemane when the meal was finished. Translated, "Gethsemane" means "oil press." This was the garden where the olives were pressed by a large stone; it was a place of intense pressure. This was the place Jesus chose to pray to the Father in Heaven to let the cup of His crucifixion pass from Him, if it were possible. A place of metaphorical significance, as this would be Jesus' most pressing hour, as He struggled in prayer with the flesh He had put on to fulfill His intended purpose (Matthew 26:36; Mark 14:32; Luke 22:39).

Jesus selected Peter, James, and John from the group to accompany Him a little farther than the rest of the disciples (Matthew 26:37; Mark 14:33). Peter, James, and John, as this study has shown before, were His inner circle of disciples. They experienced His transfiguration upon the mountain and witnessed Jairus' daughter being raised from the dead (Mark 5:41; Luke 8:54). Jesus took them a little farther than the rest of the group and told them "His soul [was] exceedingly sorrowful, even to death" (Matthew 26:38; Mark 14:34). He then asked them to stay where they were and "watch with [Him]" (Matthew 26:38; Mark 14:34). He went a little farther Himself and prayed.

Jesus went back to Peter, James, and John three times. The first time, He awakened them and told them to "pray that [they] not enter into temptation" (Luke 22:40). He also explained to them "the spirit is willing but the flesh is weak" (Mark 14:38). He knew, for example, Peter's confession of loyalty, which all the disciples followed, was earnest. Peter's spirit was willing; however, his flesh would not hold out through the night. The second time Jesus came to the disciples, He found them sleeping and left them to sleep as He went to pray again. The final time, Jesus woke them to go out to meet His betrayer (Matthew 26:45, 46; Mark 14:41, 42; Luke 22:45, 46).

Day Five: The Denial

Read: Matthew 26:47–56; Mark 14:43–50; Luke 22:49–51; John 18:10–11.

1. Did Peter keep his promise to die for Jesus? What did he do?

2. How did Jesus respond to Peter's valiant efforts?

3. In whose power and understanding was Peter still trying to do things?

4. What did all the disciples do then? Why?

Read: Matthew 26:57–58, 69–75; Mark 14:53–54, 66–72; Luke 22:54–62; John 18:15–18, 25–27.

5. What did Peter and John do after Jesus' arrest?

6. How did Peter get into the high priest's courtyard?

7. What things gave Peter away to those around Him?

8. According to the Matthew verses, how did Peter's denials progress? ("Swearing and cursing" here does not mean using foul language.)

9. What reminded Peter of Jesus' words?

10. Who looked at Peter after this happened? How did Peter respond to this? Why?

Peter Acts out His Loyalty

When the mob of people led out by Judas confronted Jesus, Peter followed through with his commitment to stand with Jesus even to the death. He drew his sword, lunged at whoever was closest, and thrust his weapon. The almost humorous thing is this sanguine fisherman merely cut off the ear of a servant of the high priest (Matthew 26:51; Mark 14:47; Luke 22:50; John 18:10). However, two miraculous things happened afterward: First, Jesus picked up the ear and placed it back on the man's head. Second, Peter's actions did not incite a riot. No one retaliated. All obeyed Jesus when He told Peter to put his sword away (Matthew 26:52–54).

Peter had proclaimed his loyalty and the extent to which his loyalty would take him. He was not being boastful, for he followed through with his commitment. However, his commitment was not part of God's plan for him. He had suffered the ultimate disillusionment in ministry. He knew he was called to stand with Jesus, for Jesus told him so when He gave him the keys to the kingdom. However, Peter continually had the wrong vision of what it was to be and continued to do it all in his own understanding and strength. He continued to follow what he thought the Lord wanted, and when the moment came to fight for the kingdom he expected, Jesus said no. Peter's world came crashing down around him, and he ran away like the other disciples, just as Jesus said he would.

Peter Fails His Loyalty

Peter and John may have run away, just like all the other disciples did, but they did not run far. They followed the mob and Jesus to the high priest's courtyard. They went in to see what would become of Jesus (Matthew 26:58; Mark 14:54; Luke 22:54). John's Gospel reveals Peter could not get in without John's assistance. John said he was known by the high priest and was let in, but he had to vouch for Peter to get him in too (John 18:16). Peter was recognized in the courtyard as one of Jesus' disciples. First, his speech gave him away as Galilean (Matthew 26:73; Mark 14:70). Then something about his appearance gave him away (Luke 22:56). Finally, he was recognized from the garden earlier in the night (John 18:26). Remember, he would have stood out as the guy who wielded the sword and cut off the ear of the high priest's servant. Those in the courtyard were trying to point Peter out as a follower of Jesus.

Whenever Peter was recognized, he denied knowing Jesus. His denials were progressive. He began by simply deflecting the comments: "I don't know what you are saying" (Matthew 26:70). Basically, Peter's response was a modern-day saying, "I don't know what you are talking about." The next progression in Peter's denials was taking an oath: swearing he was not a disciple of Jesus, nor did he know the man (Matthew 26:72). The third and final denial progressed to "cursing and swearing" (Matthew 26:74). This did not mean Peter began to use vulgar language. It meant his oath-taking had progressed from a positive to a negative. The first time Peter swore he did not know Jesus, there was a positive note in the affirmation of his lie. However, the second oath was affirmed by calling down a curse. He was affirming his lie this time by calling heaven and earth as his witness; he was calling down a curse upon himself if he were lying.

Peter's final denial was met with a rooster's crow, which snapped him back to what Jesus had told him would happen. Peter immediately realized he *had* failed his commitment to Jesus. At the same, exact moment, Jesus (who was being struck by the guards) turned his face, maybe red and swollen, probably bloody, and His eyes met with Peter's (Luke 22:60-62). Peter met face to face with the Lord and Savior he proclaimed and yet believed in, and realized the depth of his failure. What was the look Jesus gave Peter? Was Jesus' look one of disappointment? Most likely, it was not. We know Jesus had already warned Peter it would happen, so it was not a disappointing surprise to Jesus. Instead, Jesus said He had already prayed for Peter and knew he would return (Luke 22:31, 32). Jesus' look must have been one of compassion for His friend, Peter, who would now struggle through his faith crisis and suffer the anguish of failing Him and the torments of Satan, who would remind him of his failure probably for his lifetime. Jesus sorrowed for His friend.

Fear of man led Peter to his desperate act. Peter knew he was lying, and he knew he was being weak in lying. However, he had also been completely disillusioned about who Jesus was. He was lost, not knowing what to do, and just trying to survive the night. Jesus said Satan had asked to sift him. While this was a devastating moment in Peter's life, the man who would come out of this experience would be a man who could lead the dawn of the church age.

Are you going through an unbelievable struggle right now? Have you ever felt like you failed the Lord in a big way? Isn't this lesson good news? Peter became one of the greatest church leaders ever, and he failed the Lord miserably. This should give every believer hope. We learn a valuable truth here. We will be sifted, but we can come back and still fulfill God's desired destiny if we bend our knees and bow our hearts before Him. When we humble ourselves and yield to His plan, He will always receive us back and place us back on plan A.

Whatever disillusionment you have suffered, whatever failures you have experienced, the Lord has prayed for you, and He has a plan for your return. So take heart. Let the past fade into history, take up your cross again, and follow Jesus into your kingdom destiny.

Day Six: Service and Denial

1. Review this week's lessons and highlight your big takeaways. Be prepared to share these if you are meeting with a group.

2. Did you learn something about Peter this week? Share your thoughts.

3. How do you see your big takeaway(s) relating to the world around you today? To the Church in the broader sense, or the local church?

4. How might you apply one of these takeaways this week?

Commission, Fishin', and Power

Days One and Two: Peter Receives the Great Commission and Goes Fishin'

Read: Matthew 28:1–10; Mark 16:1–8; Luke 24:1–12; John 20:1–10.

1. What did the angel tell the women to tell Jesus' disciples? Thinking back to the last lesson, how long ago had Jesus told them this Himself?

2. Which disciple did the angel specifically name to tell? Why do you think this might be?

3. Who ran to the tomb? Who got there first? Who went in first? What did they find? How were they affected by what they saw?

Peter Runs to the Empty Tomb

The story continues with Peter on Sunday morning, when Jesus' tomb was found empty. The first to meet the risen Lord were the women who had followed Him closely: Mary Magdalene and the other Mary (not to be confused with Jesus' mother: Matthew 28:1). When they arrived at the tomb with the stone rolled away, and the Lord missing, they found an angel there, waiting with a message.

The message the angel gave to the women was for the disciples. His message was for them to go into Galilee, and they would see Jesus there. Jesus had told the disciples the same thing Himself three days before, during the Passover dinner (Matthew 26:32). Yet much had happened in those three days. As far as the disciples knew, the Man who sent this word via the angel was dead. Even if they remembered His words, they may have thought things hadn't worked out the way Jesus had intended. In the natural, we all tend to believe someone is not coming back after their death. The disciples could not fathom what was happening because there was no precedent. Therefore, the angel gave the message to Jesus' disciples via the women who went to the tomb.

According to Mark's Gospel, the angel mentioned Peter specifically by name when giving the women the message for the disciples (Mark 16:7). It is possible Peter was explicitly mentioned to assure him he was still considered one of the disciples. Peter had denied his Lord and probably felt like a terrible failure. He had been sifted and most likely was experiencing the depths of disillusionment. He thought he was serving his Lord with the best he could offer. Unfortunately, he was doing so in his own understanding and strength. He most likely thought his blunder cost him the keys to the kingdom (Matthew 16:19). He had forgotten Jesus said he would come back (Luke 22:31). Peter was utterly lost in his failure, possibly equating his denial with Judas' betrayal. However, there is a distinct difference between denial and betrayal. Peter's denial carried with it a note of self-preservation, whereas Judas' betrayal was a direct assault upon Jesus, in which he decided to follow Him no longer.

The women brought the message to the disciples, and Peter and John ran to the tomb. John outran Peter but stopped short of going into the tomb. Peter, however, did not stop running until he reached the spot where Jesus had been laid. Inside the tomb, Peter found the linen cloths and the handkerchief which had been wrapped around His head. The handkerchief was folded neatly (Luke 24:12; John 20:4–7). What is interesting to note here is the neatly folded handkerchief. Later, those who sought to discredit the resurrection suggested Jesus' disciples stole His body and took it away. Roman guards outside the tomb at all hours should have been enough to discredit this tale, but the handkerchief also discredits it. What thief would take the time to remove the grave cloths and neatly fold the handkerchief before stealing the body? Wouldn't a robber just grab the body and run? It makes no sense for the cloth to be neatly folded unless Jesus did it Himself. Peter left the tomb "marveling to himself," wondering what had happened (Luke 2:12). He did not have to wait long for an answer.

Read Matthew 28:16–20; Mark 16:14–18; Luke 24:33–48; John 20:19–23.

4. When did Jesus appear to the disciples?

5. Why did Jesus rebuke the disciples? What reason did the disciples have for acting the way they did? (See Matthew 24:23.) Are there other reasons?

6. What did Jesus say had been given to Him? Why is this important?

7. What did Jesus command the disciples to do?

8. Where were they to begin?

9. What signs will follow those who believe?

10. How were the disciples made to understand these things?

Peter Runs from His Calling

Peter and John returned to the disciples in Jerusalem. They met up with the other disciples and shut themselves in a room (John 20:19). They feared the Jews would come for them next, since they followed the Messiah, who died. To the world, it said Jesus was, in fact, not the Messiah, and the disciples had all been led astray. They were sheep without a Shepherd and were lost for what to do. This is the point at which Jesus appeared to them behind closed doors (John 20:19, 20). Jesus spoke peace to the disciples, and all could see Him alive from the dead; His wounds were proof it was no hoax. He had died and He rose again.

Jesus rebuked them for allowing doubts to rise in their hearts while He stood before them. He allowed them to touch Him and look closely at Him to determine it was Him (Luke 24:38, 39). It is difficult to imagine how the disciples of Jesus could doubt, with Him standing right in front of them, with His wounds real, but not bleeding. Of course, it would be difficult to understand this moment, which broke the natural laws of life and death. This moment required them to fundamentally change their thinking about death, life, and the Savior.

Jesus announced He had received all authority in heaven and on earth (Matthew 28:18). He claimed His right as the Messiah. This was important to the disciples because He confirmed His word, command, and promises stood firm for all who followed Him. What He says, He will do. What He commands His disciples to do is doable, in Him. His word will not return to Him void; it will accomplish what it was sent forth to do (Isaiah 55:11). This revelation would (and should) give Jesus' disciples courage and strength to receive His following command and promise on faith.

Jesus gave His disciples what we now refer to as the Great Commission. He commanded them to go and make disciples in all the earth. They were to baptize them in the name of the Father, the Son, and the Holy Spirit. Jesus also said they should teach these new disciples to observe all things He had commanded them (Matthew 28:19, 20). Jesus told them to begin in Jerusalem, then go to Samaria, and then to the outer reaches of the world. Why start in Jerusalem? It is where God chose to put the temple, representing His presence in Israel. It was the place where people were to bring their sacrifices for sins. What better place to begin than the house of God, where worshipers already had an expectation of the Messiah?

Jesus' promise to His disciples who choose to heed His commission is "these signs will follow those who believe: In [His] name they will cast out demons; they will speak with new tongues; they will take up serpents; and if they drink anything deadly, it will by no means hurt them; they will lay hands on the sick, and they will recover" (Mark 16:17, 18). This promise has not passed away. The ends of the earth have yet to be reached with the gospel. If "Jesus Christ is the same yesterday, today, and forever," then these promises are still alive and expected today (Hebrews 13:8). Jesus' disciples today still believe in the necessity of making new disciples; they also need to continue to believe His promises follow them.

Where was Peter during all this excitement? He was not explicitly mentioned after running to the empty tomb. Yet we know he was in their midst. Did he avoid eye contact with the Lord? The last time their eyes met, Peter had just failed miserably. Did he stand outside of the group, avoiding Jesus, feeling unworthy? Was he worried he might be asked to leave? The angel had mentioned him in particular to tell of Jesus' resurrection, so he was there.

Jesus had just said they should go and make disciples, but Peter did not. Peter went fishing. Still disheartened after his failure, Peter did not appear to believe he could remain in his first calling. He did not believe he could be a fisher of men anymore, so he returned to the Sea of Galilee; he returned to fishing. Peter went back to what he knew, not what he hoped. As John's Gospel relays this story, we can see Peter was still a leader, whether walking in his calling or not. We see this by "Thomas, the twin; Nathaniel, James, John, and two others" went with him (John 21:1–2). Six of the eleven disciples followed Peter back to the Sea of Galilee. He was meant to lead, but could not see it in his despair. He must have been convinced he was not worthy of the calling of Christ on his life.

This is good news for us. Peter was *not* worthy of the calling, and neither are we. Romans 3:23 tells us we "all have sinned and fall short of the glory of God." Paul explains this in Romans. Each one's right standing before God is only found "through faith in Jesus Christ … being justified freely by His grace through the redemption that is in Christ Jesus" (Romans 3:22–24). Peter was still beating himself up for failing in ministry. He had taken the calling away from himself. Jesus had not. However, Peter went back to what he knew best, fishing, until he was able (with the Lord's help) to figure it all out.

Many in God's kingdom today are suffering this same way. We think failing in ministry is synonymous with losing our calling. Yet in the next section, we will see the glorious truth of how these are all teaching moments Jesus will use to mold us into His image. We easily think failure is unacceptable, and we must be perfect in ministry. However, Jesus did not expect us to always get it right. He does expect us to run to Him, to seek His forgiveness, to accept forgiveness, and to learn from our failures. The end goal is Christ-likeness. There will be imperfections along the way. Disciples of Jesus must remember we are all in the process of becoming Christlike; we are not there yet.

Day Three: Peter Receives the Great Commission and Goes Fishin'

Read: John 21:1–23; Luke 5:1–11.

1. Where did Peter go after the Great Commission, and who was with him? Why do you think he went there instead of Jerusalem?

2. What parallels do you find in the John and Luke stories? What differences?

3. Why might Jesus have chosen to meet Peter in this context?

4. Who knew the Man was Jesus? How did Peter react when he realized this?

5. What was on the fire? What is significant about this?

6. What three questions did Jesus ask Peter? What was different in the first question?

7. Why do you think Jesus asked Peter this question three times? What happened in Peter the third time? Was this what Jesus was going for?

8. What had Peter done three times before Jesus was crucified?

9. What did Jesus tell Peter to do three times? According to Matthew 4:19, what did Jesus tell Peter He would make him?

10. What was Jesus telling Peter in John 21:18?

11. What would Peter's death do for the Lord?

12. What was Peter's reaction to this news, and what was Jesus' response?

13. Think about Peter from his boasting at the Passover dinner table, through his denials, and up to this moment. Discuss the emotions and thoughts you think he may have had. Why might Jesus' actions have been necessary?

Peter Runs to the Risen Lord

Peter and the disciples who followed him back to the Sea of Galilee fished all night without a catch. The dawn had risen. A Man was on the shore inquiring if they had any food, not if they had caught anything. They had to admit they had no food. The Man on the shore instructed them to cast their net again on their right side. They did so without argument or complaint and were rewarded with a catch too big for their net (John 21:3–7).

Peter and John locked eyes, for they could not help but realize the similarities to their first calling. They had fished all night. A Man, Jesus, came to them on the shore and commanded them to pull out into the deep and cast their net after a whole night of fishing with no catch. The first time Peter had argued and complained, he was the fisherman. He pulled out into the deep to prove the Man wrong, but instead was incredibly humbled by the large catch. The catch was so large he had to call his business partners James and John over to help haul it in (Luke 5:1–11).

John said, "It is the Lord." Peter did not wait. He jumped out of the boat and ran to Jesus (John 21:7). What a beautiful picture the Lord painted for Peter of his redemption. Peter thought he had failed in his calling, and there was no return. Only Jesus knew how to reach Peter in a way he would understand his calling was still the same, and he was still the one. He did so by repeating the moment Peter was first called.

When Peter arrived on the shore, Jesus had a fire going with fish on it and bread. These were what Jesus miraculously fed the multitudes with (John 6:1–14). It was an object lesson for Peter. He may only have a few fish and some bread spiritually, but it was enough with Jesus' miraculous touch. When Jesus fed the multitude, He followed up with a teaching on the Bread of Life. Jesus said He was the Bread of Life. He told them anyone who came to Him, He would not cast out (John 6:37). Jesus had also encouraged the crowd, saying whoever "believes in Him [would] have everlasting life" (John 6:40). He went on to say, "Unless you eat the flesh of the Son of Man and drink His blood, you have no life in you.… For My flesh is food indeed, and My blood is drink indeed. He who eats my flesh and drinks my blood abides in Me, and I in him" (John 6:53, 55, 56). This saying caused many to walk away from following Jesus. However, one has to wonder if all this teaching had come flooding back to Peter and the other disciples with understanding, in light of the Cross. No rituals or works can satisfy the debts we each owe on account of our sin. Jesus is the Bread of Life. Eternal salvation is found only in Him. Peter would later write, "Nor is there salvation in any other, for there is no other name under heaven given among men by which we must be saved" (Acts 4:12).

John recorded this first conversation between Jesus and Peter. Since Peter had professed greater loyalty to Jesus than any other disciples. His loyalty was not in question, as he was the one who lunged forward with his sword. He did show himself loyal. However, the issue was with his proclaiming to be *more* faithful and to have *more* love for Jesus than all the rest. There was nothing wrong with Peter's zeal for the Lord, except he esteemed his zeal to be greater than anyone else's (Philippians 2:3).

Jesus referenced their last conversation in His first question: "Do you love Me more than these?" (John 21:15). Jesus' question used the word for "love" which "denotes to take pleasure in [Jesus], prize [Him] above other things, be unwilling to abandon [Him] or do without [Him]" (Thayer 2000). This love signifies choice, such as a moral decision to love.

Peter knew he could not answer Jesus with a simple yes, because he recently proved his lack of loving Jesus this way in the high priest's courtyard. Peter realized the context of the question and responded, "Yes, Lord, You know that I love You" (John 21:15). However, he used a different word with a different meaning for "love." Peter acknowledged Jesus' ability to know the answer to the question already. The truth was, Peter had an affectionate and brotherly love for the Lord. He had fallen short of the moral, sacrificial love. It must have pained him to say it, to admit his shortcoming, when he had been such a proud man.

Jesus asked Peter a second time, in the same context, whether he loved Him, and Peter responded with the same brotherly affection. The third time Jesus asked Peter if he loved Him, He changed His question. He asked Peter using the same brotherly affectionate word for "love." Jesus lowered His form of love to Peter's confession of brotherly love. John tells us Peter was grieved because Jesus asked a third time (John 21:17). Peter's response acknowledged Jesus knew all things, and he knew Jesus already knew the depth of Peter's love for Him, and it was brotherly affection.

Three times Peter denied Jesus, and now three times he humbly proclaimed his love for Him. He did not claim to love Jesus more than any other, as he had come to understand his humble but equal position to his fellow disciples. He had not been given the keys of the kingdom because he was more special than anyone else, but because it was simply his calling. Jesus placed Peter in the position because it was the place He chose to mold Peter into His likeness.

Jesus asked three difficult questions of Peter. However, He also gave Peter three commands. Upon each confession of brotherly love, Jesus commanded Peter to feed or tend His lambs (depending on the translation). Jesus commanded Peter with a metaphor of feeding sheep. Sheep need constant care; they need to be led to places to graze, and they need persistent looking after. There, by the lake, Jesus re-commissioned Peter to his first calling to be a fisher of men (Luke 5:10). He was to preach, teach the gospel, and lead the church. Jesus affirmed Peter's call was still the same, and he was still the one.

Jesus revealed to Peter the way he would die. He would be martyred on a cross, just like his Lord. He told Peter his death would glorify Him. Peter's response to this news was to point at John and ask about *his* destiny. Like a sibling rivalry, Peter wanted to know he was being treated fairly and equally, like the others. Jesus' response was pointed. He essentially told Peter to worry about his calling alone. He was told to keep his eyes fixed on Jesus and follow Jesus for himself, not worrying about another's walk with Him. He was not to compare himself with others but walk with the Lord where He led him. We must have this same confidence in Christ for our walks with Him.

Day Four: Receives Power from on High

Read: Acts 1:1–26; Luke 24:49–53.

1. What promise of the Father did Jesus speak of? How would the apostles receive it?

2. Where were the apostles supposed to wait for the promise?

3. What question did the apostles have for Jesus?

4. Why do you think they were still asking this question?

5. What was Jesus' response?

6. Can you apply this response to your life? What should disciples of Jesus keep their focus on?

7. What happened as Jesus was speaking to them? What was their response?

8. Who spoke to the apostles, and what did they tell them?

9. Where had they been? Do you think this is significant? Why or why not?

10. Where did the apostles return to, and who was there with them?

11. What were they doing in the upper room?

12. What did Peter do in those days? (Challenge) Why was this? What did Peter do first? Why?

13. How did they pick? Why was this acceptable? Did they give God an option of neither?

14. Was Matthias God's choice? Why or why not? (See Acts 9:4–6, 15–22.)

Jesus Went Up

Jesus' last earthly conversation with His disciples occurred on the road from Jerusalem to Bethany (Luke 24:50). This was the road they walked daily during the week leading up to His crucifixion. Jesus cursed the fig tree on this same path, and it withered, allowing Him to speak to His disciples about faith and moving mountains (Matthew 21:21). Along the way this time, Jesus spoke His final earthly words to His disciples. Jesus explained to them they would receive power when they received the promise of the Father, which was the Holy Spirit (Luke 24:49; Acts 1:8). He commanded them to stay in Jerusalem until they would be baptized with the Holy Spirit (Acts 1:5).

The disciples' first question was whether Jesus would restore the kingdom to the Israelites after their Holy Spirit baptism. They were still trying to make what was happening around them fit into their box of expectations for the Messiah. They thought Jesus would overthrow the Roman government when He made His triumphal entry into Jerusalem. Instead, He died. Yet He rose again. Jesus' victory was over sin and death, a much greater victory than overthrowing an earthly government, yet the disciples still could not shake their ideals and grasp the magnitude of what He had done. They were still seeking an earthly reward. Jesus replied, it was not for them to know. The Father in heaven is the only one who knows these things (Acts 1:7). This answer appeared to silence the disciples.

Jesus told His disciples, they would be "witnesses to [Him]after the baptism of the Holy Spirit came in Jerusalem, Judea, Samaria, and then to the end of the earth" (Acts 1:8). The disciples would first carry the message of salvation in Jesus, the Messiah, to the place where God's priests resided and studied the scriptures. They would then radiate outward throughout Judea, the home of Jewish people and faith. Then they would bring the gospel to Samaria. The Samaritans were Gentiles who believed in the God of the Hebrews but mixed other religions in their faith. Jews despised them. Finally, Jesus would send them to the ends of the world, to all peoples: Jew and Gentile. These were Jesus' last words to His disciples, which are recorded in scripture.

When Jesus was finished speaking, He was taken up to heaven in their sight, and they saw Him sit down at the right hand of God (Acts 1:9; Mark 16:19). Luke wrote his account as though the disciples were frozen in place, staring upward in amazement, unable to pull their eyes away (Acts 1:10). Were they stunned by what they had just seen, or were they waiting to see if something else might happen? Luke does not tell us. However, "two men in white apparel" spoke to them to pull them back to their senses. The men were clearly understood as angels, messengers from heaven. They told the disciples Jesus would return as He went up (Acts 1:10, 11). This was good enough for them, as they turned and returned to Jerusalem in direct and immediate obedience to what Jesus had commanded them. They would go and wait for the promised Holy Spirit baptism.

This scene occurred at Bethany on the Mount of Olivet, or Mount of Olives (Luke 24:50; Acts 1:12). This was significant. Everything Jesus did was significant. The Mount of Olives and Bethany were where Lazarus was raised from the dead. This was the place where Lazarus lived with his sisters, Mary and Martha, and where Mary anointed Jesus' feet and wiped them with her hair (John 11:43–45; 12:3). The Mount of Olives was where Jesus sat with His disciples overlooking Jerusalem and spoke of the end times. It was where He prayed in anguish over the pending crucifixion. It was where Judas betrayed Him with a kiss (Matthew 26:39–42, 49). What a beautiful and poignant scene, as Jesus ascended back to where He came from, seated at the Father's right hand.

Day Five: Power from on High

Read: Acts 2:1–47, 1:14–15; Luke 11:11–13.

1. How many were there altogether on the day of Pentecost? What happened?

2. Have you received the baptism of the Holy Spirit described here? Is it a gift for today? Explain your answer. (See Luke 11:11–13 and Hebrews 13:8.)

3. Where were the crowds from? What did they hear? What was their reaction?

4. What did Peter do?

5. According to Peter's sermon, what understanding did the Holy Spirit reveal about Jesus?

6. How did the crowd respond to Peter's message? What did Peter tell them they must do?

7. How many were added to the church?

8. In whose doctrine did the church continue? What else did the church do together?

9. What happened when fear came upon every soul?

10. What culture of the church allowed souls to be added daily?

Personal Reflection

11. Has the Holy Spirit encouraged you to make any change(s) based on this week's study? If so, what?

The Holy Spirit Went Down

The disciples did as the angels and as Jesus told them. They went to Jerusalem to wait. The eleven disciples of Jesus were not alone in Jerusalem, however. Mary, Jesus' mother, the other women who had followed Jesus closely, and Jesus' brothers were there with them (Acts 1:12, 13). They were together, male and female, spending their time praying with like minds (Acts 1:14; Galatians 3:28). Jesus had instructed them to wait for the baptism of the Holy Spirit before spreading the gospel, but He did not tell them to wait to begin acting like a church body. So Peter stepped up and began to lead the church.

Peter's first act of business in leading the church was to find a replacement for Judas, who had betrayed Jesus. Peter led the church to find a twelfth disciple in response to scripture. They believed twelve disciples would reign over the twelve tribes of Israel after the Messiah's reign came into place. The disciples created parameters to choose a replacement: The man must have followed Jesus since John the Baptist. Two men were selected, lots were cast, and Matthias was chosen to replace Judas (Acts 1:15–26). This was Peter's first recorded act as leader of the church.

Scripture later reveals Paul as Jesus' choice to replace Judas. Paul was directly called by Jesus (Acts 9:4–6). Paul evangelized much of the known Gentile world at that time, and his letters comprise most of the New Testament today. Though evidenced in The Book of Acts and the epistles, Paul appears to be Jesus' choice to take Judas' place, but Peter's act does not seem sinful. Peter was head of the church and maybe thought he was supposed to do something other than wait for the Holy Spirit.

So much of the time, Christians fall into this same trap. They know what the last thing the Lord told them was, but they become bored or think they've missed something. This is when disciples walk out of God's strength and into their own. This is when people begin to figure things out for themselves to feel they are doing something. They forget that waiting *is* something; it is obedience. People will quote, "Behold I will do a new thing," and use it as an excuse to do something other than wait on the Lord (Isaiah 43:19). It is an easy trap to fall into. However, the only thing Christians ought to be doing is obeying scripture to love God, love their neighbor, and do the last thing they heard the Lord tell them until He tells them something new. Whenever you get lost in what you are to be doing, ask yourself what the last clear direction the Lord gave you and go back there and wait some more.

The good news is, Peter was human. He didn't always do things according to God's plan, but he did seek to please the Lord like the rest of us. He also grew into a greatly admired and respected Christian and church leader, just like the rest of us can. The key is to continue seeking Jesus, learn from failures and mistakes with humility, and continue to be molded into the image of Christ. Remember, these are the times God's grace truly is sufficient (2 Corinthians 12:9).

Peter's choice did not hinder the Holy Spirit from descending. On the day of Pentecost, the entire church was together: the twelve disciples, Mary (Jesus' mother), the other women who had followed Him, Jesus' brothers, and more. There were one hundred and twenty men and women together in "one accord" (Acts 1:14). "Accord" means to be like-minded or of the same passion. These disciples experienced the miraculous baptism of the Holy Spirit, the sound of a rushing wind, tongues of fire, and speaking in other languages (Acts 1:14–15, 2:1–4). It was obvious, and it was spectacular.

The Gospel Went Out

Men from all over the known world were in the city on this day. Scripture says they were devout men, which tells us they came for Jewish religious purposes. These men were astonished by the one hundred and twenty disciples speaking their own languages. They recognized all those speaking with other tongues as Galileans and marveled at their speaking these languages. Others mocked them as though they were drunk (Acts 2:5–7, 12).

Peter, newly baptized in the Holy Spirit, stood up to speak. All turned their attention to the uneducated Galilean and listened to him preach the gospel news to them. Jesus said they would have power when the Holy Spirit came upon them, and they would witness of Him beginning in Jerusalem

(Acts 1:8). This was precisely what happened here to Peter. He had been locked behind closed doors for fear of the Romans, but now, filled with the Holy Spirit, Peter had the boldness of Christ living in him, and he spoke the truth to the crowd (Acts 2:14–36).

We see Peter's Holy Spirit-filled transition (Acts 2:14–39). Throughout Peter's story, up until this point, he had been looking for Jesus to "restore the kingdom to Israel" (Acts 1:6). His understanding of the Messiah was completely finite. When the gift of the Holy Spirit was sent, his understanding changed by revelation from the Helper: the Infinite dwelling within the finite. Jesus said, "But when the Helper comes, whom I shall send to you from the Father, the Spirit of truth who proceeds from the Father, He will testify of Me. And you also will bear witness, because you have been with Me from the beginning" (John 15:26–27). Peter testified of Jesus from the moment he was baptized with the Spirit.

By revelation of the Spirit, Peter understood they were experiencing the fulfillment of Joel's prophecy, which said God's Spirit would be poured out on all people (Joel 2:28–32). He understood the Holy Spirit was no longer reserved for prophets and priests. He was now pouring His Spirit on all who believed in the Name of Jesus Christ of Nazareth, the Messiah. There were no more distinctions between men and women because all the disciples, all one hundred and twenty, received the baptism of the Holy Spirit, and both genders were heard speaking in other tongues. Peter spoke of signs and wonders, both those already done by Jesus and those to come.

Peter understood Jesus' crucifixion was the foreordained plan of God. The very night all the disciples stumbled was meant to be. What healing this must have brought to Peter, as he heard the words travel from his mouth to the ears of the people from every nation under the sun. Peter understood Jesus' death and resurrection loosed the pains of death. Finally, Peter knew Jesus' death restored Him to glory, as He took His seat at the right hand of God. This was the kingdom restored, not in the bounds of country borders, but fulfilled beyond every border of humanity by the gift of the Holy Spirit. His kingdom of grace and the dispensation of the Holy Spirit awakened the church age in which we now live: a kingdom without boundaries, where all are welcome to call upon the Name which is above every name, Jesus, Lord, Master, and Savior-King.

When Peter finished, the crowd was deeply convicted of their sins and sought what they could do. Peter told them to repent and be baptized for the remission of sin, and then he said they would also receive the Holy Spirit. Peter explained that the promise of the Father was to them, their children, and those who were far off. The promise of the Father was to all who repent of their sins and receive Jesus as their Lord and Savior (Acts 2:37–39). Peter, filled with the Holy Spirit, witnessed to the crowd, and the church grew by three thousand people: "They steadfastly continued together in the apostles' doctrine and fellowship, in the breaking of bread, and in prayers" (Acts 2:42–43). Scripture also tells us new believers were added to the church daily; they shared meals in each other's homes and continued in one accord (Acts 2:45–47).

Jesus ascended to the Father so the Holy Spirit could descend to His followers. A miraculous and obvious sign accompanied the baptism of the Holy Spirit: the sign of speaking in tongues, which also led to sharing the gospel. Peter, filled with the promised Holy Spirit power, shared the gospel boldly, and new believers were added daily to the church. He had been given the keys to the kingdom. He had failed much and failed miserably, but he caught his stride and was walking in his calling, and it was affecting the world for the kingdom of God.

Day Six: Commission, Fishin', and Power

1. Review this week's lessons and highlight your big takeaways. Be prepared to share these if you are meeting with a group.

2. Did you learn something about Peter this week? Share your thoughts.

3. How do you see your big takeaway(s) relating to the world around you today? To the Church in the broader sense, or the local church?

4. How might you apply one of these takeaways this week?

A BEAUTIFUL HEALING DISTURBS ELDERS

Day One: Healing at Gate Beautiful

Read: Acts 3:1–10; Luke 5:5–10.

1. Who was going up to the temple? Had they been partners before?

2. What were they partners at before? What were they partners of now? Did Jesus fulfill His words to them?

3. Who did they meet, and what does scripture tell us about him?

4. What did he seek?

5. What did Peter ask him to do first? Why do you think the man complied?

6. What did Peter say to him, and in whose name?

7. How did Peter help the man receive what he was no longer asking for?

8. Was his healing gradual? How did he respond after the healing?

9. In whose name was he healed? To whom did he give the glory?

Personal Reflection
10. What have you grown weary of hoping for? Where are you seeking help from?

Peter Heals a Lame Man in Jesus' Name

When we first met Peter and John in this study, we found they were business partners and fishermen. They had most likely been together since childhood in Capernaum. Their fathers, being fishermen, were most likely friends. In this week's study, we find Peter and John together as partners again. This time, however, they were fishers of men, just as Jesus had promised (Luke 5:5–10). Peter and John were going up to the temple. They had continued in Jerusalem, as Jesus had commanded.

When Peter and John reached the gate called Beautiful, they came upon a man who was lame from birth. He was brought to the temple daily to ask for alms from those going to temple (Acts 3:2). Peter and John did not appear to have been paying attention to the man. They were about to enter the temple, passing by him. The lame man was the one who called their attention to himself when he asked for charity from them. He saw them and asked alms of them, but he was not looking at them. Maybe he expected them to continue, passing him by. Perhaps he was accustomed to temple-goers ignoring his plea for help. However, he caught Peter and John's attention.

Peter and John stopped and turned back to the man. They saw he was not looking at them. We know this because Peter told him to look at them. The man looked at them, hopeful of receiving financial support. His hope for anything more, such as healing, never existed (or he had given up long ago). He turned his eyes toward them, maybe even holding a hand out to receive what they might give him. Peter informed the man he did not have silver or gold. One has to wonder if the man's heart sank at this point. Was he expecting another speech from another pious Jew or a lame prayer for a lame man? Yet Peter's speech did not go there; instead, he offered the man what he had. He spoke words of healing in Jesus' name. Peter not only spoke a command of healing to the man but also reached forth his hand to help the man up. Peter restored the idea of a hope for healing in a man who was lame from birth. Peter restored a sense of worth to a man whom most people passed by and ignored. By invoking Jesus' name, Peter brought healing to a man lame from birth (Acts 3:4–7).

The man rose with Peter's helping hand and immediately was able to walk and even jump around (Acts 3:8). He entered the temple with Peter and John on his own two feet, praising and giving God the glory for what had been done to him, for he knew only God could have done such a healing miracle. He was healed in Jesus' name, but he gave the glory to God and made no small stir about it. He was animated and loud enough to draw attention to himself and to what God had done (Acts 3:8–9).

Day Two: Healing at Gate Beautiful

Read: Acts 3:10–26.

1. How did the other people at the temple react? Who were they amazed by?

2. What did the man's healing provide Peter and John with? Was this Peter's plan when he spoke healing words to him?

3. What did Peter say was not a factor in the man's healing? What characteristic does this show in Peter?

4. What names did Peter ascribe to Jesus?

5. What did Peter say made the man strong or healed?

6. What did Peter say this crowd had done?

7. According to verses 17 and 18, why did the crowd do this?

8. What did Peter say was the remedy for their actions? What comes after this?

9. How long must Jesus be received in heaven?

10. What did Moses say about the Prophet?

11. What had the prophets from Samuel on spoken of?

12. Who were Peter's audience sons of? What was the promise to them?

13. What was the blessing Jesus was sent to give?

Peter Preaches Jesus to the Amazed Crowd

The crowd in the temple could not help but notice the stir. Curiosity caused them to take a closer look. Many had passed this man by daily. All who knew him knew he was lame from birth. There was great prejudice concerning birth defects in their culture. Hebrews believed a birth defect was a sign of sin for either the affected person or their parents. So when the crowd saw the man lame from birth, the fixture at the Gate Beautiful, not only walking but jumping around, they were amazed, wondering how this could have happened (Acts 3:9–10). While the healed man praised God, the crowd of worshipers looked at Peter and John with amazement. They sought what was special in Peter and John.

Here lies a trap of temptation for many who minister in Jesus' name. When onlookers begin to think they are special, the temptation is to think of themselves as special. They forget the glory belongs to Jesus alone. It is spiritually dangerous to think too highly of God's ministers, for this brings a snare to them. It is also spiritually dangerous to begin to believe our unique qualities cause ministry to be effective in our lives. Peter explains this beautifully to the crowd of awestruck onlookers. Peter first recognized where the crowd was going and quickly began to remedy the situation. He immediately declared that his and John's godliness and power did not heal the man. He absolved himself from any part of the man's healing. He took no credit and no glory for himself. The fisherman we met in the beginning was no longer the same man. He had become a humble fisher of men. He was no longer his own boss but a willing servant of Jesus. He sought only to glorify his Savior (Acts 3:11–12).

Peter went on to tell the crowd about Jesus, the One in whose name the man was healed. He used several names for Jesus as he spoke of Him and to the crowd about their guilt for His bloodshed. Peter called Jesus God's Servant, the Holy One, the Just, and the Prince of Life. Peter explained Pilate's desire to free Jesus was curbed by their cries for His crucifixion. The Man they murdered was responsible for the healing of the lame man and for the praise and glory to God.

Think how the crowd must have felt. If the Man, Jesus, had the power to heal this lame man from beyond the grave, they were guilty of killing the Messiah (Acts 3:13–16). They must have had a deep sinking feeling as they realized they were complicit in the murder of their Savior. They must have felt there was no forgiveness before God for them. Peter had set them up to feel the depths of despair, just as the lame man felt at the gate called Beautiful, then he turned them to the gospel. Peter told the crowd he understood they did this in ignorance, which was part of God's redemptive plan (Acts 3:17–18).

Peter had their full attention, just as he'd had the lame man's before the healing came. Now Peter would speak the healing *they* needed. They were primed and ready to receive the gospel, the good news. The gate name, Beautiful, meant "belonging to the right hour or season." This was the right hour to preach the gospel. Peter said the suffering of the Messiah had been fulfilled. What they needed to do was repent and be converted. They were to believe Jesus was, in fact, the Messiah. Peter said repentance and conversion were the keys to receiving forgiveness for sins. He also said these actions would bring "refreshing from … the presence of the Lord" (Acts 3:19).

Peter went on from ministering repentance and salvation to a condensed version of future events in light of history. He said Jesus would remain in heaven until the restoration of all things. He said this aligned with what the prophets spoke through the centuries. He reminded the crowd of Hebrews how Moses prophesied of this Prophet and said those who follow Him would be saved, but those who would not hear Him would be destroyed. He was speaking to them of eternal salvation or eternal damnation: the difference being whether they received Jesus as their Savior or not. It is really this simple. Salvation is a free gift to all who would repent and be converted through Jesus (Acts 3:20–23).

Peter went on to remind his audience how the prophets had foretold the very days they were in. They all prophesied of the days of Jesus on the earth and the birth of the church (Acts 3:24). Those in Peter's audience were sons of the prophets and were of the covenant God made with Abraham and his descendants. The promise being, all families of the earth would be blessed through

Abraham's offspring: Jesus, the Messiah (Deuteronomy 18:15, 18, 19; Genesis 22:18, 26:4, 28:14; Acts 3:24–26). Peter said the blessing Jesus was sent to give was to turn each one away from their iniquities (Acts 3:26). This did not just mean a turning from past sins but an actual change in the compulsion toward sinning.

Peter and John were not out peddling the gospel but rather heeding the opportunities presented. There is a difference between walking out the door with a mindset to serve Jesus and a mindset to save sinners. There is a difference between sharing with someone ready and sharing with someone because you want them to hear your message. With Christlike compassion, Peter saw an opportunity to serve a man in great need, and he did. He did not serve the man hoping to draw a crowd to preach to. Instead, his kindness toward the man drew a crowd and presented an opportunity Peter chose not to miss.

Peter and John did not see the man at the Gate Beautiful; he drew their attention to himself. They did not ignore his plea but saw an opportunity to glorify Jesus by helping the man. This act of mercy attracted a crowd, which became awestruck by Peter and John. They seized the opportunity to turn their eyes away from them and onto Jesus. Their Christian service lifestyle opened up opportunities to minister healing and share the gospel message.

What a great lesson for Christians today. Live life seeking to serve Jesus and have a lifestyle of worship, and then opportunities will present themselves. Seek opportunities to serve, and opportunities to share the gospel and glorify Jesus will present themselves. Today's trouble Christians have is trying to glorify Jesus without a lifestyle of worship or service. Jesus came as a sacrificial servant. He said we must take up our crosses and follow Him (Matthew 16:24). This is not a picture of comfort and ease. Rather, it is a picture of serving and sacrifice. Peter would write in his letter how we are supposed to follow Christ's example, and Christ suffered (1 Peter 1:21–23).

Day Three: Peter Disturbs the Temple Elders

Read: Acts 4:1–4.

1. Who were Peter and John speaking to?

2. Who came upon them? Why were they disturbed?

3. What did the church leaders do in response to the disciples' teaching?

4. How many were added to the church on this day?

Peter and John Arrested

Peter and John were in the temple, speaking to the large crowd gathered after the lame man was healed. Peter did not miss the opportunity to teach them what Jesus had done for them. The leaders of the synagogue were the very same leaders who plotted against Jesus and incited the crowd to cry out, "Crucify Him!" (Matthew 27:20–22). They expected His disciples to scatter and His teachings to die with Him, so they were incensed when they heard what was happening in the temple. They knew they stood guilty of Jesus' blood and most likely did not desire to be reminded of it. So they set out to put an end to His disciples' teachings.

The temple guard alone was not sent to arrest Peter and John. The priests, the captain of the temple, and the Sadducees were the ones who were "greatly disturbed" by Peter's teaching (Acts 4:2). They arrested Peter and John and placed them in custody overnight, because it was too late in the day to call the council together. The Sadducees did not believe in the resurrection of the dead, and they were worried Peter might convince others of what they did not believe. They probably thought they were doing the crowd a favor, as they were convinced there was no resurrection from the dead. However, the others were not as opposed to the resurrection of the dead as they were to Jesus.

Peter and John were arrested in front of the crowd to whom they preached. The body of believers (men) grew to about five thousand-plus that day. This does not include women and children, so about two thousand men were added (Acts 4:3–4). Peter's first two sermons, recorded in the Book of Acts, reveal the church's growth to be over five thousand, which include those added daily (Acts 2:41, 4:4). Peter may have spent a night in jail, but it looks like he thought the souls of five thousand people were worth it.

Day Four: Peter Disturbs the Temple Elders

Read: Acts 4:5–14; Matthew 10:16–20, 12:23–27, 21:23, 42–46; 26:3–4, 27:62–66.

1. Who did Peter and John stand before on the next day?

2. What question did they begin with? When had they heard this question before?

3. What had Jesus told His disciples about this very thing?

4. How did Peter find the words to speak?

5. For what were Peter and John being judged?

6. To whom did Peter give the credit for the man's healing?

7. When had the council heard the words regarding the chief cornerstone recently? What revelation did Peter share when he repeated it?

8. Memorize Acts 4:12. What did Peter explain to the church leaders about Jesus' name?

9. Why did Peter's audience marvel? Does this have application for you today?

10. Why could they say nothing against it?

Peter and John on Trial

The next morning, Peter and John were retrieved from the jail and brought before the elders for questioning. Those who were in attendance to question them included Annas, the high priest, Caiaphas, John, Alexander, and the family of the high priest as well as their rulers, elders, and scribes (Acts 4:5, 6). It seems no one would miss the questioning of Jesus' disciples.

Two names in this group stand out: Annas and Caiaphas. They were high priests when John the Baptist began his ministry in the wilderness (Luke 3:2). Caiaphas was married to Annas' daughter. He was acting high priest when Jesus was arrested (John 18:13). Scripture tells us the chief priests (Annas and Caiaphas) perceived Jesus' parables were about them, and they wanted to take Him but could not because they feared the people (Matthew 21:25, 26). These were the chief priests Judas made a deal with to betray Jesus (Matthew 26:14–16). When Jesus was arrested, He was brought to Annas first, and then Annas sent Him to Caiaphas. Caiaphas was the one who questioned Jesus about whether or not He was the Messiah. Then he tore his clothes and accused the Savior of blasphemy (Matthew 26:65). He turned Jesus over to Pilate and, in chorus with Annas and the others mention above, incited the crowd to cry out for His crucifixion; these men had blood on their hands and therefore had a keen interest in stopping the disciples of Jesus from preaching any more in His name.

The elders led off with a question the disciples had heard before: "By what power or by what name have you done this?" (Acts 4:7). They had heard the very same chief priests and elders ask the same question of Jesus after He had cleansed the temple: "By what authority are You doing these things? And who gave You this authority?" (Matthew 21:23; Mark 11:27–33; Luke 20:1–8). In this case, Jesus promised to give them the answer to their question if they could tell Him whether the baptism of John the Baptist was from God or not. They refused to answer, and so did Jesus (Matthew 21:24–27). The disciples had the example of Jesus' response to draw on, but there was something else they had to help them. Jesus told them this would happen; they would be brought before the authorities. He told them not to worry about how or what they would speak at those times. He promised the Holy Spirit would give them the words (Matthew 10:17–20).

Scripture tells us this was precisely what happened when Peter spoke; he was full of the Holy Spirit when he responded to the question posed (Acts 4:8). Peter began by pointing out the audacity of being on trial for doing something good for someone in need (Acts 4:9). He went on boldly to say it was in the name of Jesus Christ of Nazareth the man was healed. Peter, emboldened by the Holy Spirit, said, Jesus was the Savior they had all been waiting for, and He was Jesus from Nazareth. Just to be clear, Peter pointed out, He is the Jesus they had crucified (Acts 4:10). He added God raised this same Jesus from the dead, a point they knew already, as they were involved in the cover-up (Matthew 28:11–15).

Peter went further to explain to the assembled crowd Jesus was the Chief Cornerstone, which they rejected (Acts 4:11). This statement of Peter's would burn in the hearts of his audience, who heard Jesus say to them, "Have you never read in the scriptures: 'The stone which the builders rejected has become the chief cornerstone. This was the Lord's doing, and it is marvelous in our eyes'? Therefore, I say to you, the kingdom of God will be taken from you and given to a nation bearing the fruits of it. And whoever falls on this stone will be broken; but on whomever it falls, it will grind him to powder" (Matthew 21:42–44). When Jesus had spoken those words, the chief priests and Pharisees sought to lay hands on Him, but because they feared the multitude, they did not (Matthew 21:45, 46). Indeed, those in Peter's hearing who had heard Jesus speak those words would remember. They would either be convicted by their actions and fall on the Stone, or they would yet harden their hearts further and be destroyed by their vehement hatred of Jesus of Nazareth, the Chief Cornerstone.

Peter's final statement, recorded in Acts 4:12 was, "There is no other name under heaven given among men by which we must be saved." Peter spoke a mere three-sentence reply. Yet in those few sentences, volumes were spoken to his audience. The healing of one man brought him before a large crowd of Jewish leaders, both religious and political, to testify to Jesus as the long-awaited Messiah. This statement was not only volatile in Peter's day, but it is the core of conflict between Christian belief and all others today. Knowing Jesus is the only way to salvation makes Christians seem intolerant to a world filled with religions catering to human desires. Jesus said well, "Narrow is the gate and difficult is the way which leads to life, and there are few who find it" (Matthew 7:14). Jesus is the gate, for He said, "I am the way, the truth, and the life. No one comes to the Father except through Me" (John 14:6).

Peter's audience marveled at his words. They were intelligent, precise, and knowledgeable. They marveled because they understood Peter to be an uneducated man, which was correct. He was a fisherman turned fisher of men. He was not trained like his audience was in the scriptures, but he had spent a few years with Jesus, the Word (John 1:1). Peter spoke with a boldness and authority only the Holy Spirit could give him. This is why it does not matter what any person has to offer; with the Holy Spirit, Jesus can meet the need through any willing vessel. Peter's audience not only marveled but were rendered speechless, as it was clear a miracle had taken place. There was no argument they could form against a man lame for many years now standing in their presence.

Day Five: Peter Disturbs the Temple Elders

Read: Acts 4:15-31.

1. What did the council admit in private?

2. What did the council conclude as their plan of action? Why?

3. What was Peter and John's answer to their demand?

4. Peter and John could have agreed and gone on and done what they pleased. Why didn't they?

5. Why were they let go?

6. Where did Peter and John go after their release? Why? What was the response?

7. What did they pray for? What happened after they prayed?

Peter and John Sentenced and Released

The council sent the apostles out of their presence so they could deliberate about what to do. They admitted to the miracle privately, and it was widely spread public knowledge. They had no room to argue against it (Acts 4:16). Therefore, since the council could not publicly deny the miracle done in Jesus' name, they instead chose an attempt to silence the apostles. Their plan of action was to intimidate the apostles enough to cause them to cease their activities (Acts 4:17). The council chose to reject Jesus, the Chief Cornerstone. They had seen the miracle, had again been confronted with Jesus the Messiah, and had again chosen to reject Him.

The council called the apostles back into their presence and shared their plan. They were to stop teaching and preaching Jesus and discontinue using His name (Acts 4:18). Peter and John responded to the council. Both stated they were answering to a higher authority than the council. They were answering to God alone, and man would not sway them, not even these powerful men— the men who crucified their Lord. They committed and confessed to the council their commitment to continue (Matthew 4:19, 20).

Peter and John could have just agreed with the council and gone and done their own thing anyway. They would have had much less risk. However, they were men of integrity, filled with the Holy Spirit, and were emboldened to speak truth. The beauty of their telling the truth was the council's inability to punish them and had to set them free (Acts 4:21). Even though the disciples said they would not yield to the council's threats and commands, they were let go without punishment.

Peter and John made haste to rejoin the others and report what had happened. When the church heard their testimony, they could only praise, exalt, and pray to the Lord for continued support, such as they had just heard. When they were finished praying and exalting the Lord, the place they were in shook, as God answered their prayer to fill them, and they continued to speak the Word of God with boldness (Acts 4:24–31).

Peter had been a fisherman who spoke his mind fearlessly. Now, a fisher of men, he yielded his confident voice to the Lord and spoke by His authority and the power of His Holy Spirit. The gift was already in him. He just needed to submit it to the Lord's use and glory instead of his own.

Day Six: A Beautiful Healing Disturbs Elders

1. Review this week's lessons and highlight your big takeaways. Be prepared to share these if you are meeting with a group.

2. Did you learn something about Peter this week? Share your thoughts.

3. How do you see your big takeaway(s) relating to the world around you today? To the Church in the broader sense, or the local church?

4. How might you apply one of these takeaways this week?

One Accord and Second Arrest

Day One: Peter Leads the Church in One Accord

Read: Acts 4:32–37; 9:27.

1. How generous were the individuals of the first church? Why might this be?

2. How did the apostles give witness to the resurrection of the Lord Jesus?

3. Why did no one lack?

4. Who distributed to the needs of the people?

5. (Challenge) What noteworthy thing did Joses do? Who was he? Why is this significant?

All Things in Common

The story of the believers in the first church Peter led is a beautiful picture of brotherly love and affection. Those who possessed material things did not consider them their own. They held onto everything they owned very loosely because they were so sold out to Jesus. They cared about their fellow believer and their needs. They were attached not to the stuff of life but to the Giver of Life. Even those who owned large items, such as land and houses, sold them and gave all the money to the apostles. Today, we would say they gave it all to the church. They lived, ate, worshiped, and cared for one another's needs. They were a true *family* of believers (Acts 4:32–37).

This giving activity of the first church raises a question today: Why would they sell everything and give it all to the church? Why would they give up their homes and possessions? Wouldn't they still need a roof over their heads? Where did more than eight thousand believers live together? First of all, they were sold out to Jesus. The Great Commission commanded them to spread the gospel. If you traveled from Jerusalem to Judea, to Samaria, and then to the ends of the earth, you would not need a home or property, but finances to support the journey. They may also have thought Jesus was returning soon and did not need such things. Or maybe they became believers in Jerusalem while there to celebrate a holiday, and therefore sold holdings in other parts of the country so they could remain in Jerusalem. Whatever the reason, we see a deep faith in the Lord and trust in the apostles to care for their needs and lead them. Scripture says the apostles distributed to the needs of the people (Acts 4:34, 35).

Joses received special honor in scripture for selling all he had and laying it at the apostles' feet. We are told this was the activity of the entire church, so why would Joses receive special acclaim by Luke (Acts 4:36)? While laying the money at the apostle's feet was an extravagant act, there was more to Joses' acclaim. As Luke pointed out, he was Barnabas, a Levite from Cyprus. Barnabas was a descendant of Levi, whose tribe God chose to minister to Him in the temple. Barnabas, being a priest, would know the scriptures well. He acknowledged Jesus as the long-awaited Messiah and did not demand his priestly position remain intact. Instead, he submitted himself to the uneducated apostles who walked with Jesus and trusted them to lead him in the ways of the Messiah. Barnabas was also the one who later introduced Paul (Saul) to the elders at the church in Jerusalem. Paul had become known as a persecutor of Christians, and church leaders feared him. However, Barnabas had met him and attested to his conversion to Christianity (Acts 9:26, 27). Barnabas also accompanied Paul on missionary journeys. God called Barnabas and Saul to missions at Antioch (Acts 13:2).

Day Two: Peter Leads the Church in One Accord

Read: Acts 5:1-10; Ephesians 6:12; Colossians 3:18.

1. What did Ananias and Sapphira sell? What did they do with the proceeds?

2. What did Peter understand about what was happening? Who did Peter say Ananias was lying to?

3. What did Peter say about Ananias' possession? What is the lesson here?

4. What happened to Ananias? Why do you think such a severe consequence was warranted?

5. What was Sapphira's sin?

6. Who did Peter say she was testing? What did he mean by this?

7. What was different about Ananias' death and Sapphira's death?

Ananias and Sapphira Hold Back

Luke strategically placed the story of Joses' generosity just before the story of Ananias and Sapphira to give a severe contrast in the giving actions of each one. Ananias and Sapphira also sold all they had but gave only a portion to the apostles. However, they lied and said it was the full amount. Imagine the pressure they must have been under in a church where all these faithful believers were selling all they had and giving it all to the church, leaving themselves utterly dependent upon the apostles and Jesus. Peer pressure only got the better of them. They felt a need to appear as spiritual as the others, but as of yet, they were not. They did not have to sell all (or even anything) they owned and give it to the church. The church was not requiring this kind of sacrifice from anyone. People who were moved to sell all did so. However, looks like Ananias was concerned about appearing just as spiritual as everyone else, so he faked it. Worse yet, Ananias got Sapphira, his wife, to agree to the plan (Acts 5:3).

Ananias and Sapphira did not expect the Holy Spirit to tattle on them. They had seen the Holy Spirit at work through physical miracles and giving words when needed, such as Peter and John's recent imprisonment. However, they clearly did not understand the Holy Spirit. He was always with them and Peter and the other disciples. He was present when they made their sinful plans, and He was also present with Peter when they brought their lie to his feet.

Peter was confident he heard the Holy Spirit reveal what Ananias and Sapphira had done, because he had spent so much time experiencing Him in prayer and ministering. He was not timid about it at all. Peter was straightforward in his confrontation with Ananias and spoke the words the

Holy Spirit gave him to speak, just as he'd done before the assembly of priests and elders. Peter said Ananias had allowed Satan to fill his heart with this scheme (Acts 5:3).

Since the beginning, in the garden with Adam and Eve, Satan has worked to undermine what God has been doing through human history. Satan may have lost the war when Jesus rose from the grave, but he is still fighting the battle until Jesus' final triumphant return. Satan, of course, attacked the fledgling church. He did not want the gospel to spread even more than the Jewish leaders did not want it to spread. Satan is now in a race to destroy as many souls as possible before Jesus' return. He will use any willing vessel, preferably a churchgoer, a family member, someone least expected, or someone the least bit disgruntled. Ananias was a church member dealing with a prideful sin. He left a door open for Satan, and he came in with full charge. Satan wanted to use his foothold on Ananias to gain a foothold in the church (1 Peter 5:8).

Peter revealed the level of Ananias' foolishness when he said Ananias did not have to sell his possessions; they were his to do with as he pleased. Neither God nor the disciples had called the church to sell all and live in poverty. Scripture does not say poverty is a gift or a calling, nor does it laud it as an admirable quality. God did not ask church members to live in poverty. While one might be able to fool people sometimes, God is never fooled. He sees the true but hidden motive of the heart in every choice a person makes. He will judge in the end (1 Corinthians 4:5). The church must see the seriousness of lying to the Holy Spirit (Ephesians 4:25–32). The result of Ananias' sin was to fall dead at Peter's feet. This might seem rather severe. Scripture does not elaborate on why he had to die. However, this was the church in its infancy. God the Father would have been exceedingly protective of her. Just like an earthly father protects his children from predators, our heavenly Father protects His baby to set a sure foundation for the rest of the world, for the rest of time. This was a clear sign of how the Lord feels about hypocrisy.

Sapphira entered the scene, not knowing what had just transpired and what the result was for her husband. Luke tells us Sapphira agreed to her husband's scheme (Acts 5:8). One might question whether Sapphira had a choice other than to obey her husband. Sapphira's sin was in obeying her husband more than God. Her husband may have had an earthly authority over her, but he did not have an eternal one. When it comes to moral action, a woman must obey God first. Colossians 3:18 says, "Submit to husbands as is fitting in the Lord." Ananias' plan was not fitting in the Lord, and therefore Sapphira's duty was to either talk sense to her husband or refuse to comply with his ungodly plan. A woman can disagree with her husband while allowing him to remain in authority and still giving him respect.

Abigail bowed before David, the king, and gave him the honor due him while yet confronting him about his unrighteous plans to kill her husband. David, moved by her respectful confrontation, turned from his evil intent. Abigail's husband died at God's hand, and she later became David, the king of Israel's wife (1 Samuel 25:1–42). Sapphira had the opportunity in the Lord to speak truth to her husband and obey God rather than man, but the way scripture tells the story, she did not choose it; she chose the lie. Her sin was her silence and her partnering in the deception.

Peter said Sapphira was testing the Holy Spirit. She and Ananias did not fathom anyone knowing what they had planned in secret. They did not understand the powerful workings of the Holy Spirit (1 Corinthians 4:5). Jesus told the disciples, speaking of the hypocrisy of the Pharisees, that plans and schemes made in secret would be revealed openly. He said His disciples ought not be afraid of men who can do physical harm, but fear God, who is powerful to grant or deny eternal life (Luke 12:2–5). Ananias and Sapphira did not believe the Holy Spirit was a revealer of secrets. The outcome for them was fatal. While Ananias' death came suddenly and without warning, Sapphira's death came at Peter's prophetic word; she and Peter both knew it was coming (Acts 5:5, 9). She, too, fell at Peter's feet and was carried out to be buried with her husband.

Day Three: Peter Leads the Church in One Accord

Read: Acts 5:11-16.

1. What resulted from Ananias and Sapphira's deaths for the church?

2. Who else was affected by the story of Ananias and Sapphira? Why?

3. What was done through the hands of the apostles?

4. What state was the church in at this time? Where was the church meeting? Where was this located?

5. What kept people from joining the church? How did those people feel about the church? How will this affect them eternally? (See Romans 10:9–10.)

6. How many believers were added to the Lord?

7. Why were the streets lined with the sick? What does this say about their faith?

8. How many people came from the surrounding cities and why? How many were healed?

9. How far had Peter come?

Ananias and Sapphira's Effect on the Church

While this might seem too severe a punishment, we cannot know the mind of the Lord (Isaiah 40:13, 14). We will not always understand the things the Lord does. He does not answer to us and is infinitely more intelligent than we are. He sees the whole picture, while we measure things through our finite knowledge and thinking. "For as the heavens are higher than the earth, so are [His] ways higher than [our] ways, And [His] thoughts than [our] thoughts" (Isaiah 55:9). What we do know resulted from the Ananias and Sapphira saga was, great fear fell upon the church. Furthermore, their story was witnessed outside of the church and greatly affected every soul who heard the story (Acts 5:11). God used Ananias and Sapphira's story to witness to His and His church's disdain for hypocrisy. What a refreshing thought it must have been to a Jewish population overwhelmed by the hypocrisy of its leaders. Righteousness was what Jewish believers expected of their leaders, and they were seeing it in the church, but not in the synagogue, where they refused to recognize Him. Maybe Jesus really is the Messiah, must have been a thought in not just a few minds then. God took a potential scandal for the church and turned it around to glorify Himself.

The church was meeting in the temple area at Solomon's Porch. They were in "one accord" or unified agreement, and many signs and wonders were witnessed through the apostles (Acts 5:12). Many people thought highly of the church but would not join because of fear. There were many things to fear about joining the church: rejection from one's own family, loss of friends in and out of synagogue, and becoming an enemy of Jewish leaders and elders, to name a few (Acts 5:13). Conversely, God's judgment of a person was the difference between eternal life and death; it was worthy of sacrifice and even persecution. You cannot be saved by highly esteeming the church or Jesus. You can only be saved when you confess Jesus as Lord and follow Him. Too many today confess they believe Jesus is the Son of God, but they do not invite Him into their heart to be Lord and Master of their life. Even Satan believes in Jesus, but is not submitted to Him and is guaranteed a place in eternal hell (Revelation 20:10).

The church was now innumerable. Luke's account of believers goes from three and five thousand saved, making eight thousand church members, to "multitudes" (Acts 5:14). There were so many people turning to faith in Jesus as the Messiah, they could no longer keep count. The fame of Peter had spread, and a multitude of people were coming from all over, lying themselves or their sick in the streets, just hoping to be touched by his shadow and believing it would be enough to receive a touch from God. Luke tells us all who came were healed, whether from illness or demonic activity (Acts 5:16).

Peter was not just the leader of the church of the multitude; he also had another multitude coming to seek healing. They were no longer going to the priests at the temple but to Peter at the temple and in the streets along the way to the temple. Healing moved from the meeting place to the streets. Jesus also took His healing and teaching ministry to the streets. What an excellent lesson for churchgoers today. Too many Christians think the ministry call for them is found inside a building, but Peter's example teaches believers to take their ministry to the streets, where the sick and tormented are found.

Look how far Peter had come. Peter and James, who wrote the book of James, were co-leaders in Jerusalem. James wrote, "Humble yourselves in the sight of the Lord, and He will lift you up" (James 4:10). One has to wonder if he was thinking of Peter when he wrote it. Peter, the man who was a boastful, proud business owner turned humble servant of Jesus, was no longer seeking a position in the kingdom; he was just glad to have been allowed back after his blunder. He was a different man: a man under authority. He was a man who understood the saving grace of Jesus and was determined to share it with all who would receive it. Whenever attention was paid to him, he redirected it to the Lord Jesus Christ and invited onlookers to share in the salvation he too had found in Him. Peter was humble, not timid. Through his humility, he was exalted to lead the world's first megachurch, and his fame spread throughout the land and history.

Day Four: Peter's Second Arrest

Read: Acts 5:17–21.

1. How did the high priest feel about the apostles? What sect did he and his friends belong to?

2. What do you know about this sect? Look in a Bible dictionary for help.

3. Why do you think they were so indignant over the apostles?

4. Where did the high priest have the apostles placed?

5. Who came to the apostles' aid, and what were they told to do? How do you think they felt about this command? How would you feel?

6. What do you think is meant by "all the words of this life"?

7. How quick were the apostles to obey? What did they do?

The Apostle's Second Arrest

The high priest had gone from being greatly disturbed over what the apostles had been teaching and doing to indignant because of their activities (Acts 4:2, 5:17). These verses shed a little more light upon why the high priest was filled with such punitive zeal toward the apostles. We know the high priest was active in the sect of the Sadducees. The word "Sadducee" means "the righteous." They believed their doctrine was the only doctrine. They did not believe the Law was revealed by God to the Israelites; they saw the Law as their complete and only viable authority. They did not believe in the body's resurrection, the soul's immortality, predestination, free will, or the existence of angels.

No wonder the Sadducees sect was indignant (punitively zealous) toward the apostles' teachings. Everything the apostles taught went against what the Sadducees believed. They were casting out demons, which the Sadducees did not believe existed. They also preached a resurrected Jesus. Isn't it interesting? Many saints rose from their graves, went into town, and were seen by many when Jesus died (Matthew 27:52, 53). Jesus even remained for days before ascending to heaven. How did the high priests and Sadducees miss seeing any or all of them (Acts 1:3)? How could they hold so tightly to their doctrine in light of these revelations?

Can you imagine what people would do who do not believe in the resurrection, the immortality of the soul, or God's intimate activity in humanity? Look around your world today. Many people believe Jesus is the Son of God and rose from the grave, but they do not believe in demons, nor do they believe Jesus is actively involved in humanity. If people thought Jesus was actively involved in their lives, their walk would be more prudent. Their lifestyle reveals their disbelief.

The high priest gained much wealth in his position and clearly had some political power with the Roman government, which wanted to keep the Jews friendly toward them. When people believe the only authority over them is words on a page, they are less likely to obey those mere words. However, when people believe there is a God and He is intimately associated and active with each person, they are more likely to obey Him. These men, the Sadducees, were convinced of their doctrine and determined to keep their authority (on paper), so they killed Jesus. Jesus, the one who taught resurrection, cast out demons, and behaved as though God *was* intimately involved in humanity. They came against Him because He threatened their core beliefs, and they were unwilling to change their minds. They thought their troubles were gone with Jesus. They must have felt He was haunting them from the grave through the teachings of His apostles, who preached Jesus the Messiah raised from the dead. This wouldn't be so troublesome, except great signs and wonders followed their ministry, and they were losing thousands of people to this doctrine.

The apostles, not just Peter, were placed in the common prison. Luke tells us they were put into custody. This reads as though they were placed under house arrest the first time, but they were housed with common criminals this time. There had been a progression or escalation of the Sadducees' zeal against them. According to Luke, they were first greatly disturbed, and then they became indignant. They were first put into custody and are now placed in the common prison. As the Jewish leaders' aggression toward the apostles increased, so did heavenly support for them.

The Apostles Released from Prison

The apostles found themselves together in the common prison. At the very least, they were all together and could pray and support one another. When the apostles were locked away with no ability to save themselves, God sent an angel to aid them by night. In the darkest hours, locked away in a prison, God sent help to His apostles. He did not save them from the arrest, but delivered them in His perfect timing. Luke tells us the angel opened the door to the prison and "brought them out" (Acts 5:19). The angel was active in leading them out of the prison and into the open. What a beautiful picture of the Lord meeting our need. When we feel like all doors of a situation are locked and cannot see our way out, God brings deliverance. However, with the deliverance also came a command for the apostles. The angel said they were to return to the temple and continue teaching. Specifically, they were to tell "the people all the words of this life" (Acts 5:20).

We soon see the apostles' obedience to the words of the angel sent by God. However, imagine for a moment what they might have felt as they heard the angel speak those words. On one hand, you rarely expect to be delivered from the lion's den, only to be sent back into the lion's territory. Deliverance usually connotes being set free of the entire ordeal. Yet the apostles were told to return to where they had been arrested and continue speaking to the people. However, receiving clear direction after a miraculous deliverance must have been exhilarating. They must have gained a great deal of confidence from the angel's actions and words. How beautiful it is to realize God's intimate involvement in your life. Whether the apostles understood God's grand plan or not, they obeyed (Acts 5:21). What a great lesson for all disciples of Jesus. We do not need to know the grand scheme or why Jesus asked us to do something. We are to obey His leading, trusting Him with the grand scheme and outcome. Even when we end up in prison, we must trust Him with the result.

Day Five: Peter's Second Arrest

Read: Acts 5:22-42.

1. Who did the high priest call together before sending for the prisoners?

2. Reading verses 22 and 23, what is this a picture of? Do you think this was a purposeful visual for the Sadducees? What was their initial response (verse 24)?

3. How did the officers bring the apostles in for questioning? Why? How do they compare and contrast with the apostles at this point?

4. What was the high priest's complaint?

5. How did Peter and the other apostles respond to this?

6. Is there a point in your life where you fear man more than God? What will you do about it?

7. What are the words of life Peter preached to the council?

8. How did the council respond to the words of life?

9. Who stood up in the midst of this? What sect did he belong to? Is this significant?

10. What did he tell the council to take heed of?

11. What was his advice regarding the apostles?

12. How did the council part with the apostles?

13. How did the apostles leave the council? Why? What was their daily activity after all of this?

The Apostles Lost and Found

The scene was somewhat comical, as the apostles were sent for from the prison and were nowhere to be found. The high priest had called together the council and all the elders. He was in a rage against the apostles of Jesus and was primed to silence them once and for all before a crowd. He had assembled his peer group and sent for the apostles, only to have to admit to his friends and peers they were not where he left them. The visual reference to the empty tomb was even more comical and poignant. The guards went, found the other guards standing outside the locked door, opened the door, and found an empty room. One does not have to wonder if the high priest got the visual metaphor of the risen Lord, this Sadducee who did not believe in resurrection. All who heard it took pause and wondered how this would turn out. They felt the illusion of control slip from their grasp.

When the apostles were found, they were in the temple, preaching the words of this life. The officers took pause in regard to how they apprehended their suspects. They were afraid of the crowd because the apostles were popular with them (Acts 5:26). The contrast between the officers and the apostles is stark. The officers feared the people more than they feared their earthly employers, whereas the apostles feared God more than man. This kind of confidence can only be found in the saving knowledge of Jesus Christ.

The Apostles Released and Rejoicing

The apostles were finally brought before the assembly of the high priest, council, and elders, and the complaint against them was heard. The high priest's complaint was against the apostles teaching in Jesus' name, their doctrine, and the blood of Jesus upon their own hands (Acts 5:28). The high priest was also angry because he had warned Peter and John not to teach in Jesus' name and they were doing it anyway (Acts 4:18). We learned in an earlier lesson, when Jesus gave Peter the keys to the kingdom, He was giving him the right to produce doctrine in light of the Messiah's work. The high priest found these disciples of Jesus to be as uncontrollable as Jesus had been.

Peter and the apostles responded the same way they had responded the first time, saying they would obey God rather than man (Acts 4:19, 5:29). This was the doctrine they taught, the doctrine we hold to today as Christian believers. They are the words of life the angel commanded the disciples to speak. The words of this life are this. Jesus was resurrected and exalted to God's right hand to be Prince and Savior, to give repentance to Israel, and for the forgiveness of sins. The apostles added they were witnesses to these things, but the Holy Spirit was also a witness to those things, and the Holy Spirit was given to those who obey God (Acts 5:30–32).

The high priest was the religious leader of the Jews. Above all people, he should have been obedient to God. Yet he had not heard these things or received the Holy Spirit. He was a Sadducee who did not believe in resurrection or life after this earth. The apostles had insulted every aspect of his belief system. They had boldly told him he was not in obedience to God (nor were any of the other leaders and Sadducees in attendance), and his disbelief in the resurrection was wrong. This, of course, infuriated their audience and caused a violent rage to well up in them, and they began to make plans to kill them as they did Jesus (Matthew 12:14; Acts 5:33).

A man named Gamaliel was in the audience. He was a Pharisee. Pharisees believed in a resurrection. When the disciples were taken out so the group could deliberate, Gamaliel spoke words of wisdom and spared the disciples' lives. Gamaliel warned those with murderous rage to heed what they were considering. If this were the Lord, they could do nothing; if it were not, the disciples of Jesus would fade away sooner or later (Acts 5:36–39). The council heeded Gamaliel's wise words, and instead of seeking their death, they merely beat the apostles and commanded them to no longer preach in Jesus' name (Acts 5:40).

The disciples, having just been beaten and released, left rejoicing. They were honored "that they were counted worthy to suffer shame for His name" (Acts 5:41). They then returned to the temple and preached all the more in Jesus' name. They preached it in the temple and in His name in every home. They did not obey man, even with the threat and experience of violence against them. Instead, it inspired them to greater service for Jesus. We have seen Peter and all the disciples change from self-seekers to men willing to suffer any price for Jesus. They had abandoned Him in the garden because of the threat of violence and His willingness to accept it. Now they accepted the violence against them in His name with great joy.

Day Six: One Accord and Second Arrest

1. Review this week's lessons and highlight your big takeaways. Be prepared to share these if you are meeting with a group.

2. Did you learn something about Peter this week? Share your thoughts.

3. How do you see your big takeaway(s) relating to the world around you today? To the Church in the broader sense, or the local church?

4. How might you apply one of these takeaways this week?

Prayer, Ministry, and Partiality

Day One: Peter Given to Prayer and Ministry

Read: Acts 6:1–7.

1. Upon the complaint, what did the apostles do?

2. What was not desirable for the apostles to do?

3. Who did they place in charge of finding workers? What were the job requirements?

4. What was it the apostles wanted to give themselves to?

5. Do you see this formula in the church today?

6. What did the apostles do with the men chosen by the church?

7. What happened to the word of God and the church after this?

The Church Scatters

The apostles were leading a megachurch. The twelve ran into complaints regarding the care of widows. The Jews who took on Greek culture and spoke Greek (Hellenists) felt their widows were being slighted in favor of the traditional Jewish widows. The apostles' reaction to this was not a sermon on regarding others more highly than yourself, or any other number of teachings to silence complaints. Instead, the apostles met the problem head-on. They realized they could not manage the entire church and study to teach God's Word alone. They needed to appoint leaders to help with the works of the church (Acts 6:1, 2). Moses in the desert experienced a similar situation. He realized he could not keep up the pace of judging all of Israel alone; upon his father-in-law's advice, he set up other leaders to help carry the burden of caring for Israel (Exodus 18:13–26).

While Moses chose men according to a set of standards, the apostles laid the responsibility upon the church members. They gave guidelines for the characteristics the men should possess. The men chosen were to have a good reputation, they were to be filled with the Holy Spirit, and they were to be full of wisdom (Acts 6:3). If the disciples had chosen these men, they would have selected from those closest to them and missed an opportunity to promote godly men they didn't know, due to the size of the church. However, by giving the church the responsibility to elect these men, everyone was given an equal chance to serve in ministry.

The apostles did a wise thing by appointing other leaders to head the food distribution. They had probably experienced their inability to do it all on their own. They were not opposed to the work, but could not give proper time to studying God's Word and prayer, as those charged with preaching the gospel required. These men were charged with expounding God's Word to the church and the community. This does not exclude ministers from helping in various areas of the church, but it does mean the bulk of what they are to do is study and expound God's Word.

These are beneficial lessons for the church today. Ministers must be given to prayer, studying, and ministering the Word of God. They need church members to rise up and take on ministry roles within the church and without, whether a special title or paycheck comes with it or not. Ministers need to be supported by their congregations to do the work of ministering inside and outside of the church walls. This is not the intended role of the pastor's spouse. We don't see any of the disciples' wives being mentioned as setting up communion, cleaning the church, or running the Sunday school (okay, they didn't have Sunday school or church buildings back then, but you see the point).

Another good lesson for the church is the requirements for service. For the first church, those serving in the kitchen were to be people of good reputation, filled with the Holy Spirit and wisdom. Sometimes, a church will become too desperate to fill a position. They take whoever volunteers, without consideration for the spirit they bring to the position. This is not to slight anyone; we all belong in the kingdom. However, believers who fill positions at any level in the church ought to meet some standards. The first requirement is to receive Jesus as their Lord and Savior. Some churches hire musicians who don't know Jesus to lead their congregations into worship. How can someone lead where they cannot go? Furthermore, if we believe the Bible to be infallible and authoritative, we must agree on standards for serving. First, they should have a good reputation (most employers require this in the secular realm). They must be filled with the same understanding as the first church, being baptized with the Holy Spirit. Lastly, according to Peter and the apostles, those who desire to serve in the church must display the characteristics of wisdom (Acts 6:3). However, I will add this disclaimer: people grow when they serve. Church leaders must use wisdom.

When the congregation chose the men, the apostles prayed and laid hands on them. The apostles prayed first. Prayer reveals they were dependent upon the Lord in all things. Scripture doesn't tell us what they prayed specifically. However, it is not a far stretch of the imagination to think of what they may have prayed. They sought God to bless them in the ministry they were setting out to do and for Him to lead them, guide them, and give them wisdom for the task at hand. The laying on of hands is symbolic of transference. It is a visual aid for a spiritual reality. As the men offered themselves to ministry, God imparted the necessary gifts to carry out ministry. The apostles were not transferring the gifts through their touch but giving a visual conduit for what the Lord was doing in the spiritual realm.

Luke makes an important point. The gospel spread when the apostles were freed to spend more time praying and studying after appointing others to serve tables. The apostles were free to speak and teach more, as they did in the beginning, before they had such a large congregation to care for. They were back speaking and teaching salvation in Jesus the Messiah, and the church continued to grow. Luke tells us many priests were not just believers but obedient to the faith, which means they openly followed the teachings of Jesus' apostles (Acts 6:7).

Day Two: Peter Given to Prayer and Ministry

Read: Acts 8:4–25.

1. Where did Philip go, and what happened there?

2. What do we learn about the man called Simon? What was he amazed by?

3. Who did the apostles send to minister to the new believers in Samaria?

4. What did Peter and John do for the new believers? How did they do it?

5. How did Simon respond to the miracle of Holy Spirit baptism?

6. What did Peter say was wrong with Simon's request? What was Peter's diagnosis of Simon's problem?

7. What did Peter say was the remedy for Simon?

8. Did Simon follow Peter's advice? Why or why not?

9. Where did Peter and John go after ministering in Samaria?

The Gospel Spreads to Samaria

Jesus' command to the disciples before He ascended was for them to witness in Jerusalem, Judea, Samaria, and to the ends of the earth (Acts 1:8). They were doing an excellent job in Jerusalem; scripture clearly shows this. However, up to this point, scripture has not shown us they had yet ministered in any of the following places. While this was meant as a picture of the gospel spreading out from Jerusalem to the ends of the earth, there was also a strategy here. It took the church being persecuted to scatter the church and make way for the gospel to spread (Acts 8:3).

Philip went to Samaria to preach the gospel there. Believers in Samaria grew to a multitude amidst Philip's preaching, which came with signs and wonders (Acts 8:4–7). However, while they became believers, the Holy Spirit had not yet been poured upon them, even amid all the miraculous occurrences. These miracles got the attention of one man in particular. Simon was a man who manipulated crowds with the use of sorcery. Of course, this brought him some fame and awe with people, especially in this time in history. Simon sold himself through his sorcery to be a great man of God. He was a con artist and probably made a good living at it. He became a believer through Philip's ministry and continued with Philip (Acts 8:9–13).

The apostles at Jerusalem sent Peter and John to Samaria to partner with Philip and establish the hearts of the people there. Peter and John were again laying hands on people as a sign of impartation. They prayed for many new believers to receive the Holy Spirit (Acts 8:14–15, 17). This was more than Simon, the new believer and former sorcerer, could take. He was saved, but he was also a baby believer recently released from an occult lifestyle. He sought to purchase from Peter and John the ability to impart the Holy Spirit to others. He may have had to pay someone to teach him the sorceries he performed, and approached them from this understanding (Acts 8:18, 19).

Peter's response to Simon may remind you of Jesus' comment to Peter some time ago: "Get behind me, Satan" (Matthew 16:23). Peter's response to Simon was pointed. According to Luke's Gospel, the Holy Spirit was a free gift to anyone who asked for it (Luke 11:13). Simon saw things in the context of his world before Jesus. He was saved and being transformed, making blunders along the way. The beautiful thing Peter did here was not just rebuke Simon, but he spoke to his core issue. Peter was looking for healing and restoration of the man's soul. He pointed out how Simon was a man driven by bitterness and iniquity (Acts 8:20, 23). While Peter's statement came across as harsh, if Simon had responded humbly, he would have received greater healing than a lame man walking; he would have been a broken-souled man, made whole. Scripture does not tell us the outcome for Simon except for his asking Peter to pray for him (Acts 8:24). Peter could not repent on Simon's behalf. Simon would have to come to a place to repent for his actions and open those wounded and wicked areas to Jesus to forgive, cleanse, and heal.

Peter spoke the truth to Simon, then returned to Jerusalem (Acts 8:25). There is a great lesson to be learned here. Peter spoke the truth to a man who needed to hear the truth, and then he left him in God's hands. Peter did not stay around and debate with him or become emotionally involved in his salvation process. Peter knew his and others' salvation was wholly between them and Jesus alone. He could do nothing except obey what Jesus had called him to do, and he was called to preach the gospel. We often become too desperate for other people's salvation, even to the point of getting in the way of letting the Lord deal with them. There is much wisdom in speaking truth and then remaining silent or getting out of the way completely. Jesus will not grade you on how many souls were saved at your hand, because He is the Author and Finisher of each person's faith. However, He will judge according to your obedience.

Day Three: Peter Given to Prayer and Ministry

Read: Acts 9:32–43.

1. Where did Peter travel to minister?

2. Who did Peter meet at Lydda? What did he do for him?

3. What was the result for Lydda and Sharon from Peter's work with one man?

4. Why did Peter go to Joppa? What did he do there?

5. What was the response from the people in Joppa?

6. How long did Peter stay in Joppa, and with whom did he stay?

Peter Ministers around Judea

Peter began traveling throughout Judea, ministering the gospel. He was most likely visiting the Christians who had taken up residence elsewhere (Acts 9:32). Many who believed in Jerusalem did so at Peter's preaching. He was intimately involved with their salvation process and probably felt a kingdom responsibility toward them. Jesus, after all, said to feed His sheep. Jesus didn't say, "just the ones in your city." Jesus said from Jerusalem to Judea and Samaria, and then to the ends of the world (Acts 1:8). Peter's letters were also written to the Diaspora, the Jews who were scattered about the region. This reveals why we see Peter traveling in Samaria and Judea, ministering to the saints and preaching the gospel.

When Peter arrived at Lydda, he met a man, Aeneas, who had been paralyzed for eight years. Peter spoke healing to Aeneas in Jesus' name, and the result was not just Aeneas' healing but salvation for all those in Lydda and Sharon who saw him (Acts 9:32–35). They turned to the Lord when they saw the healed man. While healing may be happening inside the church, Peter was taking healing to the streets and using it as a very effective tool to minister the gospel.

While Peter was still in Lydda, the saints at Joppa sent for him to come to them. One of their beloved sisters in Christ had died. Peter went with them, without question or argument. He did not attach himself to the believers as though he were necessary to minister to their Christian walk. He knew and trusted the Holy Spirit to minister to them through another willing soul. Peter was no longer the man who thought too highly of himself. He was free to go where God called him to and minister where the Holy Spirit led him. Peter did not have a heightened sense of who he was in the kingdom. He would later write, "Therefore humble yourselves under the mighty hand of God, that He may exalt you in due time" (1 Peter 5:6). He certainly showed he understood this in the way he carried out his ministry calling.

Peter arrived at Joppa to find the widows mourning Tabatha, who had been laid in an upper room. As you read the story, the thought of Jesus attending Jairus' daughter may come to mind

(Mark 5:38–42). The stories are similar. Tabatha was confirmed dead, as the mourners were already at the house. She had been dead long enough for two men to walk to Lydda, find Peter, and return with him. Peter, like Jesus, put everyone out. He then knelt and prayed. When he was finished praying, he looked to Tabatha and commanded her to arise, and she did (Acts 9:40). One has to wonder what Peter was praying. Was he, too, thinking of Jairus' daughter? He was there and witnessed her rising to life at Jesus' words. Was he asking Jesus to give him the faith for this mission? We cannot know, because scripture does not tell us, but what would you be praying about?

News about the dead having risen to life spread, and many became believers in Jesus. Peter chose to stay in Joppa for a while. We are told he stayed with a man named Simon, whose occupation was a tanner (Acts 9:43). Peter probably stayed to establish the church there. He also had a divine appointment with a vision atop Simon's house. (We'll look at this tomorrow.)

What a beautiful transition Peter made. He went from being a disciple of Jesus who makes the rest of us look good to one who challenges us to get outside of our comfort zones. While we are not all called to travel the world and preach the gospel, we are all called to seize every opportunity the Lord gives us to share the gospel. This takes humility. If we humble ourselves and minister God's Word to the world hurting around us, Jesus will lift us up. We fear rejection by our peers, but Peter suffered physical abuse by his peers and yet continued ministering. As Peter did, the church needs to get its priorities straight and share the good news. Won't you pray right now and ask Jesus to open up opportunities for you to share and ask Him to help you not miss them? Humble yourself, step out in faith, and rejoice in what the Lord will do through you.

Day Four: Peter Learns God Shows No Partiality

Read: Acts 10:1–23.

1. What does scripture tell us about the man, Cornelius?

2. What happened to Cornelius while praying? Why did it happen?

3. Why was Cornelius told to send for Peter? How quickly did he obey?

4. When did Peter's vision come to him?

5. What did Peter see in his vision? Why did it upset him?

6. What did the voice tell Peter? How many times did this happen?

7. Who was at Simon's gate when Peter's visions were concluded?

8. When did Peter know the men were at the door? How could Peter trust the voice he heard?

Cornelius Sends for Peter

Cornelius is introduced in the Bible as a Gentile soldier. He was not just any soldier; he was a centurion, which meant he commanded over a hundred men. He was a believer in God who was given to prayer and charity. He lived in Caesarea, just north of Joppa along the seacoast. Scripture tells us everyone in his household was a God fearer. The term "God fearer" was used to describe Gentiles who believed in God but fell short of circumcision to join the synagogue. They were not given full fellowship in the synagogue without circumcision, because for the Jews, this was the outward sign God had commanded those who claimed His promises. We are introduced to a Roman soldier who feared God and did what was godly in prayer and giving, and was yet not fully received into the synagogue (Acts 10:1–2).

Cornelius prayed and saw a vision of an angel. The angel told him God had noticed his faithful lifestyle. God had noticed his generosity in giving and had heard his many sincere prayers. This may have been a surprise for Cornelius. He had been told by the synagogue he couldn't have full fellowship, because he did not bear the outward sign (circumcision) of the inward condition of his heart. However, the angel showed up during Cornelius' prayer and told him his lifestyle and prayers were acceptable *and* pleasing to God (Acts 10:3–4). God told Samuel, when he was seeking the king in Jesse's house, He does not look upon the outward appearance but upon a person's heart (1 Samuel 16:7). This was a period in history when the Jews, at least the leaders of the Jews, were much more concerned with keeping up the religious appearances of their faith rather than practicing a true religion from the heart. They put more worth in the circumcision of their flesh than in the condition of their hearts (Romans 2:28–29).

The angel spoke to Cornelius, who had been quite surprised and frightened by his appearance. The angel told him to send for Peter in Joppa. Scripture makes it clear. Cornelius had not heard of Peter before, as the angel did not say to send for the apostle Peter but instead gave his name, Simon Peter. The angel went as far as to tell him where Peter was staying and the name of the person he was staying with. The angel told Cornelius Peter would "tell him what he must do" (Acts 10:5). The angel shared his message and was gone as quickly as he came. Cornelius wasted no time. He immediately called for men to send to Simon the tanner's house in Joppa to invite Simon Peter to his home. He sent two household servants and a soldier (Acts 10:6–8). His immediacy in obeying the angel's command was another sign of his devotion to the Lord.

Peter Sees a Vision and Goes to Cornelius

Peter had a vision the day after Cornelius' experience with the angel and his sending the men out to find him. Peter's vision came to him on the top of Simon the tanner's home, just as the men Cornelius sent reached the city of Joppa (Acts 10:9). Peter had gone up to pray while he was hungry and waiting for the next meal. There was no mistaking why the vision had to do with food. This would catch Peter's attention more intensely in the moment.

Three times, a vision came to Peter. He was offered many varieties of animals, birds, and more to eat. He was told in the vision to get up, go and kill, and eat. Peter was not a little disturbed by this command coming from the Lord in the vision. Peter knew the things presented were unclean (against the Law of Moses) to eat. The vision made the Lord appear to contradict His own law. Sometimes, God seems to contradict scripture, but if we take the time to pursue it, we will always find He does not contradict Himself, nor does scripture contradict scripture: ever. Peter cried out to be released from such a command. He had not back-talked to the Lord like this in a long time. He was being asked, in his mind, to defile himself before God, *by* God. Peter was not trying to prove himself smarter than Jesus but was seeking truth in a confusing situation (Acts 10:11–14).

Peter finally got relief after the third time the vision came, and he proclaimed he had never defiled himself with the unclean. Jesus commanded Peter not to call unclean what He had called clean (Acts 10:14, 15). When the visions concluded and the Lord's point was made, Cornelius' men were at Simon's gate to call on Peter (Acts 10:16, 17). They arrived as Peter was still on the housetop, contemplating the visions he'd just had. He was confused by them and was trying to find understanding. The Holy Spirit told Peter to go with the three men at the gate, for God had sent them. Three visions, three men; Peter obeyed the Spirit, even when he did not understand. He went with three Gentiles who were considered unclean to go to a Gentile's home, which was unfathomable for a pious Jew to do. Yet he followed where the Spirit led him, even when it was beyond his understanding (Acts 10:17–23).

Day Five: Peter Learns God Shows No Partiality

Read: Acts 10:24–48.

1. What was Cornelius doing when Peter and company arrived?

2. How did Cornelius greet Peter? What was Peter's response?

3. Do modern Christians do this today with Christian celebrities?

4. What did Peter say was the lesson he had learned?

5. Who were they present before, and who did they expect to hear from?

6. What was the first lesson Peter confessed to learning?

7. How did Peter describe the ministry of Jesus?

8. What were Peter and the disciples witnesses to? When were they chosen?

9. What were they commanded?

10. What happened while Peter was speaking?

11. Who was astonished? Why?

12. What did they hear them speaking?

13. What was Peter's response to what had happened?

14. How did the Gentile experience compare with the Jewish one?

Peter Ministers at a Cornelius' Home

The scene of Peter arriving at Cornelius' house shows what a faith-filled man Cornelius was. He had already gathered all his family and close friends to his home. They were waiting for Peter to arrive (Acts 10:24). Many people might wait to see if Peter would come before calling so many people together. Not Cornelius, he had faith in what the angel had said to him, and he prepared himself and everyone he loved to receive what Peter was bringing. He didn't sit around, second-guessing the vision he saw. He did not give himself time to doubt. Instead, he acted immediately and then waited with patience.

When Peter did arrive the next day, Cornelius put himself on the floor and worshiped him (Acts 10:25). He was a Gentile; maybe he did this out of the context of his culture to worship Caesar. He may have been trying to honor Peter in the highest way he knew how. We cannot understand what was going through Cornelius' mind, because scripture does not tell us. However, we can look at the typical human behavior and draw some possible conclusions. Whatever the reason, when Peter arrived, Cornelius worshiped him at his feet.

Peter quickly corrected him. Scripture says Peter lifted him up, giving the word picture of Peter physically reaching out to Cornelius and assisting him to his feet. Peter explained to him he, too, was just a man (Acts 10:26). The old Peter may have enjoyed the attention a little, but the new Peter refused to share in any of Jesus' glory. He stepped aside by saying, "I am only a man, but look to Jesus; worship Him." In Cornelius' Roman culture, Caesar was treated as more of a god than a man. If this was indeed why Cornelius bowed to Peter, maybe there was a correction to Cornelius' cultural thinking in realizing Caesar was also just a man.

Peter continued speaking, and this is where we learn what he understood from the vision he received on Simon the tanner's housetop. Peter announced what he understood. God does not consider Gentiles unclean. He does not require segregation of Jew and Gentile, because in Jesus, they are equal in God's eyes (Acts 10:28). Peter explained this, maybe even for his own benefit, because Jews were not allowed to fellowship in Gentile homes. They were considered unclean. Peter found a large crowd waiting for him inside, and he repeated the lesson he had learned from God and explained it was why he had come to them without hesitation (Acts 10:27–29).

When Peter finished explaining why he had come, Cornelius recounted why he had called for him. Then, a most beautiful example is shown to us in Cornelius' household. They expected Peter to come to them, but they anticipated hearing from God (Acts 10:33). They were not wowed and amazed by Peter, the great and famous apostle. They were excited to hear from God via His messenger, Peter. Sometimes, we do the opposite of this. Sometimes, we think we need counseling from our pastor, not our small group leader. Why? We put more stock in men than in God and in His ability to use any vessel He chooses. Maybe if our hearts were bent on hearing God's words through whatever vessel He chooses, we might hear more and more clearly from Him.

Peter began to speak to the assembled crowd. He started with Jesus' baptism by John and walked them through His life and ministry. He told them of the events he witnessed: Jesus' life, ministry, death, and resurrection (Acts 10:39–40). He said they were chosen before by God to preach to the people and teach them Jesus was indeed the Messiah and what it meant for them (Acts 10:41–42). As Peter spoke these truths to the Gentile audience at Cornelius' house, the Holy Spirit came upon all of them (Acts 10:44). The Jewish believers who had accompanied Peter to Cornelius' home were astonished by the event taking place, because all of those who received the baptism of the Holy Spirit were Gentiles (Acts 10:45–46). They had always been taught Gentiles were unclean and not to be associated with. However, this was never God's intention. The separation was always based on faith, not ethnicity (Genesis 18:18; Exodus 12:48). The Jewish believers with Peter were astonished. The same Holy Spirit indwelling them had also indwelt the Gentile believers.

They knew the Holy Spirit had come upon the Gentiles because they heard them speaking in tongues and were glorifying God (Acts 10:46). Peter, always leading, spoke out, and realized if God poured the Holy Spirit upon them, then, they should offer them the rite of water baptism as an outward sign of their inward faith, but also as a sign the church accepted their fellowship (Acts 10:47). There was no difference between the Gentile experience and the Jewish experience. The

Holy Spirit fell on the Jews, just as He did the Gentiles. They were the same because their salvation and Spirit-filling were from the same Source: Jesus.

Peter was blessed to be included in the first group of disciples to receive the baptism of the Holy Spirit and then preach to a large crowd the saving grace of Jesus. Here, he was honored to preach the gospel to Gentiles and witness the first outpouring of the Holy Spirit to the Gentiles. His humble, obedient service to the King of Kings afforded him many unique opportunities in the kingdom. We never see Peter begin to believe his own press. He no longer got impressed with himself, nor did he require anyone else to be impressed by him. Instead, he quickly corrected anyone who esteemed him too highly, not wanting to take any part of Jesus' glory unto himself.

Day Six: Prayer, Ministry and No Partiality

1. Review this week's lessons and highlight your big takeaways. Be prepared to share these if you are meeting with a group.

2. Did you learn something about Peter this week? Share your thoughts.

3. How do you see your big takeaway(s) relating to the world around you today? To the Church in the broader sense, or the local church?

4. How might you apply one of these takeaways this week?

JEWS, HEROD, AND PAUL

Day One: Confronted by the Jews

Read: Acts 11:1–18.

1. How was Peter received in Jerusalem after ministering the Holy Spirit to Gentiles?

2. How did Peter respond? Was this the Peter we've known from the beginning?

3. What did Peter say he remembered Jesus telling them about baptism?

4. What silenced those who opposed Peter?

Peter Defends Gentile Visit

Not everyone was pleased with Peter's visit to a Gentile home. Some of the Jews who followed Jesus still held to the importance of following the Law of Moses and the circumcision of Abraham (Genesis 17:11–14; Leviticus 11:44–45, 18:24–26; Exodus 12:44). The group who confronted Peter did not seem as angry about the Gentiles hearing the Word of God as they were about Peter going into their home and eating with them (Acts 11:1–3). According to the Law of Moses, the Israelites were commanded to separate themselves to God and not defile themselves by associating closely with those of other nations. However, they were also commanded to be kind to foreigners who lived among them (Exodus 22:1). Somewhere along history, Israel made it a practice not to enter a Gentile's home or to eat with a Gentile, making this an unclean act. However, the Lord has always made room for Gentiles to enter His kingdom before and after the Cross (Genesis 18:18; Exodus 12:48).

Peter responded to this confrontation with great calm and great patience. He was possibly expecting this, as even he and his associates were surprised when the Holy Spirit fell upon the Gentiles. The Judean Jews did not have the whole story. They only heard Peter had gone to the Gentiles with the gospel; they had not heard the entire account, beginning in Joppa with the vision to the outpouring of the Holy Spirit. He then recounted what Jesus had said about them baptizing with the Holy Spirit (Acts 1:4, 11:4–16). The disciples did not understand what Jesus spoke of at the time, since they had not yet experienced the baptism of the Holy Spirit. In hindsight, Peter could see and understand the meaning clearly.

The Holy Spirit had come on the Gentiles the same way He had come upon them. Peter's final response to his confronters was a commitment not to resist God but to go wherever He led. This silenced those questioning Peter. When they fully understood what had happened and the experiences were the same, they agreed not to resist what the Lord was doing. They understood God was also giving the Gentiles the same opportunity to be reconciled to Him as the Jews were (Acts 11:17–18).

Peter's calm demeanor helped his confronters accept his answer. The Peter we first met along the shores of Galilee, who made sure to let Jesus know He was wrong about the fish, was nowhere in sight (Luke 5:5). The old Peter would not have been so patient to explain the facts to them. He would most likely not have stood for the questioning. He knew what he was doing and was a man of integrity, who didn't need to explain himself to anyone. At least, this was how he came across in those places when we first met him in scripture. He was not a perfect man, but he was a submitted man. He had submitted his life fully to Jesus. He had let the Holy Spirit lead and guide him. He chose humility, which opened the door to making these things possible. In His life example, we see Jesus transforms lives.

Day Two: Arrested by Herod

Read: Acts 12:1–5; Matthew 26:4–5, 17; Mark 4:37–41; John 21:18.

1. From previous lessons, who was James to Peter?

2. Why did Herod arrest Peter?

3. What festival was being celebrated at the time?

4. What festival was being celebrated when Jesus was arrested?

5. How did Peter's imprisonment mirror Jesus' final day? What might Peter have been thinking?

6. Why do you think four squads of soldiers were commanded to guard Peter? (Think of earlier lessons.)

7. What was the church doing during Peter's imprisonment?

Arrested by Herod

Luke tells us it was around the time the Holy Spirit had been given to the Gentiles when Herod began to persecute Christians. Luke said he did this because he saw it pleased the Jews. Herod arrested and killed James, childhood friend and business partner of Peter and his brother Andrew (Acts 12:1). James was there the day Jesus asked Peter to pull his boat out and drop his net to fish. James and his brother John, Peter and Andrew's business partners, were called over to help haul in the excessive load of fish (Luke 5:7–11). James was also among Jesus' inner circle of disciples, along with Peter and John (Mark 5:37, 14:33; Matthew 17:1). James and Peter had been close their entire lives. They had met the Messiah together and left all to follow Him on the same day. They walked with Jesus throughout His earthly ministry; they watched Him die, rise to life, and ascend into heaven. Together with the other disciples, they planted the first church and began the very first work of the Christian church.

Peter, while mourning the loss of his longtime friend, business associate, ministry partner, and brother in Christ, was also arrested by Herod. Luke tells us Herod did this because killing James put him in good standing with the Jews who did not accept Jesus as the Messiah (Acts 12:3). Every secular king or ruler of the city knew the Jews of the temple held significant political power in the region and were more than eager to remain on their good side to keep order under their rule, even if it meant murdering a few Christians to obtain it. When Herod realized the favor he garnered with the Jews from attacking Christians, he went after Peter, the visible head of the church.

Peter was arrested during the Feast of Unleavened Bread (Acts 12:3). He certainly did not miss the significance of the timing. Jesus, too, was arrested during the Feast of Unleavened Bread. However, those who sought Jesus' arrest chose not to arrest Him during the Passover feast (Mark

14:1, 2). Instead, Jesus was arrested after the feast, late at night in the Garden of Gethsemane (Mark 14:32–46). Peter and Jesus were both arrested at the time of the Passover celebration. Those who sought Jesus' life waited to arrest him until after the meal, whereas Peter's arrest came before the meal, and he was placed in prison to deal with after the Passover. Jesus' foes were Jewish leaders who manipulated a Gentile government to murder Jesus. Peter's foe was a Gentile king seeking to please Jewish leaders. They were all the same players: the leader of the Way, Jewish leaders, and Gentile rulers; even the feast was the same. One cannot imagine Peter would have missed the significance and similitude of the times.

Peter found himself in the Roman prison, attached by chains to two Roman soldiers, with two more Roman soldiers just outside the door. Roman soldiers were a war machine. They were trained to kill and far outnumbered Peter. There was nothing he could do. It seems silly to assign four soldiers to Peter, even to attach two of them to him by chains. Peter was not trained for battle, nor did he have a violent reputation, yet Herod seemed to believe four soldiers were necessary to keep him secure. Maybe Herod had heard how Peter escaped custody before and caused his captors to appear foolish (Acts 5:19, 20).

Many scholars believe Jesus' statement of how Peter would be led where he did not want to go and would have his hands stretched out alluded to the fact Peter would die a martyr's death upon a cross (John 21:18). Peter, being arrested at Passover, must have thought of Jesus' arrest and trial. He must have remembered Jesus' words to him and thought it too high an honor to be killed at the same time, during the same festival, and even in the same way as his Savior. All the signs pointed to Peter not surviving this arrest. Whatever thoughts may have gone through Peter's mind, he was found sleeping just before Herod was going to send for him (Acts 12:6). Peter knew his Lord and Savior more than anything, and he slept with a trust and peace which surpassed all understanding. Peter's slumber amid this life-storm reminds us of Jesus in the boat on the sea, sleeping during the tempest at the stern of the boat (Matthew 8:23–27). During the storm, Peter was in a panic and, along with the others, yelled at Jesus because of His calm sleep when the rest of them were sure they were going to die. Here, Peter, sure to die, slept as his Lord slept during the storm just a few years before. Again, we glimpse the spiritual growth and maturity of our friend and example, Peter. We also see the church offered constant prayers for him throughout this ordeal (Acts 12:5).

Day Three: Arrested by Herod

Read: Acts 12:5–19.

1. How well was Peter secured in prison?

2. Who stood by Peter in the prison?

3. What did he have to do to wake Peter up? What lesson had Peter learned from Jesus about riding out a storm?

4. How many instructions did the angel have to give to Peter? Why?

5. How did Peter exit the prison? When did the angel depart from him?

6. What did Peter say he was delivered from? Do you think he was surprised by this? Why or why not?

7. Where did Peter go when he had come to himself?

8. Why wouldn't Rhoda let Peter into the house? Who did the church believe it to be? Was the church's faith shaken in this trial? How did they respond when they saw it was Peter?

9. What instructions did Peter give to the church? Where did Peter go?

10. How did Herod respond to Peter's disappearance?

Peter Escapes Prison

While Peter slept, chained to a guard on either side of him, a light burst into the jail, and an angel appeared. The angel had to strike him physically and raise him to his feet because Peter's faith-filled slumber was so good and deep (Acts 12:7). The angel had to go further, giving Peter step-by-step instruction to help him prepare to leave. He told Peter to put on his clothes, outer garment, and sandals. He further had to hurry Peter along, telling him to move quickly. One might think Peter was stunned by the vision of the angel, but this was not the case. Peter thought he was seeing a vision and therefore did not believe he was participating in the moment (Acts 12:7, 8). This attests to the vividness of the visions Peter was accustomed to experiencing. He followed the angel out of the cell, out of the prison (as the prison doors miraculously opened), and down the street a safe distance. Then, as miraculously as the angel appeared, he disappeared (Acts 12:9–10).

Peter did not come to his senses until the angel disappeared, and he found himself standing on the street. His revelation was this: "Now I know for certain that the Lord has sent His angel, and has delivered me from the hand of Herod and from all the expectation of the Jewish people" (Acts 12:11). While Peter was in prison, he realized the gravity of his situation. He understood death loomed. However, he also understood Jesus could deliver him if it were His will to do so. Peter's comments regarding the expectation of the Jewish people referred to the Jews who also called for Jesus' crucifixion; those who did not accept Jesus as the Messiah. Peter knew they were connected to Herod's persecution of the church, just as they had played a part in Jesus' story. Yet while Jesus had not saved Himself, He did deliver Peter. This was possibly what helped Peter sleep so soundly. He was at peace with the Lord's will for him. He knew the Lord's will for him was to continue teaching, preaching, and healing in His name. Peter headed to where the church members met.

The church gathered and prayed at Mary's house (Acts 12:12). Mary is the mother of Mark, who later became Peter's interpreter and the writer of the Gospel of Mark. Peter's arrival at the house reads like a comedy sketch. However, Rhoda's not letting Peter in the house, and the church's belief in Peter's ghost over the physically alive Peter says some unfortunate things for the church. What does it say about the church's faith, believing Peter's ghost would come knocking, rather than the physically alive Peter? The church, which prayed constantly on Peter's behalf, did not appear to have the faith for the miracle they were seeking. They had more faith in Herod's power and the Roman soldiers; they had difficulty seeing how God would grant such a miracle, especially in light of what had just happened to James. However, the book of Hebrews reminds us, "Faith is the substance of things hoped for, the evidence of things not seen" (Hebrews 11:1). We do not need to be able to see how God can work a miracle, just pray and believe He is able.

One has to realize this same church was most likely praying the same way for James, and he died. Their faith had taken a hard blow with his death. Why does God rescue some and allow others to suffer? Some things we cannot know on this side of heaven. We must rest our finite minds on faith, knowing our heavenly Father is always good, loving, and kind. Sometimes, our infinite God heals by taking His children home; sometimes, the healing does not happen upon the earth but in the transition from this life to the next.

When the church finally let Peter into Mary's house, they were all astonished at the extraordinary miraculous answer to their prayers. God had delivered Peter from the mighty hand of Herod and his Roman soldiers (Acts 12:16). Peter instructed the church to share the news of his deliverance, and he left to go somewhere else (Acts 12:17). Peter could not risk staying in Jerusalem any longer. His arrest made it clear he was a hunted man, and his deliverance made it clear it was not yet his time to die. He must continue preaching the gospel, just not in Jerusalem.

Another great miracle came for the church in Jerusalem through Peter's deliverance: Herod left town, too. The shame he experienced over Peter's escape caused him to move to Caesarea. Scripture tells us he stayed in Caesarea, meaning the Jerusalem church was safe from his sport of Christian-killing (Acts 12:19).

We see Peter walking in his calling. He was being noticed by those who despised Jesus, and they were persecuting him, yet he remained meek and mild, just as his Savior had done. He stood up without fear and spoke the truth to those who accused him regarding Gentiles. He knew his Lord and his Lord's will and fearlessly shared it with the Jewish Christians to enlighten them. He was well received. We also saw him sleeping between two guards on the anniversary of Jesus' death on the Cross, knowing he was to die in the same way. He slept the peaceful sleep of a man who knew his God would neither leave nor forsake him. He was content to live or die, as long as he was within the will of God. He had spent three intimate years with Jesus. For Peter, death meant he would be restored to Jesus' presence (2 Corinthians 5:7, 8). He did not fear death. Peter understood Jesus had gone to prepare a place for him, and this place is the goal of every Christian, not life on this earth.

Day Four: Moments with Paul

Read: Acts 15:1–12; Romans 2:11; 10:12–13; Galatians 3:28; Ephesians 2:8–22.

1. Who were Paul and Barnabas going to see and why? Where did they have to go?

2. How were they treated by the church when they arrived?

3. Who disagreed and why?

4. Who came together to discuss the matter? Did they always agree?

5. Who among this group rose up to speak?

6. What gave him precedence to speak?

7. Why did God give the Holy Spirit to the Gentiles?

8. How did God purify the hearts of the Gentiles?

9. Is there a distinction between Jew and Gentile any longer?

10. How did Peter refer to the requirement of the Law for the Gentiles? How had the Jews done with obeying God's laws?

11. How will the Jews be saved?

12. How did the multitude respond to Peter's words?

Paul Submits His Gospel to Peter

Paul wrote of a visit to Jerusalem to see Peter in his letter to the Galatians. Paul journeyed to Jerusalem three years after his Damascus road conversion and stayed with Peter for fifteen days (Galatians 1:15–18). Paul did not return to Jerusalem again after this visit for fourteen years (Galatians 2:1). Paul's purpose in going to Jerusalem was to meet with the church leaders and to see if his gospel lined up with theirs (Galatians 2:2). It appears the specific topic Paul was addressing was circumcision for the Gentiles (Galatians 2:3). This is the same visit recorded in Acts chapter 15.

During his second meeting, everyone determined Peter as the apostle called to the Jews, and Paul to Gentiles (Galatians 2:7). Paul met Peter, James, and John, and he described them as pillars (Galatians 2:9). Paul's respect for these men as leaders of the church was immense. He reported in his letter to the Galatians on Peter, James, and John's acceptance of him as a brother in the Lord and an apostle in the ministry (Galatians 2:9).

Paul Brings Debate over Circumcision

Peter crossed paths with Paul when he came to Jerusalem to bring a matter of contention to the apostles and elders of the faith. Paul and Barnabas were in Antioch when other believers from Judea came there. They disputed over whether Gentiles should be required to submit to the rite of circumcision, as stated in the Law of Moses. They agreed to go together to Jerusalem to submit themselves to the apostles and elders in Jerusalem to reach an agreement on the matter (Acts 15:1–7). Scripturally, this is the first time we see Peter and Paul together.

Paul and Barnabas spoke to the council about ministry to the Gentiles and how God was pouring out through their ministry. Peter would relate to this personally due to his experience with Cornelius' household. Peter knew the Lord had poured the Holy Spirit out upon the Gentiles, simply by their faith and nothing more. This was most likely Paul's argument. However, the Pharisees desired adherence to the Law of Moses, which required circumcision for the Gentile believers. This was not a surprise, as the Pharisees prided themselves on the knowledge of the Old Testament laws and customs. For them to change their thinking from earning salvation to receiving it by grace, as the Gentiles had done, would be understandably difficult (Acts 15:4, 5).

Peter was among the council and rose up to speak. He had listened for a while to the arguments on both sides, and then he stood to address the crowd (Acts 15:7). This scene, recorded for us, shows the level of respect Peter commanded with his presence. The debate had carried on with intensity, and then silence blanketed the room when Peter stood to speak. He had experienced firsthand the Gentiles not only coming to a saving knowledge of Jesus but also receiving the baptism of the Holy Spirit without adherence to the Law. Peter was also head of the church, as Jesus had placed him to be, and was front and center, speaking to the church leaders in Jerusalem.

Peter said God gave the Gentiles the Holy Spirit because He knew their hearts, and they were purified through faith (Acts 15:8, 9). Paul would later write to the church at Ephesus, "For by grace you have been saved through faith, and that not of yourselves; it is the gift of God, not of works, lest anyone should boast" (Ephesians 2:8, 9). To the Galatian church, Paul wrote, "For you are all sons of God through faith in Christ Jesus. For as many of you as were baptized into Christ have put on Christ. There is neither Jew nor Greek, there is neither slave nor free, there is neither male nor female; for you are all one in Christ Jesus" (Galatians 3:26–28).

Paul further taught there was no longer any distinction between Jew and Gentile in his letter to the Romans, but they were both one through faith in Christ (Romans 10:12, 13). This was good news for the Jews as much as it was for the Gentiles; as Peter pointed out in his speech, the Law is a burden too heavy even for the Jews to bear. He pointed out the Jews were not able to keep the whole Law perfectly, so why should they lay the same impossible burden on the Gentiles? The Jews were not being saved by the Law; they were saved the same way the Gentiles were: by faith in Jesus, the free gift of God. When Peter finished, the room was silent. There was no rebuttal to be made for the way God chose to save both Jew and Gentile (Acts 15:10–12).

Day Five: Moments with Paul

Read: Galatians 1:15-18; 2:1-16.

1. Who did Paul go to Jerusalem to see, and who did he stay with?

2. How long after Paul's conversion did he make this trip?

3. How long was it before Paul returned again to Jerusalem?

4. Who did Paul go to see this time? What was his purpose for going?

5. What was concluded regarding Paul's ministry and Peter's ministry?

6. Who gave Paul the right hand of fellowship, and how did Paul describe them?

7. Did Paul fear Peter? How do you know?

8. What did Peter do wrong at Antioch? What compelled him?

9. What was the result of Peter's action?

10. How do you think he felt being confronted openly by Paul?

11. What did Paul point out was the root of what caused Peter's actions?

12. How do you feel about Peter, after all these years, making this mistake? How will you respond to your church leaders when they fall short?

Paul Rebukes Peter

Paul and Barnabas returned to Antioch after they met with the Jerusalem elders regarding the issue of circumcision and what laws the Gentiles needed to follow (Acts 15:25–30). Peter later comes down to Antioch, and Paul confronts Peter about his behavior (Galatians 2:11). Paul is a fascinating figure. He seemed somewhat awed by Peter and the others at Jerusalem, but simultaneously, he was not afraid to speak the truth to those he admired when they were outside the bounds of their Christian agreement.

Paul's issue with Peter was Peter's eating and associating with Gentiles before the Jews' arrival. Once they came down from Jerusalem, Peter distanced himself from the Gentiles. Paul's diagnosis was fear of man. Peter feared the Jews from Jerusalem (Galatians 2:12). It is interesting because Peter was the one who brought the gospel to the Gentiles at Cornelius' house and then defended his actions in Jerusalem (Acts 11:1–18). One would not expect he would revert to Jewish custom or law when the Jews from Jerusalem came down to Antioch. Yet it shows us no matter how highly esteemed a church leader may be or how much authority they may have, they are still fallible human beings. Peter had come a long way but had not attained perfection.

Paul did not just confront Peter; he confronted him publicly (Galatians 2:14). Leadership has a price. Leaders must remember to lead by example, because people will follow their actions. Peter's actions not only led the other Jews to follow suit but also led Barnabas, Paul's missionary partner, to separate himself (Galatians 2:13). Barnabas had been with Paul, preaching the gospel and teaching the equality of Jew and Gentile. He went with Paul to Jerusalem before the council to discuss circumcision and Gentiles' requirements, and he returned to Antioch with Paul after the council. Yet he allowed himself to be awed enough by Peter to follow his example. Peter's sin was public and was causing others to stumble; therefore, Paul confronted him publicly for the sake of those being led astray by his actions.

Paul was compelled to speak when he saw the hypocrisy of their actions and "that they were not straightforward about the truth of the gospel" (Galatians 2:13, 14). Paul was a man committed to the gospel message as it related to the Gentiles. Peter came to Paul's place of ministry and countered the freedom and equality Paul had been preaching to Gentile believers there. Paul's commitment to the truth of the gospel outweighed any fear of man. We see a contrast here between Peter and Paul. Peter's actions were brought on by fear of man (something we have not seen in Peter before). Paul's actions were brought on by a greater concern for Jesus' sheep not being led away from the truth. Paul knew the truth of the gospel outweighed any social or religious-political order. The truth always comes first. Paul reminded Peter how they, too, being Jews, believed in Jesus for their salvation, and they understood the works of the law did not bring them salvation. So why would Peter live as a Gentile until the Jews arrived and then live as a Jew (Galatians 2:15, 16)? Paul's statements were true and to the point, and Peter would certainly have no argument against them.

Peter may have been shocked to be confronted, maybe a little embarrassed, and most likely convicted by the truth. He was accustomed to ministering to the Jews. He probably placed himself under the law so as not to offend them. Even Paul, in his first letter to the Corinthians, said, "For though I am free from all men, I have made myself a servant to all, that I might win the more; and to the Jews I became as a Jew, that I might win Jews; to those who are under the law, as under the law, that I might win those who are under the law; to those who are without law, as without law (not being without law toward God, but under law toward Christ), that I might win those who are without law; to the weak I became as weak, that I might win the weak. I have become all things to all men that I might by all means save some" (1 Corinthians 9:19–22). Paul understood the principle of not offending those he was ministering to; however, Peter's actions devalued the freedom of the Gentiles and even led Paul's missionary partner away from his freedoms. The act of becoming all things to all people so one might save a few is good, unless it causes others to fall away.

One great lesson to walk away from this is knowing our church leaders are not perfect people. They are human and fallible. We ought not place them on a pedestal. They are in the position they are in to be molded into Christ-likeness, just as we are in our place to be molded into Christ-likeness, but neither they nor we have attained to the full measure of the perfection of Christ-likeness. We must give each other room to make mistakes and quickly forgive and restore one another.

Day Six: The Jews, Herod, and Paul

1. Review this week's lessons and highlight your big takeaways. Be prepared to share these if you are meeting with a group.

2. Did you learn something about Peter this week? Share your thoughts.

3. How do you see your big takeaway(s) relating to the world around you today? To the Church in the broader sense, or the local church?

4. How might you apply one of these takeaways this week?

FIRST AND SECOND PETER

Day One: First Peter

Read: 1 Peter 1:1–2:5.

1. Who was Peter writing to?

2. What has God the Father begotten us again to? How?

3. How does Peter describe the inheritance of God's elect? How is it kept?

4. What does Peter state is the purpose of trials? Would he know?

5. What does Peter exhort all Christians to do? (See 1:13–16.)

6. How does Peter say Christians ought to conduct themselves? Why?

7. How had Peter's audience purified their souls?

8. What must Christians lay aside? What must they desire?

9. Jesus called Peter a rock; what does Peter call Christians? Why?

Living Stones

Peter wrote to Christians dispersed throughout Asia Minor (1 Peter 1:1, 2). In his first letter, he reminded believers of their foundation in Christ and exhorted them to own their calling and righteous living. The central focus of his letter is suffering, with insights into its purpose in a Christian's life and how to overcome it. Peter's first letter also demonstrates his heeding and obeying Jesus's commands. He first told Peter to strengthen the brethren, and later told Peter to feed His sheep (Luke 22:32; John 21:15–17). Peter did both in this letter by encouraging the church in times of trouble and giving them tools for overcoming.

Peter began by reminding his readers of their living hope in Christ. Jesus rose from the dead and is, therefore, alive. Christians are not spending their hope on a dead prophet, but on a living Savior (1 Peter 1:3). Other religions follow earthly teachers who died or false gods, the figment of someone's imagination. Christians follow a living God, not a myth or legend. Doesn't this enhance your faith, just reading and being reminded of it?

Peter then described the inheritance of God's elect and how it is kept. He said, with many colorful words, the inheritance of the elect is sure, stable, and unchanging. He concluded the elect's inheritance is such because the power above all powers protects it: the power of God (1 Peter 1:4, 5). It is encouraging to know. Nothing can rob the followers of Jesus of their inheritance. No trial or tribulation can take it away, and there is no expiration date. This is good news.

Laying the foundation of a living God and an incorruptible inheritance, Peter transitioned to speak of trials and related them to his previous statements. He explained with the voice of experience how trials challenge, refine, and prove one's faith (1 Peter 1:7). Faith is the key to salvation. Trials strengthen faith. By this time, Peter had experienced his share of suffering. He even experienced sufferings before Jesus was crucified, when he denied his Lord. As we have seen throughout this study, Peter had caused his own suffering and had sufferings thrust upon him. Peter spoke to his readers past and present with the knowledge and wisdom of one who had been through it and come out victoriously. However, Peter took no credit for his victories, pointing all praise, honor, and glory to Jesus. According to Peter, this is what the testing of faith is to produce; it should deliver each one to the promised inheritance when Jesus returns to bring His own home.

Having laid the foundation and the exhortation, Peter moved into giving tools to meet and overcome trials. He spoke about the battle of the mind, pointing out the mental determination required for spiritual faith. He didn't just talk about being separate from the world (holy) or walking in obedience to the Word; he spoke of having control over one's mind. He said Christians should decide what they will do before the trial or test comes. This is girding up the loins of your mind; it is a mental preparation before the trials come. He also said to anchor hope entirely on Jesus. The writer of Hebrews said, "Hope anchors the soul" (Hebrews 6:19). There is no room for doubt about who Jesus is or what He has done. When your hope is anchored in Christ, you can stand the test of trials. However, you must make your mind up to stand firm before the trial comes (1 Peter 1:13).

Another weighty reminder from Peter: the assurance of salvation is not a free pass for careless living. He told his readers to remember their reverence for (or fear/awe of) God, remembering He would yet judge them in the end, and He would give no one preference over His precepts (1 Peter 1:17). He further reminded Christians their souls had been purified by their obedience to the truth through the Spirit and in sincere love for one another. He then encouraged them to love their brethren earnestly (1 Peter 1:22). Paul said faith, hope, and love are what endure (1 Corinthians 13:13). Peter had spoken of faith and hope already. One cannot be a follower of Jesus without faith. One cannot continue as a believer without hope. However, one cannot love Him without obeying His commands (John 14:15–24). Peter explained to Christians of all time how their inheritance is sure through faith and enduring hope, but he also sent a reminder: God is yet to be feared and obeyed.

Peter cited a list of things Christians must leave behind with their old natures. He lists "malice, deceit, hypocrisy, envy, and all evil speaking" (1 Peter 2:1). Peter suggested they were to seek God's

Word for spiritual nourishment so they might grow into new men with the new character of disciples of Jesus. "Peter," called such by Jesus, means "rock" and refers to Jesus' followers as living stones. He had come to understand this himself. Peter, a rock upon which Jesus would build His church, was just one rock in the living, growing organism, the church. He understood all believers are living stones who together build the house of God, the church (Matthew 16:8; 1 Peter 2:4, 5).

Day Two: First Peter

Read: 1 Peter 2:6–3:9

1. What does Peter explain about God's followers in 1 Peter 2:9–10? Try to memorize it.

2. As sojourners and pilgrims, how should Christians act?

3. Peter speaks of submission. On a separate sheet of paper, list who is to be submissive to whom and why.

4. What makes a woman truly beautiful?

5. How should husbands treat their wives?

6. How ought Christians treat one another? Why?

A Royal Priesthood

One of Peter's most famous quotes explains the position of a follower of Jesus. Peter said followers of Jesus are chosen by Him. As co-heirs with Jesus, they have attained a position of royalty and ministry in God's kingdom. God sees the church as a holy nation, His own people set apart to Him. His people are to acknowledge His goodness with their lips. God did all this as He invited people to leave a sinful life behind to enter into a life of light, hope, and the fellowship of believers, through the free gift of forgiveness (2 Peter 2:9, 10). Peter expanded this thought when he wrote, Christians are just passing through this earthly experience to their eternal reward. In light of this, he exhorted Christians to give up any practice or desire of the flesh competing with the ability to worship and follow Jesus freely (1 Peter 2:11).

Christians are to live a righteous life at all times, but especially when in the presence of nonbelievers. No Christian wants to be the reason any person chooses not to follow Jesus. Believers must walk before nonbelievers in such a way as to cause them to desire to follow Jesus. Peter gives some examples of how this looks in a variety of relationships. He told all Christians to submit to the governing authorities of the land they lived in (1 Peter 2:13). He understood obedience to civil laws was a good witness to those who would seek to find reason to discredit the church by the behavior of its members (1 Peter 2:14–16).

To servants, Peter said they ought to submit to their masters but with a Christian attitude, hoping to turn them to Christ (1 Peter 2:18). He exhorted them to serve well, whether the master was kind or not. This is easily translated to employee-employer relations. Christians need to serve well regardless of how they are being treated. They must exemplify Christ so they might win their employer to Christ. When their employer witnesses them taking unjust treatment with patience, the employer will see they are different and know this is because they serve Christ. However, Peter also stated God would note and admire this behavior. He said it was exemplified by Christ Himself (1 Peter 2:19–25).

Peter then turned to the marriage relationship, exhorting wives to submit to their own husbands (1 Peter 3:1). He did not say they were to be subservient. This is not a slave and master relationship. A few short sentences away, Peter taught equality among men and women, husbands and wives, who were co-heirs of Christ (1 Peter 3:7). Their salvation was equal. Peter was not diminishing women in value or ability. He was expressing proper Christian conduct within the marriage. The man is spiritually responsible for the wife. It is right for her to submit to him for the final word or decision; it does not mean she has no voice. A wife is welcome to have an opinion and to express her view, but someone has to make the final decision when the two minds cannot meet. The woman's submitted behavior can lead to the salvation of an unbelieving spouse, but it also shows she truly has faith in God for providing and caring for her. She understands it is not her husband she depends on to meet all of her needs, but God meets her needs through her husband (1 Peter 3:2–5). Therefore, she can confidently submit to her husband because she understands God is ultimately head of her home. God does not call her to be less than, but he calls her to obedience, which means her obedience to God can only benefit her and her husband. He will grow to become the man God created him to be in this environment. Her submission is a gift she partners with Jesus to give him. He, in turn, wears a mantle of responsibility for her before the Lord.

I want to take a moment to say one vital thing here. God never calls a wife to submit to an abusive relationship. If you are being harmed, please get help. Contact your local crisis line, call the police, a trusted friend or family member, a pastor, or a church. There is no shame in reaching out and getting yourself on the road to safety and recovery.

Peter finishes his thoughts on wives by stating what makes a woman truly beautiful (1 Peter 3:3). He says what makes a woman beautiful is who and how she is, not just how she looks or dresses. He did not discount a woman dressing nicely, but relying on appearance is insufficient. A woman needs to have substance. A truly beautiful woman displays the fruit of the Spirit in her life. She does not rely on her looks or serve the latest trends to find her place in the world. Instead, she builds up her character in Christ first and cares about her outward appearance second.

Having covered civil, employment, and marital relationships, Peter then turned to relationships within the body of Christ. He said fellow believers ought "to be of one mind, having compassion for one another; love as brothers, be tenderhearted, be courteous; not returning evil for evil or reviling for reviling, but on the contrary blessing, knowing that you were called to this, that you may inherit a blessing" (1 Peter 3:8, 9). Above all, the family of God must treat one another with pure motives and receive others as though their motives are pure. Christians cannot run around being suspicious of one another or assuming the worst in each other. They must receive one another as Christ received them.

Day Three: First Peter

Read: Matthew 20:25-28; 1 Peter 3:10-5:14.

1. What advice does Peter give regarding suffering? What is his reasoning?

2. What does Peter say about the suffering of Jesus, his Friend and Savior?

3. What does Peter tell Christians to arm themselves with? Why?

4. What should Christians have above all things? Why? How does this look?

5. How are gifts to be ministered, and for what purpose?

6. Why does Peter want Christians to rejoice in suffering?

7. What exhortation does Peter give to elders? Where did Peter hear it?

8. What does Peter exhort younger Christians to do?

9. What is Peter's final exhortation to the church in verses 6–10?

Suffering Servants

Regarding suffering, Peter exhorted Christians to remain holy toward God and to be prepared with an explanation for everyone who asks. He said to do so with humility and reverence for God (1 Peter 3:15). He reasoned and understood, it is a blessing to the one who is counted worthy to suffer for the name of Jesus (1 Peter 2:13). Remember when Peter and the disciples had been beaten and released, they left praising God for being counted worthy to suffer for Jesus (Acts 5:41). In a strange way, suffering for Jesus is a compliment to the believer. If you are not walking with Jesus, the reality of anyone coming against you for your beliefs is unlikely. Peter understood it was an opportunity to witness when you suffer with a mind to exalt Jesus. He said, if we are counted worthy to participate in the sufferings of Christ, then when He returns, we can rejoice knowing He will carry us on to His reward (1 Peter 4:13).

Another sober reminder from Peter, Jesus was just (or righteous) and died for us, the unjust (or unrighteous). He exhorted the church to have the mind of Christ (1 Peter 4:1). Jesus set His mind to what He was to do for humanity, and He understood it would come with great suffering. He chose to resist temptation, to walk a perfect life, to drink the cup the Father gave Him, and in all

His ways glorify the Father. Peter told Christians to put on this mind, a mind able to make its decision before the moment arises; a mind determined not to enter into temptation and will resist it. Even if suffering comes, it will not deny Christ; instead, it will use suffering as an opportunity to witness and to glorify Jesus (Matthew 10:28).

Peter continued his discussion on how Christians ought to be prepared by stating the most crucial necessity for Christians: "fervent love for one another" (1 Peter 4:8–10). The root of love for one another, giving preference to one another, opens the door to great blessings in the church. Peter stated, "Love covers a multitude of sins" (1 Peter 4:8). This was not a new idea. The idea of love covering is seen in Genesis 9:23, when Shem and Japheth took a blanket and walked it into their father's tent backwards to cover his nakedness. In this instance, it is a covering for shame. Love covers another's shame. Proverbs also speaks of love as a covering. One who loves does not take a person's offense and use it to stir up contention but rather is gentle, forgiving, and considers the other person's feelings and embarrassment over their mistake or actions (Proverbs 10:12). Proverbs 17:9 says one who loves covers a matter rather than spreading the news of it (gossiping about it). Peter says fervent love for one another equates to caring about others as we would want them to care for us (Matthew 7:12). We would not want our failures to open the door to attacks upon us or gossip about us. Forgiveness and grace go much further to healing people's lives than our demand for justice or need to be right.

Peter gave some tangible examples of fervent love for one another. He spoke of the ministering of the gifts. He said gifts ought to be ministered "with the ability which God supplies"; this is a possible clue to things Peter had seen as he traveled to various church homes (1 Peter 4:11). He reminds the church in his comments of the purpose of the gifts, to glorify Jesus. Ministering gifts in the kingdom of God is a privilege, meant for exalting Jesus, not self. Indeed, it is easy for people to believe they are called to an office or to minister with a particular gift because they are special. It is a subtle lie from the enemy. Peter reminded the church to maintain a right relationship with the gifts, not to force them in their power, and not to begin to think too highly of themselves when they minister the gifts. Humility in ministry exudes fervent love.

Peter spoke to the elders about their fervent love for others. He exhorted the elders to shepherd the flock from the willingness of their hearts. They were to watch over the flock. Jesus only wants those who earnestly care for His flock to oversee them. He desires elders who will watch over as an extension of Himself. Jesus would leave the ninety-nine to find the one lost sheep (Luke 15:4). He seeks those who will love and serve the church with the same heart. The ones who oversee by compulsion will not care for the flock with Christ's heart. Peter understood this as he wrote. I wonder if he recalled the day on the beach when Jesus asked him if he loved Him and told him to feed His sheep (John 21:15–17).

Peter turned his thoughts toward the younger Christians. His letter, having been read in the hearing of all, meant they had heard the words to the elders, and now they would hear Peter's exhortation to them while the elders listened. The last submission Peter spoke to in his letter was for younger Christians to submit to the elders and one another. For the younger, Peter came right out and stated they ought to walk humbly in all they say and do. Did Peter think back to the day on the boat when Jesus told him to let down his net (Luke 5:5)? Did he think of the time Jesus rebuked him for confronting Him about His suffering (Matthew 16:23)? Peter learned the hard way, but he had come all the way around to the place he could minister wisdom to those who came along behind him. Maybe he could spare them some of the heartache he had suffered and the heartache he might have felt he caused his Lord.

Peter's final exhortation was to the whole body of Christ. He began with, above all things, humility. Humility is key. Peter exhorted the church to bring all their cares and worries to Jesus and give them to Him as though they were Old Testament offerings, leave them there, and allow them to burn on the altar of His love and sacrifice. Have faith to give those things to Him and trust He will do what is best with them. Peter encouraged the church to keep their mind on what was true and real, to be prepared in all things, and suffer in the flesh to overcome the evil one. To his multi-church audience, he said none were more persecuted than the other. The church suffered the same things around the world. No one had it harder than anyone else. Why tell them this? To dispel the lies of the enemy, which suggest being a Christian is too hard. Knowing others are bearing up under the same troubles gives each one strength and courage to continue. This is why sharing our story with authenticity is so important.

I don't know about you, but after walking with Peter through his lifetime of transformation, I want to hear what he has to say. I feel he understands me because he was as much of a normal, fallible, human being as I am. He struggled with character flaws just as I do, but he came to a place where he was willing and able to share his wisdom with others. Peter's life gives me courage to believe I can follow Jesus, fail, pick myself up, be transformed, and minister the love of Christ to others. What a beautiful story and example Peter's life is for all Christians.

Day Four: Second Peter

Read: 2 Peter 1:1–2:3. Acts 4:13.

1. Who is Peter writing this letter to?

2. What had God's divine power given to believers?

3. How does one partake of the divine nature?

4. What must Christians be diligent to do? What is the progression? Do you think this has been the progression of Peter's walk with Jesus?

5. What is the promise to those who abound in these Christian graces?

6. What is true of the Christian who lacks these things?

7. What does Peter tell Christians to be diligent about? (See verses 10–11.)

8. Does Peter believe in "Once saved, always saved"?

9. How can you be assured of your salvation?

10. Why was Peter intent to stir up and remind the church of these things now? Why did he put it in a letter?

11. What majesty was Peter an eyewitness to? When?

12. What does Peter mean in 2 Peter 2:19?

13. Why did Peter say prophecy is not of private interpretation? How would he know?

14. How can prophecy not be of private interpretation?

Peter Stirs up the Church

Peter wrote his second letter to Christians in the known world. He referred to himself as both bondservant and apostle of Jesus Christ (2 Peter 1:1). Peter sheds light on the transformation he had come through. He had transformed from being his own man, confident in all his ways, to a man submitted as a slave to the Lord Jesus Christ: his Lord. When we met Peter, we saw he was a man not easily swayed by another. Here, at the end of our study, we see a man completely sold out and entirely submitted to another, to Jesus. Peter was once a man who would be owned by no one, but now, in the first sentence of his letter, he proclaimed a bondservant (or slave) of Jesus Christ.

Peter's blessing, his heart for the church, was for them to grow in the knowledge of "Jesus our Lord" (2 Peter 1:2). Peter encouraged Christ followers in their ability to traverse this life and attain to godliness. He said God has given believers everything they need to meet this goal. He exhorted Christians to know they have access to what God has supplied through knowing Jesus and increasing in knowledge, reminding them they were called by Jesus' glory and virtue (2 Peter 1:3). Nothing of ourselves, no special talents on our part: He already supplied our need. Everything we are and everything we have is in Him. Take a moment and see Jesus through Peter's eyes. He is all in all; in Him, nothing is lacking for the Christian.

Peter moved on to exhort Christians to tangible steps of growth. He said faith is good, but it is just the beginning of a glorious walk with Jesus. Peter believed Jesus was the Messiah early on, but he still had to go through transformational steps to become the man, the apostle, and the bondservant he was. He said, "Add to faith virtue, to virtue knowledge, to knowledge self-control, to self-control perseverance, to perseverance godliness, to godliness brotherly kindness, to brotherly kindness love" (2 Peter 1:5–7). Peter understood the need for new believers to encounter a maturing process in the kingdom, which takes time. He knew they had faith, but faith is the beginning step of a miraculous and amazing journey to a mature life in Jesus. Peter was teaching Christians to take an active role in their growth process. Spending time daily in God's Word and getting to know Jesus more and more will lead to the rest. To know God's will and obey His Word is to grow to Christian maturity. Soon, a life of moral excellence will develop: the ability to live with moderation, the heart to stand the test of time, the will to live separated from the world, the desire to do good to others, and love birthed within and empowered by divine force, which will pour forth into a world thirsty for the truth (2 Peter 1:8).

Peter gives a warning. Christians who stop at faith or shortly thereafter will not remain where they are but will return to their old ways (2 Peter 1:9). Peter called these people short-sighted and said they would forget their sanctification. He counseled Christians to continue spiritual maturing as long as they walk upon the earth. Christians must increase in their knowledge of the Lord Jesus Christ or risk forgetting Him altogether. Peter did not believe Christians were "once saved, always saved." If he did, he would not have exhorted the church to "make their calling and election sure" (2 Peter 1:10). Peter had just given the formula for making one's calling and election sure. He said it has to do with continuing to learn about and know Jesus and growing in Christian maturity, becoming more and more Christlike.

Peter shared his urgency in reminding the church of these things. He understood he was soon approaching the end of his life. He knew he would die the way Jesus said he would (John 21:18, 19). In his letter, Peter shared from the heart of an under-shepherd who had received the charge of feeding the Shepherd's sheep and would soon be leaving them. He had attained to love, and his heart desired for the sheep he had charge of to thrive when he was gone. He wrote the letter because he believed being reminded of these things was good. This is a good example for us to follow, to remind ourselves of these things and the brethren. Encourage one another to press forward rather than pointing out shortcomings. Peter wrote the letter so the Christian community would have his teaching, his heart for them, on paper to last beyond his life. He wrote it as a farewell (2 Peter 1:14, 15).

Peter Warns the Church

Peter warned Christians of his time (and the Christians to come in the future) about false teachers. He prepared his readers for this warning by beginning with what was right and what was true. First, Peter reminded his readers of his witnessing Jesus' majesty. He walked with Jesus upon the earth, was taught by Jesus, and was chosen by Jesus. The majesty Peter referred to was his witnessing Jesus' transfiguration and the appearance of Moses and Elijah upon the mountain (Matthew 17:1–6; 2 Peter 1:16–18). Jesus fulfilled the Law and the Prophets according to Peter (2 Peter 1:19). This was seen in Moses as representative of the Law and Elijah of the Prophets. Both the Law and the Prophets pointed to Jesus, the Messiah, and in Jesus, all was fulfilled.

Peter pointed out that prophecy is not of private interpretation (2 Peter 1:20). He reminded the church that no one holds the key to prophetic understanding. The Holy Spirit witnesses to each believer. All people have the ability in the Lord through the Holy Spirit to understand these things. The Holy Spirit is the One who interprets prophecy, not a person in a church position. Peter knew what he spoke of. Jesus did not give him the keys of the kingdom because he was special, nor did it make him special (Matthew 16:19). Rather, it was his calling and anointing for service to the kingdom of God. Holy Spirit revelation and truth belong to all believers regardless of age, education, or social standing. It belongs to those who spend time with Jesus (Acts 4:13).

Peter reminded the church of his witness (2 Peter 1:18). He earnestly desired them to heed his words, knowing the depth of necessity for the church to understand this. Peter knew there had been false prophets and teachers before Jesus came, and he warned the church that false prophets and teachers would continue (2 Peter 2:1). These men would bring false teachings bent on destroying the church's foundation: faith in Jesus. This underlines each believer's need to read scripture for themselves and to have a personal relationship with Jesus through daily devotion: reading the Bible, spending time in prayer, worshipping, and having a lifestyle of devotion. The only way to know if someone is teaching false doctrine is to know the truth for yourself (2 Peter 2:2, 3).

Day Five: Second Peter

Read: 2 Peter 2:4–3:18. Acts 4:13.

1. What was true of Old Testament and New Testament times?

2. What is Peter's point for Christians regarding Noah and Lot?

3. Which souls are susceptible to false teachers? How do false teachers lure them?

4. Who might Peter have been thinking of as he wrote verse 2:21?

5. What does Peter say is his purpose for writing? What should Christians be mindful of?

6. What is the Lord's slackness toward Christians and those who are perishing?

7. How will the day of the Lord come, and what will it be like?

8. How should Christians live in light of this?

9. What is the warning Peter leaves the church with?

10. What is the final exhortation Peter leaves for the church?

God is Able and Patient to Deliver

Peter used two Old Testament examples to make a point for his readers. Noah, who found favor with God in a grossly sinful world, was delivered from the flood waters by an ark (Genesis 6, 7). Lot, who was a righteous man in a wicked town, was delivered by angels from its destruction (Genesis 19). Peter's use of these examples lends to his point. God knows how to save the godly from the influences around them. He also cautioned with another truth about God. He knows how to reserve the ungodly for punishment (2 Peter 2:9). Peter's words held promise and warning. Those who have faith but continue in carnal activities ought to beware, for they are in danger of being reserved for judgment (2 Peter 2:10). However, those who choose to walk in righteousness before their God can expect divine assistance in overcoming temptation.

Peter said he wrote this letter to encourage purity in the minds of those who follow Jesus (2 Peter 3:1). Those whose minds are set on what is pure will not be attracted by those impure things. He encouraged believers to read, know, and study the words of the Old Testament prophets and the words of Jesus' apostles for sound doctrinal understanding and protection against false teachers (2 Peter 3:1, 2). This is where Peter adds why the godly have not yet been delivered. God awaited more of the ungodly to be reconciled to Him. God is not in a hurry to judge, because rushing judgment would mean He would have to condemn the ungodly, which is not His will for them. He will give time for all to come to repentance who will come (2 Peter 3:9). This led him into the topic of the last days, when judgment becomes imminent.

Peter Prepares the Church

The final words of Peter's final letter look to Jesus' return. The theme of the letter focuses on working out salvation as a lifelong process and pursuit, the culmination of which is Jesus returning and taking His own to heaven with Him. Peter, speaking of Jesus' return, at this point, is yet another warning for the church to be ready. The church must follow Peter's prescription for holy living until the day comes. The warning here is the mystery of when it will be. No one knows. Jesus' second coming would be unexpected. Peter said all would be aware of Jesus' return, but it would be too late to make one's life right with Him. When Jesus comes again, this earth and the heavens as we know them will pass away. He said they will melt and be burned up (2 Peter 3:10).

While the ideas of the heavens passing away and the earth and everything in it burning up were fresh, Peter said it was a time to look forward to (2 Peter 3:14). The only way one can look forward to the return of Jesus and catastrophic destruction of all we have seen and known is to have lived a life which honors Christ. Peter exhorted Christians to live holy and godly lives (2 Peter 3:11). Thayer uses three words to describe "godly": "reverence, respect, and piety towards God" (Thayer 2000). If all things as we know them will pass away, then we should take our time here while the earth remains to work out our salvation. Peter added a promise for hope to hold onto. He reminded the church of God's promise to her, the Bride of Christ, new heavens and a new earth filled with righteousness (2 Peter 3:13).

Peter's finishing comments reveal his heart for the church. He was concerned they might fall prey to wicked enticement and fall from grace. He warned them to beware of the possibility and to do all to stand firm in their faith (2 Peter 3:17). He finished with a condensed summary of his letter's purpose: to remind the church to continue to mature in Christ (2 Peter 3:18a). Peter strongly desired Christians to understand this truth. As long as they walk upon this earth, there is room for spiritual growth. He exhorted Christians to pursue knowledge of Jesus Christ and seek His character traits in and for themselves.

The final words we have of Peter's to the church—to us—state his lifestyle and purpose, a lifestyle and purpose Christians ought to emulate: "To [Jesus] be the glory both now and forever" (2 Peter 2:18b). How do we glorify Jesus? Pursue Him with passion, through daily reading the Bible (all of it, not just the parts we like the best), by including Him in everything we do all day long, by reverencing Him and honoring Him in all we say and do. As Peter said, we must grow and mature in Christ, becoming more Christlike as time passes, standing firm in our faith, and continuing to grow in Christlikeness. Peter gives us all hope, knowing our character flaws do not disqualify us. He had shortcomings, but he grew in Christian grace and overcame his sin nature and became a great servant of God; so can we.

I would like us to finish with these words of Peter: "Lord, to whom shall we go? You have the words of eternal life. Also, we have come to believe and know that You are the Christ, the Son of the living God" (John 6:67–69).

Day Six: First and Second Peter

1. Review this week's lessons and highlight your big takeaways. Be prepared to share these if you are meeting with a group.

2. Did you learn something about Peter this week? Share your thoughts.

3. How do you see your big takeaway(s) relating to the world around you today? To the Church in the broader sense, or the local church?

4. How might you apply one of these takeaways this week?

Overall Study Reflections

5. Look back over the entire study and your takeaways. What has changed in you, for you, or through you in this season?

6. How would you fill in the blanks below? Where were you, and where are you now?
   a. Fifteen weeks ago, I . . .

   b. Today, I . . .

WORKS CITED

Brown, F., Driver, S., & Briggs, C. 2003. The Brown-Driver-Briggs Hebrew and English Lexicon. Peabody, MA: Hendrickson Publishers, Inc.

Carson, D. A., R. T. France, J. A. Motyer, and G. J. Wenham. 1994. New Bible Commentary 21st Edition. Downers Grove: Inter-Varsity Press.

Harris, R. Laird, ed.; Archer, Jr., Gleason L., Assoc. ed.; Waltke, Bruce K., Assoc. ed. 1980. Theological Wordbook of the Old Testament Words. Chicago: Moody Press.

Thayer, J. H. 2000. Thayer's Greek-English Lexicon of New Testament. Peabody, MA: Hendrickson.

Thompson, ed., Frank Charles. 1997. The Thompson Chain-Reference Bible. United States: B. B. Kirkbride Bible Company, Inc.

Youngblood, Ronald F., F. F. Bruce, and R. K. Harrison. 1995. Nelson's New Illustrated Bible Dictionary. Nashville: Nelson.

ACKNOWLEDGEMENTS

I am grateful to everyone who helped bring the first and second editions of this Bible study alive. Your encouragement, prayers, and yesses throughout this process have been a tremendous blessing to me. You are my tribe, and I am better in every way for knowing you.

To my VCC family, pastors, and staff, thank you for seeing me, loving me, and releasing me to do what I love. Specifically to Pam Sand, Kristen Weatherford, Tina Colwell, Felicia Hart, Jeni Leeson, Bonnie Allen, Nicole Cade, Martin Hoekstra, Jolene Rogers, Kelly Lehto, Clay and Donna Dhluehosh, Jimmy Pownall, Diane Bartlett, Vicki Harris, and Casey Perry. Thank you for your quick yes to doing one chapter of this reformatted study—and for your prayers, encouragement, and support. This study is better because of you. I appreciate you, and I am honored to call each one of you my friend.

ABOUT THE AUTHOR

Jacquie Hoekstra is an author and speaker who has written Bible studies for healing and transformation, as well as a short biblical fiction story for inspiration. Her passion is teaching the Word, recognizing and calling out gifts in others, and releasing them to fulfill their purposes.

Jacquie's thirty years of experience in leading groups, Bible studies, and various ministry roles shine through her written works. She teaches with humor and authenticity. Her journey with inner healing and overcoming trials makes her studies relatable.

Jacquie has degrees in Bible study from Life Pacific College and Theology from Canyon College. She was ordained by The International Church of the Foursquare Gospel in 2008, though she does not currently hold a specific appointment. She writes a column, *Mountaintop Reflections: A Faith Perspective*, for her local newspaper, The Brownsville Times. She continues to serve through preaching, teaching, and serving on her church's inner healing team.

Jacquie lives in Brownsville, Oregon, a small historic town in the Willamette Valley. Brownsville is famous for two things. It is where the movie *Stand By Me* was filmed, and it is located in the grass seed capital of the world. Jacquie enjoys the ever-changing views of the farmlands and watching lambs and calves frolic in the pastures. She often spies Bald Eagles and other birds of prey. The air is fresh, and the pace of life is peaceful.

Jacquie and her husband enjoy their home in the foothills of the Cascade Mountains. They have a westerly view of the valley, grass-seed and hazelnut tree farms, and the Coast Range Mountains in the background. Jacquie especially enjoys watching and photographing sunsets and thanks God daily for the blessings.

WORKS BY JACQUIE HOEKSTRA

Bible studies:

Peter: A Life Transformed
Becoming Israel: Jacob's Struggle
Nehemiah: Build That Wall

Biblical fiction:

This Servant's Hands